SPACING DEBT

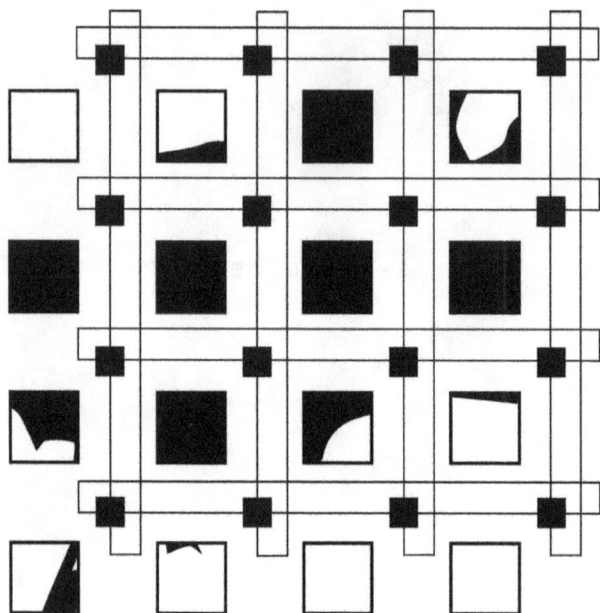

CHRISTOPHER HARKER

spacing debt

OBLIGATIONS, VIOLENCE,
AND ENDURANCE IN
RAMALLAH, PALESTINE

duke university press durham and london 2020

© 2020 Duke University Press
All rights reserved
Designed by Aimee C. Harrison and Drew Sisk
Typeset in Minion Pro and IBM Plex Mono
by Westchester Publishing Services
Library of Congress Cataloging-in-Publication Data

Names: Harker, Christopher, [date] author.
Title: Spacing debt : obligations, violence, and endurance in Ramallah,
    Palestine / Christopher Harker.
Description: Durham : Duke University Press, 2020. | Includes
    bibliographical references and index.
Identifiers: LCCN 2020017125 (print)
LCCN 2020017126 (ebook)
ISBN 9781478009900 (hardcover)
ISBN 9781478010968 (paperback)
ISBN 9781478012474 (ebook)
Subjects: LCSH: Consumer credit—West Bank—Rām Allāh. |

    Palestinian Arabs—Economic conditions—21st century. |
    Debt—Palestine. | Debt—Political aspects—West Bank—Rām
    Allāh.
Classification: LCC HG3756.P 19 H375 2020 (print)
LCC HG3756.P19 (ebook) | DDC332.7/430956942—dc23
LC record available at https://lccn.loc.gov/2020017125
LC ebook record available at https://lccn.loc.gov/2020017126

Cover art: Arab Bank ATM in Ramallah. Photograph by Christopher Harker.
Illustration and design by Aimee C. Harrison and Drew Sisk.

For Sue, beloved wife, daughter, sister, mother.
Our sadness at your passing knows no limits.

CONTENTS

ACKNOWLEDGMENTS

First and foremost, this research would not have been possible without Reema Shebeitah and Dareen Sayyad. Their contribution went well beyond research assistance. I'm grateful for their hard work, numerous insights, patience, and good humor throughout. Many thanks to both of their families too. Islah Jad introduced me to Reema and Dareen while she was Director of the Institute of Women's Studies at Birzeit University.

Many thanks to all the families that participated in this research, welcomed me into their homes, and shared what were often very intimate details about their lives. A special thank-you to my landlord, Abu Hussam, and his entire family, who looked after me and my partner in the fullest sense of that term when we lived in Um al Sharayet.

I have benefited immensely from the friendship, guidance, and support of Lisa Taraki and Rema Hammami, both at Birzeit University. My thanks to everyone else who helped me in various ways during my time in Palestine. This includes Nasser Abourahme, Yazan Al Khalili, Diana Alzeer, Zaid Amr, Yazid Anani, Hanna Baumann, Lisa Bhungalia, Simon Davis, Faris Giacaman, Samir Harb, Omar Jabary Salamanca, Craig Jones, Kareem Rabie, Yara Saqfalhait, Omar Tesdell, and Dorota Woroniecka-Krzyzanowska. Particular thanks to Maha Sammam at the Centre for Jerusalem Studies, Al Quds University; Samir Abdullah at the Palestine Economic Policy Research Institute–MAS; Khaldun Bshara at Riwaq; Mandy Turner at the Kenyon Institute, Jerusalem; Lisa Taraki at Birzeit University; and George Giacaman at Muwatin: Palestinian Institute for the Study of Democracy, for the invitations to talk about my initial findings and get feedback on the project at an early stage. A special mention also for the 2015 International Conference in Critical Geography organizational team: Nura Al Khalili, Natasha Aruri, Andreas Brück, Muna Dajani, Omar Jabary Salamanca, Lana Judeh, Punam Khosla, Anna Secor, and Christina West.

Most of the writing for this book was done in three libraries: the Ramallah Municipal Library, Kingston University's Knights Park Library, and the British Library. Three cheers for publicly accessible libraries! The writing took a long time, and during that period I've benefited from critiques from too many people to thank personally. However, I have to mention the amazing contributions Vanesa Castan Broto, Mateo Capasso, and Walaa Al Qaisiya made by commenting on the entire manuscript, and sincerely thank Hanna Baumann, Amy Horton, Sohini Kar, Sam Kirwan, Lizzie Richardson, and Krithika Srinivasan for commenting on individual chapters. All of their insights were really invaluable and helped me at a time when I couldn't see the forest for the trees. The two reviews from the publisher also significantly improved the book. Courtney Berger and Sandra Korn at Duke University Press have been wonderfully supportive.

I've been blessed by the companionship of Gerry Pratt, Will Bragg, Ben Lampert, Jess Dempsey, and Kevin Gould since my UBC days. Sandy, Muna, Salma, and Yousef, and Lauren, Oliver, Dorothy, and Liam were my families away from home for a number of years. I'm eternally grateful and overwhelmed by how much they gave me. Lynn Staeheli was a wonderful mentor and friend while I was a lecturer in the Department of Geography at Durham. Colin McFarlane was always supportive. My PhD students at Durham were a constant source of inspiration: particular thanks to Semra Akay, Walaa Al Qaisiya, Olivia Mason, and Vicky Butterby. Many thanks to all my other Durham colleagues too. Abed Al-Zuweiri provided wonderful Arabic language instruction. Thanks also to all my friends at the Durham Palestine Educational Trust. Ryan Davey, Joe Deville, Deborah James, Sam Kirwan, Paul Langley, and Johnna Montgomerie have been wonderful inspirations and companions as I've learnt more about debt. The final "push" to the finish line occurred after I moved to the Institute for Global Prosperity, UCL. My thanks to all my colleagues and the PhD cohort for your support. Particular thanks to Henrietta Moore for helping me reach a conclusion, Matthew Davies for help with all other aspects of my job, Pat Gabalova for catching my typos, and my writing lab companions Tracey Campbell and Catherine Hodge.

The Leverhulme Trust Early Career Fellowship provided financial support for this research. That application was written while I was a Senior Visiting Research Fellow at the British Institute, Amman, where the hospitality of Bill Finlayson, Carol Palmer, Daniel Neep, Veronique Bontemps, and Myriam

Ababsa in particular got me through a very cold winter. I've presented parts of this work at events at UCL, LSE, University of Birmingham, Catholic University of Eichstätt-Ingolstadt, Queen Mary University of London, Goldsmiths University of London, Cambridge University, the University of Edinburgh, and Durham University. I also contributed to sessions at the annual meetings of the American Association of Geographers in 2015 and 2017, the Royal Geographic Society in 2014 and 2015, the 2018 European Association of Social Anthropologists Biennial Conference, and the 2018 Middle Eastern Studies Association Conference. Many thanks to everyone who organized those events/sessions and invited me to speak. Portions of chapters 1 and 3 were previously published in Christopher Harker, "Debt Space: Topologies, Ecologies and Ramallah, Palestine," *Environment and Planning D: Society and Space* 35, 4 (2017): 600–619. Portions of chapter 5 were previously published in Christopher Harker, Dareen Sayyad, and Reema Shebeitah, "The Gender of Debt and Space: Notes from Ramallah Al Bireh, Palestine," *Geoforum* 98 (2019): 277–285.

Finally, this research project was originally called Families and Cities, and my own family have been the one constant throughout. Love as always to Mum, Dad, Patricia, Chris, Poppy, Betsy, Lucy, Tom, Emma, Rich, Sue, and Alfie. My grandmother died while I was writing and meant more to me than a sentence can express. Tears are still my only response to Sue's passing. Sonya spent months in Palestine, read the entire manuscript, and did so much more besides. Thanks, love!

debt/space/ramallah

"LIKE ONE OF THE FAMILY MEMBERS"

The loan is like one of the family members. It eats and drinks with me, and it sleeps and wakes up with us. It is like a nightmare!
—Interview with Im Ghassan, 31 August 2013

■ Im Ghassan and her family live in a modest apartment in the neighborhood of Um al Sharayet, part of the Ramallah–Al Bireh conurbation (hereafter Ramallah) located in the center of the Occupied West Bank.[1] Her husband, Abu Ghassan, began renting this apartment in 1995, when he moved from Hebron to Ramallah to work as a security guard at one of the newly opened Palestinian Authority (PA) ministries. After six months his family joined him, and after three years of renting they began the process of buying the apartment. The building belonged to one of Abu Ghassan's relatives, so he was able to convert the rent he had already paid into a down payment. Since the purchase price was relatively modest, he had little trouble paying the remaining amount. The following decade his eldest son, Ghassan, went to university. This time Abu Ghassan borrowed money from a bank to pay the tuition fees and ensure that his son could graduate. When I met Abu Ghassan in 2013, he was still paying back this loan. In the five years prior, he had taken another loan from the bank to cover the costs of emergency medical

---

1 Throughout the text, all residents of Um al Sharayet have been assigned a pseudonym, and details that might identify them (e.g., village of origin) have been omitted. Expert interviewees have been named, with their permission.

treatment for himself and one of his other sons. Once this loan was paid back, he borrowed more money to buy a new car and some power tools. When Im Ghassan describes her intimate life with *the* loan above, she is actually referring to multiple debt contracts, many of which are with a bank.

Abu and Im Ghassan's experiences of indebtedness are far from unique in present-day Ramallah. Their experiences might also strike the reader as unremarkable, given the pervasiveness of financial debt across the contemporary world (Graeber 2011; Lazzarato 2012, 2015). If place is thought about as extrovert—open and always in process rather than closed and static (Massey 2005; see also Haddad 2016), then the similarities between the economic situation in Ramallah and those elsewhere in the world (Ross 2014) will not be surprising. Globally, debt played a crucial role in causing the 2008 financial crisis (Blyth 2013; Langley 2014; Lazzarato 2015), and in the aftermath levels of private debt have continued to grow, reaching "an all-time high" (IMF 2016, ix). Consequently, debt has become a key concern for both politicians and scholars across the world. In response to high levels of sovereign (i.e., state) debt, many Western countries have imposed regressive austerity measures (Blyth 2013; Langley 2014). As Laura Bear's (2015) study in India illustrates, once scholarly attention moves beyond the global North there is a long history and more extensive geography of debt and austerity. Scholars have also focused on the problems created by private forms of credit. For instance, some might argue that Abu and Im Ghassan's situation provides an example of how debt, as a structural redistribution of wealth, is a form of predation upon the poor (Graeber 2011; LeBaron 2014; Roberts and Soederberg 2014). These arguments are intended to counter a more orthodox economic understanding of debt, which explains its proliferation through recourse to the (neo)liberal language of financial inclusion, free choice, and individual responsibility (cf. Foucault 2008; Povinelli 2011; Joseph 2014). Critical and (neo)liberal understandings of debt are quite different, but one thing they have in common is an underpinning conceptualization of debt as a temporal relation. Debt is about borrowing in the present and repaying in the future. In both cases it is the future that is at stake when debt is thought about as a political problem (Lazzarato 2012).

The important role that space plays, alongside time, is less well understood. However, it is crucial to understand debt's geographies if we want to understand the process of becoming indebted, the experience of being indebted, and the broader social, economic, and political consequences of those debts. For instance, the way Abu and Im Ghassan became indebted, and the way they live with and through their debts, are closely tied to their move to Ramallah. This in turn is bound up with the specific ways in which the geography of

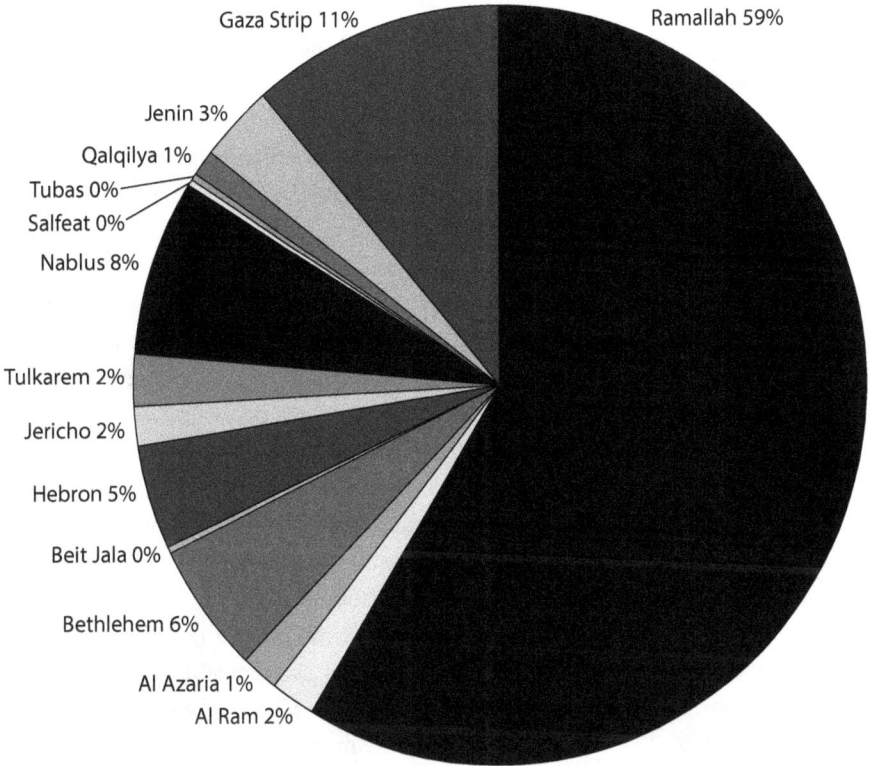

1.1 Distribution of credit/debt by Palestinian governorate, 2013. *Source: PMA 2014a, 23.*

the Occupied Territories has been produced over the past twenty-five years, largely by and in relation to the Israeli Occupation. Unlike in other places, while there is a long history of bank credit/debt in Palestine, it only became widely available (again) in the Occupied Territories after 2008. By 2013, when this research began, almost two-thirds of all bank credit in Palestine was sold in the Ramallah governorate (see figure 1.1), and most banks in this governorate are concentrated in the Ramallah–al Bireh conurbation.

This concentration of debt is often cited to support the contention that Ramallah is a bubble (Rabie 2013). This geographic metaphor, widely used in both everyday life and academic analysis, emphasizes a space that is cut off from its surroundings and a fantasy that is liable to "pop" at any minute. It is used to describe the changes that have occurred in Ramallah since the Oslo Accords were signed in 1993. As part of this process, Ramallah became the de facto capital of Palestine, as access to Jerusalem was severely curtailed and ultimately severed (Taraki 2008b). All of the Palestinian Authority ministries, bar one, are currently located in Ramallah, and the PA elites are widely seen as cut off from most Palestinians. The migration of many PA employees (i.e., public sector workers) to Ramallah during the second intifada (uprising) also played an important role in stimulating the city's housing economy and businesses. The growth in the number of employees, who account for a quarter of the jobs in the Occupied Territories, is part of a much broader economic shift from agriculture and industry to service sector employment since the 1970s (UNCTAD 2012, 2018), which has a distinct urban bias. These changes are said to represent a shift from resistance to profit generation (Grandinetti 2015), claims tied to growing levels of conspicuous consumption (Abourahme 2009; Rabie 2013) and the construction of large-scale urban developments such as Rawabi, Al Reehan, and the Ersal Center in or around the Ramallah–Al Bireh conurbation (Grandinetti 2015; Arpan Roy 2016; Khatam and Haas 2018). Such changes are narrated through the cultural life of the city: as new modes of subjectivity that focus on practices of individual consumption at the expense of political liberation (Taraki 2008b; Rabie 2013).

However, the metaphor of the bubble takes us only so far. While debt contracts are concentrated in Ramallah, this book shows that there is a more complex geography of debt at play (cf. Rabie 2013). Money taken from banks in Ramallah is spent elsewhere, and there are many debts that are not represented in the figures provided by the Palestinian Monetary Authority (PMA) because they do not involve banks. This geography of debt's proliferation, concentration, and dispersion provides the contours for the broader argument I advance in this book. In short, it is vital that we understand debt as a spatial as much as a temporal and social relation. More specifically, I will make the case that debts are topologies.

Topologies are a particular type of spatial relations, which tie indebted residents to people and institutions that have lent them money. They are like an invisible bit of string that can stretch quite far. Exactly how far depends on the two parties connected. In Ramallah, bank debts can only be enforced within the Occupied Palestinian Territories, but family debts might cross these borders. These debt topologies are practically made by practices of visiting. They are also entangled with other topological relations, particularly kinship and friendship. To continue with the image of the invisible bit of string, multiple debt topologies are like a cat's cradle, the game in which a piece of string becomes twisted in increasingly complex figurations. Each strand retains its specificity, but the whole becomes elaborately interconnected. In Palestine direct access to wages ensures the strength and endurance of debt topologies tying people to banks, while social closeness maintains debt topologies between relatives and friends. These entanglements mean that different relations can transform each other, sometimes strengthening, weakening, or even breaking connections. Topologies also enfold and become enfolded in topographic spaces within cities (including housing) and infrastructural networks. Such topographic spaces govern the possibility of debt, create demand for debt, and are spaces in which debt topologies are created.

To describe entanglements of topological and topographic time-spaces I use the concept of debt ecologies. Debt ecologies are ongoing practical achievements that are generative. In other words, they have an impact on the world. The growth of the Ramallah debt ecology has clearly enabled financialization, understood as "the growing power of money and finance in contemporary processes of economic, political and social change" (French, Leyshon, and Wainwright 2011, 814) and the creation of financial subjects (Kear 2016; Langley 2008). However, this is a contingent rather than a necessary outcome. The Ramallah debt ecology is also reworked and/or refused by other obligations, commitments, and desires. The research in this book challenges broader theoretical accounts of financialization that only examine how (debt) finance shapes broader worlds, without taking into account how those broader worlds shape finance in turn. As I argue in the concluding chapter, already existing alternatives and moments of refusal are important starting points for challenging the power of finance and the violence of debt.

It is important to foreground that this theoretical framework emerges from the particular place in which the research was conducted. Consequently, thinking about debt spatially in contemporary Ramallah not only challenges conventional accounts of financialization, but also offers unique insights into Palestinian life there. Rising levels of debt emerge from a long history of living through Israeli settler-colonialism. Settler-colonial violence has impoverished the Palestinian population over many decades, and de-developed the Palestinian economy (S. Roy 1999). The Oslo process in the 1990s shifted the nature of the Occupation in ways that led to the centralization of Palestinian political and economic life in Ramallah (Taraki 2008b). While the physical geography of the Occupied Territories became both more closed and more fragmented, Oslo also opened Palestine to foreign donor governance (Haddad 2016). The current Israeli Occupation now extends through these donor relationships, enfolding actors including the PA, the United States, the UN, the World Bank, and the EU. However, the growth of debt in Palestine was not a specific political plan or strategy. While the rationale for greater credit provision resonated with other political-economic developments in the late 2000s, debt grew because a range of technical and legislative changes enabled banks to lend more, while long-term dispossession created demand for credit. Debt has become a key means for some residents to live "modern" lives (Taraki 2008b). It has opened up a familial future of greater comfort in a context where a promised collective future of national liberation has been shut down and now seems almost extinct.

Building theory in conversation with Ramallah's residents is crucial to understand how they are active participants in their indebted lives, not simply objects targeted by banks, policy makers, and foreign states. Palestine is often comprehended through (geo)political theory and positioned as an exceptional space because of the ongoing Israeli Occupation. Palestine's history is often understood and narrated through specific events of Israeli settler-colonialism: Zionist immigration to Palestine during the Ottoman and British Mandate periods, the Palestinian *nakba* (catastrophe) beginning in 1948 with the creation of the state of Israel, the colonization of what became the Occupied Territories in 1967, the Oslo Accords in 1993, and recent transformations to Palestinian life in the West Bank following the end of the second intifada in 2007. These events have been transformational, shaping the emergence and geography of debt centered on present-day Ramallah. However, the experience of living through colonialism is not simply one of rupture nor of passive submission (L. Allen 2008; Kelly 2008; Hammami 2015). While heightened moments of violence have a great impact, Palestinians nevertheless find ways to get on with their lives. This is crucial to understand because it is through everyday practices that debt becomes folded into the shared lives of families, their practices of work and socializing, and their navigation of contemporary Ramallah as a distinctive assemblage within the Occupied Territories. In so doing, debt becomes a key means through which enduring the Israeli Occupation is capacitated. Endurance describes particular forms of agency through which Palestinians continue to continue, in the face of an increasingly pervasive assemblage of colonial violence that wears them down and out. Endurance is not a politics of resistance, which is arguably far less common in Ramallah at present. It does not describe heroic (best) practices, and it is not necessarily something that can be affirmed politically or ethically. However, to understand how people live through situations of extreme marginalization such as colonialism, it is crucial that such practices of endurance are better understood (A. Simone 2016). What is particularly striking about debt as a means of endurance in Palestine is its recent emergence.

One of the most notable features of financial credit/debt in Palestine is that there was very little of it between 1948 and 2008. The next chapter describes how the Israeli Occupation shut Arab Palestinian banks in the aftermath of 1948 and subsequently prevented new ones from opening and operating (Mitter 2014; UNCTAD 1989b). Such practices were part of a broader colonial strategy to de-develop the Palestinian economy and make it dependent on the much larger Israeli market (UNCTAD 1989a; S. Roy 1999). Only after the Oslo Accords were signed in 1993 did Palestinians acquire the political and legal tools necessary to reinvigorate the banking sector in the Occupied Territories. However, a series of policy decisions and technical changes were needed before these banks began to offer credit/debt at a significant scale.

When financial debt did begin to grow in 2008, it did so rapidly. The total amount of private credit borrowed from banks in Palestine rose from approximately US$1.6 billion in 2009 to US$3.11 billion by the end of 2013 (see table 1.1). Of this, US$1.72 billion has been borrowed for housing, land, and consumer goods (PMA 2014b, 144). This total is small when compared with that in most other territories, and the public debt to GDP ratio is also comparatively low when placed alongside that of neighboring countries. For instance, the Jordanian government debt to GDP ratio in January 2014 was 80 percent (Central Bank of Jordan 2014).

To appreciate the scale of increase in levels of indebtedness in the Occupied Territories since 2008, it is important to note that in the previous eight years (during the second Palestinian intifada), the total amount of public and private debt combined rose by just under US$500 million (from US$1.35 billion in 2000 to US$1.83 billion in 2008). This recent growth of credit/debt has had profound macroeconomic effects, as debt now plays a significant role in supporting GDP. In 2014, the PMA demonstrated that the rate of growth in credit/debt closely correlated to GDP growth and decline (PMA 2014b, 90–91). Private debt in Palestine has constituted over 20 percent of GDP since 2009, and over 25 percent since 2012 (see PMA 2014b, 90). In noting the correlation, the PMA claimed in 2014 that growth in credit was fueling growth in GDP because that credit is directed toward investment and production. However, a closer look at the statistics reveals a more ambiguous picture (see PMA 2014b, 144). Most private debt—US$1.72 billion in 2013—was spent on land, housing, and consumer goods. Far less was borrowed for industry (US$222 million), general trade (US$612 million), and services (US$373 million) that would conventionally constitute productive investment, although, as this

TABLE 1.1 Bank credit/debt in West Bank and Gaza Strip, 2013
(US$millions)

YEAR	2009	2010	2011	2012	2013
PUBLIC SECTOR DEBT	637.4	837.2	1,101.1	1,407.5	1,374.0
PRIVATE DEBT	1,596.9	2,048.7	2,449.6	2,791.6	3,106.1
TOTAL DEBT TO BANKS	2,234.3	2,885.8	3,550.7	4,199.1	4,480.1

Source: PMA 2014b, 143.

book will show, consumption spending often involves activities that produce and reproduce social relations (Graeber 2011; Bear 2015; James 2015). Palestinian Authority borrowing (public debt in table 1.1), which increased between 2009 and 2013 to make up for a shortfall in PA revenues, was largely spent on wages and social transfers (PMA 2018). Consequently, the growing public share of the total debt is not being directed at what are conventionally considered by economists as productive activities, such as support for small businesses, infrastructural investment, or education. The PMA's (2014b, 91) assessment in 2014 that credit was playing "a significant role . . . as a stimulus to economic growth in Palestine" seems rather to misread the situation. A far more plausible understanding is that debt-fueled consumption has supported a rapid increase in retail and consumer services, but not sustainable growth. By 2016, the PMA (2016, 89) publicly agreed with this argument. Debt is inflating an economic bubble, and underwriting all this consumption is donor aid.

Like all other types of economic (and noneconomic) activity in the Occupied Territories, the debt economy is ultimately shaped, governed by, and at the mercy of the Israeli Occupation (Farsakh 2008; Haddad 2016). In fact, debt provides one of the clearest illustrations of the economic impasse of living under colonial occupation. Since Palestinians have no real sovereignty, there is no Palestinian currency. All financial credit/debt is created in denominations of other currencies. In 2015, 50 percent of debt was sold as U.S. dollars (US$), 34 percent as new Israeli shekels (NIS), and almost 15 percent as Jordanian dinars (JD) (PMA 2016, 84). These currencies are controlled by other nation-states' central banks (which is one example of how the Israeli Occupation enfolds many other nation-states and supranational organizations). Palestinian politicians and bankers therefore have no control of interest rates and thus few tools for dealing with inflation. Debt-fueled economic growth in Palestine is purchased with borrowed money from donors and is tied to the contingency of donor politics (Haddad 2016). We might say that such growth is on borrowed time. And as I will show in this book, the concentration of this

TABLE 1.2 Number of Palestinians indebted and amount indebted, 2014

	NUMBER OF BORROWERS	TOTAL AMOUNT OF DEBT (US$)	AVERAGE DEBT PER BORROWER (US$)
PUBLIC SECTOR WORKERS	30,879	559,575,764	18,122
PRIVATE SECTOR WORKERS	77,930	788,961,606	10,124
ENTIRE POPULATION	108,809	1,348,537,370	12,394

Source: Statistics provided to the author by PMA in 2014.

growth in Ramallah comes at the expense of other places. Or in other words, Ramallah's growth is premised on borrowed space too.

While official PMA statistics tell one story about debt's growth, popular discourse in Ramallah tells another: "90 percent of Ramallah is mortgaged to the banks" (interview with Ahmad, 12 August 2013). "One year ago, official statistics indicated that over 80 percent of people had borrowed from banks ... I guess now it's more than 90–95 percent" (interview with Abu Omar, 12 September 2013). Statements like Ahmad's and Abu Omar's were commonly heard in Ramallah. I was frequently told that 90 percent of people or 90 percent of public sector workers ("employees") are now indebted to banks. Such statements do not correspond to statistical measures of indebtedness. Figures provided to me in 2014 by the PMA show that only 4 percent of the Palestinian population over fourteen years old, or 9 percent of the currently employed population, were indebted to banks. Only 38 percent of all public sector employees owed money to banks (see table 1.2).

However, even if statistically incorrect, residents' stories about the ubiquity of debt tell us something important about how nonelite Palestinians living in Ramallah are registering current changes there. Many see financial debt as a significant problem. For these residents, debt is an intimate part of their everyday lives rather than a statistical representation (Hall 2016). It encapsulates money owed to many different parties beyond banks, and practices that are not captured in the PMA's statistics. Residents are the experts in their own indebted lives, and as such, they provide much of the evidential basis through which we come to know debt in this book.

Im and Abu Ghassan's situation proves instructive once again. Between 2003 and 2007, Abu Ghassan had a second part-time job, and was able to gift money to his father, sister, and brother in Hebron. Im Ghassan also worked during this period. The year 2007 marks the beginning of the post–second intifada economic "boom" in Palestine, which sparked headlines in international media outlets, including "Ramallah Attracts a Cosmopolitan Crowd"

(*New York Times*, 3 March 2010), "Dream of a Palestinian Tiger: Boom Times in the West Bank" (Spiegel International, 27 April 2011), and "Ramallah Building Boom Symbolizes West Bank Growth" (*Haaretz*, 2 August 2010). However, for Abu and Im Ghassan, 2007 is when their "period of stability" ended and their personal "financial crisis" (*azma maleyya*) began. Im Ghassan stopped working, and Abu Ghassan was no longer able to work two jobs due to his poor health. This also meant that Abu Ghassan couldn't support members of his extended family (*hamula*) in Hebron anymore. Im Ghassan subsequently borrowed 1,000 JD from her brother in Amman, Jordan, to enable her immediate family (*aila*) to meet their financial obligations. In 2013, when I first met Abu Ghassan, his salary was fully or partially supporting twelve people, all of whom lived in Ramallah: Abu Ghassan, his wife, his four unmarried children; his eldest daughter and her husband (who earned only 1,000 NIS/month) and child; and his eldest son and his wife and child. His eldest son, Ghassan, had been forced to move back into his parents' house because he couldn't afford to rent his own apartment. Ghassan's university degree had not translated into a good job, and at the time of the research he was working in a supermarket. The only financial support Abu Ghassan received was from his second-eldest son, who worked as a delivery driver and gave 5–10 percent of his salary to his parents. Overburdened by this extensive duty of financial care, Abu Ghassan appeared exhausted nearly every time we visited him, partly due to ill health and stress. Paying off the loans (including interest) played a significant role in their "financial crisis," but as Im Ghassan told us, taking further loans from the bank was almost a necessity. "We know that bank loans are not blessed, but we don't have any other financial solutions. No one has the ability to lend money to others. All people are borrowers" (interview with Im Ghassan, 31 August 2013).

As Deborah James (2015) notes, increasing levels of bank debt often lead to increasing levels of informal debt: debt relations that are not with banks (see also Estes and Green 2019). Abu and Im Ghassan's story illustrates one of the ways in which bank debts are part of broader ecologies of credit and obligation. There are many others found throughout this book. The Ramallah conurbation itself constitutes, and is constituted by, the debt ecologies that are emerging there. Ramallah is not simply a context in which debt has become concentrated. It is productive too. The city is asymmetrically obligated to other places, through flows of money that are more often centripetal rather than centrifugal. Many residents, like Abu and Im Ghassan, borrow from relatives and friends living elsewhere. As I argue in chapter 4, the city can be considered indebted for its capital, population, and urban imaginaries.

These everyday geographies of debt are important because they help us understand how debt relations co-constitute particular forms of violence and agency. Geopolitical accounts of Palestinian life amid the Israeli Occupation focus on spectacular moments of military force and large-scale infrastructural violence such as the checkpoint and identity regimes (see Abourahme 2011; Harker 2011). By contrast, the growth of debt in Ramallah has created geographies of slow violence (Nixon 2011). Such practices are hard to make visible, but as I show in chapter 6, they emerge through different kinds of work and understandings of what it means to be productive. This results in a situation that might be termed financial crisis ordinariness (cf. Berlant 2011), an ongoing condition of financial hardship that is "cruddy, corrosive, and uneventful" (Povinelli 2011, 145). These geographies of slow violence fold in and out of the Israeli Occupation and its settler-colonial practices. Settler-colonialism has become an increasingly popular critical interpretative frame for understanding Israeli colonialism and its logic of elimination (Wolfe 1999; Salamanca et al. 2012). It is particularly useful for foregrounding power inequalities and the importance of decolonization (Busbridge 2018). However, like Rachel Busbridge (2018, 93), I am concerned with "the dominance of Wolfe's structural account of settler colonialism and . . . [his] vision of settler colonialism [as] effectively zero-sum, leaving little room for transformation beyond opposition." While the power and extensiveness of the Israeli Occupation clearly shape Palestinian lives across the planet in all sorts of ways, it is reductive to conceive of Palestinian life in Ramallah and elsewhere as simply the object of the Israeli Occupation. This fails to account for the agency of Palestinians and the crucially important ways in which residents of Ramallah endure occupation (cf. Hammami 2015). Debt, when seen through everyday practices, and more specifically through its intersection with obligatory subjectivity and work, is one means through which endurance is capacitated in Ramallah, as I elaborate more fully in chapter 7.

THE GEOGRAPHY OF DEBT THEORY

The connection and interplay between the conceptual argument and the empirical context that will unfold in this book are crucial. Therefore, it is important to specify exactly how theory and empirics are connected. As noted earlier, Abu and Im Ghassan's struggles with debt resonate with those taking place in many other parts of the world. They could be used to support arguments that the global explosion of sovereign debt since 2008 makes creditor/debtors of us all, the "entirety of the current population as well as the population to come" (Lazzarato 2012, 32). Such claims are far-reaching. Indeed, they cover the entire planet. However, in this book I will suggest that working through Ramallah forces us to think in more geographically nuanced ways about not just experiences and practices of debt but also its theorization.

Many recent attempts to theorize debt, such as Maurizio Lazzarato's (2012, 2015), are embedded in and reproduce Euro-America as the implicit spatial context for a series of general claims. However, if we allow Euro-American experiences of debt to pass as general or global, we risk missing (1) the diversity of experiences of debt and indebtedness (including within Europe and America); (2) the connections between different contexts through which particular forms and experiences of debt become more extensive; and (3) the different ecologies that are both constituted by debt and constitute debt in turn. All of these differences potentially provoke novel theorizations of debt. In particular, claims about debt becoming a global problem following the 2008 financial crisis risk homogenizing very different geographical and historical experiences. Such claims pass over colonialism and structural adjustment policies far too quickly (cf. Corbridge 1993; Roitman 2005; Bear 2015). These practices have created postcolonial worlds long indebted to, and thus connected and divided from, their former colonial sovereigns in historically and geographically specific and asymmetric ways (Blyth 2013). Working from and through such contexts demands a postcolonial theorization of debt.

While calls for postcolonizing theory now span many disciplines, this book has been heavily influenced by those emerging from critical urban studies (see for example Robinson 2006; Connell 2007; Ananya Roy 2009; A. Simone 2010, 2014; Comaroff and Comaroff 2012; Myers 2014). Such calls begin with the recognition that most theory is generated in, and about, Euro-American contexts. The general claims that emerge from these parochial geographies can be useful for theorizing everywhere. However, they often obscure the colonial power relations through which Euro-American specificity has come to occupy the place of the universal/general. Conventional modes of theorization also prevent other places from being viewed as sources of theoretical insight. Instead, the global South is positioned as "interesting, anomalous, different, and esoteric empirical cases" (Ananya Roy 2009, 820)—in other words, as an epistemic object that can only be thought about conceptually in relation to the global North. Calls to postcolonize theory do not deny the usefulness of Northern theory, but rather seek a "recalibration of the geographies of authoritative knowledge" (Ananya Roy 2009, 820) that open up theory to other places, voices, and practices. In relation to debt, the postcolonial theorization this book proposes is located (Robinson 2006; Ananya Roy 2009) and works from and through the contexts in which this research has taken place.

However, this does not mean that the epistemological vision of such work is limited to these contexts. It is also, simultaneously, "dislocated" (Ananya Roy 2009, 820). In other words, it retains the ability to travel and generate insights elsewhere, just as theory generated in the global North does.

Financial ways of thinking about and practicing debt have become increasingly extensive in Palestine, and thus much existing debt theory proves useful for understanding them. However, these practices and ways of thinking about debt are not all-encompassing. In Ramallah, understanding financial debt means attending to the entanglement of bank loans with other kinds of debts and obligations. The *Oxford English Dictionary* (OED 2017) defines obligation as "the constraining power of a law, duty, contract, or (more generally) custom, habit." In this book, I think about obligations as practices and relations that are understood as binding and mandatory, without the quality of necessity or absolute compulsion that acts like breathing or eating entail. Understanding intersections of various debts and obligations requires developing analytical insights through engagements with nonelite residents rather than elite financial actors. Less extensive debt relations and nonfinancial practices such as social relationships are crucial, not least because they shape how financial debt is practiced in ways that do not conform to other places. Paying attention only to more extensive debt topologies and prominent sites, such as banks and other institutions in financial centers such as London, New York, and Hong Kong, risks identifying what is general across a range of cases without examining how specific sites are ensembles of multiple processes, producing distinct debt ecologies through their recombination (cf. Collier 2011). These ecologies are financial, but also social, cultural, historical, and geographical. Specific debt ecologies thus do not add up to constitute a coherent (global) system (cf. French, Leyshon, and Wainwright 2011), even as they are constituted in part by relations that are highly extensive and move with great velocity. The impact of nondebt obligations is something that is rarely conceptualized in existing studies of debt and finance, which are primarily conducted in global North contexts. Consequently, the postcolonial theory of debt developed in this book offers new insights and avenues for scholars interested in debt everywhere.

CONDUCTING RESEARCH IN RAMALLAH

In order to develop a postcolonial theory of debt, this book draws on the expertise of residents living in one particular neighborhood of the Ramallah conurbation, combined with expert interviews and statistical data from secondary sources. Much of the impetus for my approach comes from a grounded theoretical style of conducting research. This style seeks to move or "tack" (Cerwonka and Malkki 2007) between ideas gleaned from "theoretical" texts and those that emerge from empirical research. Empirical landscapes are not thought about in opposition to theory, but rather as worlds that co-produce questions and practices of theorization. That is to say, both texts and contexts are used as sources for posing new questions about how we understand the worlds in which we move. This method treats the insights drawn from ethnography in Ramallah as being as valuable as (and sometimes more valuable than) those gleaned from theoretical texts.

The specific world that has raised many of the questions in this book is Um al Sharayet. The name Um al Sharayet, which translates as "mother of rags / washcloth," refers to a spring ('ein) where people washed their clothes. One person who does not live in the neighborhood told me it was called that because people used to dump their rags there. The first people to build in and thus establish the neighborhood were refugees who purchased land and built houses in the early 1980s. Many of these refugees, although certainly not all of them, were from nearby Al Amari Refugee Camp. Long-standing residents suggest that a number of Jerusalemites built there too, seeking to escape crowded Palestinian neighborhoods in East Jerusalem where construction and expansion had been all but prohibited by the Jewish-Israeli municipality (interview with Abu Kareem, 30 April 2013). However, subsequent changes to the Center of Life policy, which demands that Palestinian residents of Jerusalem must be able to prove that Jerusalem remains their primary residence (something usually accomplished through payment of *arnona*, the municipal tax, which is tied to residential address), meant that most Jerusalemites had to leave Um al Sharayet and move to neighborhoods within the Jerusalem municipal borders, such as nearby Kufr Aqab (Harker, Shebeitah, and Sayyad 2014).

Present-day Um al Sharayet is dominated by apartment buildings, many of which are six floors tall, although some reach ten floors. The residents of these buildings are usually migrants who have moved from other parts of the West Bank, in most cases after 2003. These people are sometimes referred to as Ahli Shamel, the people of the North, although some come from the southern West Bank. It is estimated by members of the Al Bireh Municipality that the neighborhood now houses at least 20,000 of the 200,000 residents living in the Ramallah conurbation (interview with Deema Junieh and Ala' al Deen, 4 May 2014). However, this statistic is freely acknowledged to be imprecise, and the real number of migrants is not accurately known. While censuses are conducted every ten years in Palestine, many of Ramallah's migrant residents return to their hometowns to complete them. The diversity of residents in terms of their places of origin makes Um al Sharayet in some ways a micro-cosm of the whole of Palestine. Even among the small sample of twenty-five families and individuals who participated intensively for the duration of this study, people were born in and/or had moved from nearly every West Bank governorate, as well as the '48 territories, the Gaza Strip, and various other countries. However, for all its diversity—a word that is frequently used to de-scribe the neighborhood—Um al Sharayet is also a distinct place. It is usu-ally described as either a lower-middle-class or "popular" (*shaebii* or *sha'bi*) neighborhood (Ismail 2013), often unvisited and thus largely unknown in any substantive sense by people who live elsewhere in the city. If they do come, it is usually to visit one of the many wedding halls that have been built in the neighborhood. The following description arguably embodies the sentiments of many Palestinians living in other parts of the city: "Lower-middle-class neighborhoods have become desolate places with little greenery, poor pub-lic services, and few amenities or public facilities. A new neighborhood with the unseemly name of Umm al-Sharayit is one of these areas: a sprawling settlement housing a hodgepodge of badly kept apartment buildings, public facilities such as PA ministries, commercial establishments, sha'bi restaurants, automobile repair shops, and wedding halls" (Taraki 2008a, 15).

Um al Sharayet can look very different when viewed from the vantage point of people living there. While Lisa Taraki's (2008a) claim about services may have been true in 2008, this was not the case by 2012. All buildings have access to water, waste disposal, and electricity, and public transportation (e.g., *servees* taxis) is frequent. Many residents note the benefits of being close to the city center (only a twenty-minute walk from the northern edge), and there is little unemployment in Um al Sharayet despite consistently high levels nationally (26 percent in 2017; PCBS 2017). This is largely because most residents migrated to Ramallah when they got jobs, and presumably relocate to the cheaper and more intimate surrounds of their familial homes elsewhere in the West Bank should that employment be terminated. Consequently, even families like that of Abu and Im Ghassan, who were experiencing a self-proclaimed financial crisis, were thought to be well off by relatives elsewhere. Relatively low levels of unemployment may also change in future as a generation of younger residents who have largely grown up in Um al Sharayet reach working age.

The population of Um al Sharayet can usefully be thought about as what Abdoumaliq Simone and Vyjayanthi Rao (2012) term a majority. This term is not deployed as a quantitative measure of population—as it might be used for the purposes of governance—but rather as a qualitative description of "the possibilities that individuals and households exist in cities in ways in which they come to share certain similarities in how they conduct everyday life and manage their livelihood" (A. Simone and Rao 2012, 317). A majority are "in-between," something Um al Sharayet resident and research participant Nadia (interview, 29 September 2013) also noted: "Sateh Marhaba is more beautiful than here but I guess Um al Sharayet is more vital than other neighborhoods. It has many markets, schools, and transportation. It is very close to the center of Ramallah. The rich neighborhoods don't have good social life between neighbors. Um al Sharayet is a better place to live in. Not very rich, and not very poor, in between."

As Simone and Rao (2012) state, for some of those "in-between" there may be large measures of either precarity or accumulation. Neither (extremely) affluent, like residents of gated communities or villas, nor (extremely) poor, like many residents of refugee camps, we might also understand in-between as that which falls between the cracks analytically: the in-between as a space of difference in relation to conventional stories about urban space and Palestine. These in-between spaces are "composed of heterogeneous stories and situations, and thus part of their relative invisibility in contemporary narratives of cities can be attributed to this heterogeneity. There is an absence of clear story lines, of stable class formation, ideological orientation, overarching territorial identities or ongoing institutions that embody specific collective interests and aspirations" (A. Simone and Rao 2012, 319). Residents of Um al Sharayet may be thought about in relation to a particular class profile or migrant history, as I have outlined above. Positioning them as a majority and in-between alongside these descriptions holds open what residents of this neighborhood might be, and perhaps more importantly, how collectively they constitute themselves as a neighborhood.

The account of Um al Sharayet developed in this book is based on ethnographic research conducted while living in the neighborhood for a number of periods totaling twelve months between 2010 and 2015. In addition to participant observation, during the most sustained period of research, six months in the spring, summer, and autumn of 2013, I worked with two Palestinian research assistants, Dareen Sayyad and Reema Shebeitah. Using their social networks, we recruited a number of families and individuals to participate in a series of repeat interviews that were conducted every two weeks over the six-month period. Consent was obtained verbally at the beginning of every interview, all of which were digitally recorded. Interviews covered a range of topics about migration, economic and social life, and understandings of the city. The repetitive nature of our visits and discussions enabled stronger relations of trust to be established, crucial in a context where a British researcher embodies the legacy of a former colonial power, and when the research seeks to explore sensitive topics such as personal finances and indebtedness (James 2015). In addition to interviews, participants were also asked to complete daily financial diaries during the six months of repeat interviews. These diaries were used to inform discussion in the interviews. Twenty-five of the thirty-two participant families and individuals we initially recruited continued to participate in interviews for the entire six months. Interviews were transcribed and translated shortly after they were conducted, and then subsequently coded and analyzed using qualitative analysis software (TAMS Analyzer). In the spring of 2014, we met all twenty-five participants once again to outline initial research findings and get their feedback on the interpretative analysis that emerged from coding the interviews. Building analysis from a detailed and sustained engagement with specific lives stands in contrast to studies that aggregate the heterogeneity and diversity of the everyday into the spatial subject of the household (e.g., Langley 2008; Montgomerie 2013; Soederberg 2014). Consequently, this book offers a distinct contribution to understanding the impact of debt on individuals (cf. Bear 2015).

Research with residents of Um al Sharayet was complemented by a number of expert interviews in 2014 and 2015 with policy makers working for the Palestinian Authority Ministry of Local Government, the Palestinian Monetary Authority, the Ramallah, Al Bireh, and Beitunia Municipalities, the Arab Bank, and members of the Popular Committee of Um al Sharayet. Numerous informal conversations with scholars based at Birzeit University; Al Quds University; MAS—the Palestine Economic Policy Research Institute; Riwaq—Centre for Architectural Conservation; Muwatin—the Palestinian Institute for the Study of Democracy; the Institute for Palestine Studies, Ramallah; and with colleagues affiliated with institutions outside Palestine also assisted in the development of the analysis. I collected statistical data from publicly available secondary sources including the Palestinian Monetary Authority, the Palestinian Central Bureau of Statistics, and the UN Conference on Trade and Development. Collectively this data has helped create a more nuanced spatial account of debt and obligations.

OVERVIEW OF THE BOOK

Chapter 2 provides a historical contextualization of present-day Ramallah, by narrating how the Israeli Occupation has impoverished Palestinian families and created a dependent and de-developed Palestinian economy. The chapter identifies key political and economic transformations since the Ottoman era that have shaped how—and crucially where—debt has emerged in the present-day Occupied Territories.

Chapter 3 develops a spatial theory of debt in detail. The chapter elaborates on the concept of debt topologies, examining how such topologies are entangled with other topological and topographic relations to create debt ecologies. The chapter then explores how the Ramallah debt ecology is produced and performed through a range of practices.

Chapter 4 extends the spatial theory of debt to the city. By focusing on the urban, rather than the individual, the corporation, or the state, this chapter not only offers a novel way of theorizing debt's spatiality, but also generates new insights for urban theory. More specifically, the chapter argues that Ramallah is an asymmetrically obligated city, an argument that is substantiated through a detailed discussion of flows of capital, people, and imaginaries. Thinking debt space as urban space in this manner discloses how topological spatial relations that are more extensive than the topographic city lead to inequality within and beyond Ramallah. The chapter contributes to recent attempts to think the city through the concept of assemblage, by showing how such an approach can foreground urban inequalities.

Chapter 5 moves from urban discourses to the lived experience of the city among residents of Um al Sharayet. This chapter is interested in thinking through entanglements of indebted subjectivity and space. It builds on and broadens existing scholarship on the production of subjectivity through debt, by foregrounding the role families play in this process. The concept of obligatory subjectivity is used to capture the importance of more-than-individual forms of personhood when living amid diverse social ties. The second half of this chapter examines how in Palestine gender is a key differentiator of how obligated subjectivity is lived and experienced. Rethinking indebted subjectivity in relation to different experiences of obligation also demonstrates more fully how theories of debt might respond to postcolonial critique.

Chapter 6 examines experiences of obligated subjectivity in relation to violence. While many residents view life with debt as harmful, policy elites in Ramallah deny this is the case. This chapter explores this problem, deploying the concept of slow violence geographically to understand how debt transforms life lived amid colonial occupation into what I term financial crisis ordinariness. In particular, the chapter focuses on paid and unpaid work, stress, and understandings of productivity as key dimensions of the current impasse. However, while effective at illustrating harm, the chapter concludes with some reservations about the concept of crisis, whether "ordinary" or not. These hesitations emerge because while many—perhaps most—debt topologies can be violent, this is not always the case.

This discomfort with a crisis lens becomes the starting point for the penultimate chapter of the book. In response, the chapter focuses on practices of endurance, and the ways in which endurance is capacitated in contemporary Ramallah. Debt is one such means through which residents capacitate endurance. I argue that endurance offers a theoretical language for understanding forms of agency beyond the dual frame of power (victimhood) and resistance (heroism). Endurance, a source of neither ethical good practice nor political inspiration, conceptualizes the ways through which many residents live with and get by in the face of colonial duress (Stoler 2016). Such practices incorporate continual evaluations by those involved in them and offer scholars a different entry point for thinking about Palestinian politics more generally.

The final chapter reflects on the book's ambition to spatialize and postcolonize debt theory in light of decolonial critique. Decolonial critique reminds us that anticolonial struggles are primarily for sovereignty and land. Attempts to challenge epistemologies must therefore be aligned with efforts to transform the socio-material worlds in which those understandings move and operate. In Palestine, those who challenge existing debt ecologies must necessarily do so in relation to decolonial struggles to end Israeli settler-colonialism. The chapter explores what such transformation might look like from the perspective of Ramallah's policy elites and through the "ordinary" practices of Um al Sharayet's residents. Ultimately, I argue that residents' practices of endurance may prove more salient for dealing with the current impasse.

Throughout this book, I often refer to Palestine. Such use follows my participants' deployment of the term, to refer to both the territories of historic Palestine pre-1948 and the territories now referred to as Occupied (i.e., the West Bank, the Gaza Strip, and East Jerusalem). I repeat their use in the full knowledge that these terms do not reflect the spatial extent of Palestinians, whose lives in exile extend across the Arab world and beyond. Nor does this usage reflect the lack of political coherence since the Oslo Accords were signed and the displacement of the Palestine Liberation Organization by the Palestinian Authority as the de facto representative of the Palestinian people. With these caveats in mind, I nevertheless argue that it is ethically and politically important to continually (re)assert the presence of Palestine and Palestinians on lands they have occupied for centuries. Where it is important to distinguish, I follow my participants in using the term "'48 territories" to name the lands occupied by Israel in 1948, and the term "Occupied Territories" to specify the lands captured by Israel in 1967. The latter term is used to denote the spatial extent of Palestinian Authority and Palestinian Monetary Authority governance. I use the term "Apartheid Wall" to describe the structure that is elsewhere termed the Occupation Wall or Israel's Security Barrier, because this was a term most of my participants used.

a history of debt in palestine

This chapter offers a historical contextualization of the growth of debt in Ramallah, focusing on the most salient economic, social, and political processes that have provoked, enabled, and co-constituted debt's reemergence. Consequently, the narrative focuses on political and economic developments that have shaped the provision and demand for debt, and the growth of the Ramallah conurbation where geographies of debt have become centered. The chapter is organized chronologically, according to widely accepted periodization of Palestinian history: the Ottoman and British Mandate eras; the beginning of the nakba (catastrophe) after the violent creation of the state of Israel in 1948; the expansion of the Israeli Occupation into the West Bank, the Gaza Strip, and East Jerusalem in 1967; the ratification of the Oslo Accords in 1993; and the beginning of the second intifada in 2000. I have added a final period, from 2008 onward, when financial debt began to grow rapidly (cf. Haddad 2016). While such historical delineations provide a useful means for thinking through significant transformations in Palestinian life in the Occupied Territories, as I argue later in the book it is important that the events that structure these temporal divisions do not occlude everyday life and forms of slow violence that never quite add up into something as clearly distinct as an event.

The story of debt in Palestine begins in the nineteenth century. At this time, 70 percent of the Palestinian population lived in rural areas (Khalaf 1997, 94). Urban centers, largely on the coast, grew during the nineteenth century as trade hubs, shipping the products of commercialized agriculture to Europe. As Issa Khalaf (1997, 93) notes:

> Beginning in late Ottoman times and throughout the British Mandate period (1918–48), the [Palestinian] agrarian social economy had been slowly undermined by the urban landowning class and oppressive tax and land-tenure systems. Peasant dispossession, begun in the 19th century and aggravated by Zionist land-buying in the 20th, created a significant landless rural population that was increasingly dependent on wage labor in scattered rural locations and in the cities. During the British Mandate, as Palestine was rapidly incorporated into the world market, communal harmony and social integration were further strained by urban-rural and peasant-landowner tensions, disjointed urban working-class development, unemployment, and overcrowding.

During both the Ottoman era and the British Mandate, debt became a key mechanism for the dispossession of rural land (Stein 1987; Yazbak 2000). *Fellahin* (peasants; sing. *fellah*), faced with poor crop yields and drought, took loans from largely urban-based landlords and moneylenders. Interest rates were often usurious. According to Kenneth Stein, "It was not uncommon in Palestine for the fellah to pay interest rates of 30% to 60% on money borrowed over periods of three months to a year" (Stein 1987, 28). Defaults were frequent, particularly during bad harvests when crops that were used as repayment failed. This led to the transfer of land ownership to creditors, with peasants continuing to work on the land as tenants. Credit was provided by commercial banks, and the British Mandatory Government attempted to introduce cheaper forms of credit through state-supported bank lending and agricultural cooperatives (Nadan 2005; Mitter 2014). However, most lending during the Ottoman and British Mandate periods was informal (Nadan 2005). The role of debt in the loss of land ownership was particularly problematic because creditors—urban elites and moneylenders—began to sell land to Zionist organizations. The new owners replaced the Palestinian peasant workforce with Zionist immigrants (Khalaf 1997, 95). As Patrick Wolfe (2012) argues, such practices can be understood as the beginning of Israeli settler-colonial dispossession, which then intensified in 1948. Many of the newly unemployed peasants migrated to urban areas and were one of the primary reasons for the anticolonial uprising against the British Mandate forces between 1936 and 1939 (Yazbak 2000).

1948-1967

If systematic impoverishment is one of the most significant drivers of demand for debt in contemporary Palestine, this has largely been caused by the massive dispossession of land and political sovereignty that began in 1948. This was the beginning of the ongoing Palestinian nakba (Sa'di and Abu-Lughod 2007; Alqasis 2013). After Britain renounced its Mandate for Palestine in 1947, the United Nations (UN) proposed creating two independent states, allocating 56 percent of the land for a future Jewish state, even though the Jewish population constituted a third of the total population at the time (Gregory 2004). On the day the Mandate officially ended, 14 May 1948, David Ben Gurion declared the founding of the state of Israel. The following day, the surrounding Arab states invaded, and war waged for fourteen months. During this war, Israeli fighters displaced over 700,000 Palestinians from their homes and made them refugees (Morris 2003), while partially or fully destroying over 400 Palestinian villages (Falah 1996). When armistice lines were established in 1949, Mandatory Palestine had been violently transformed into the state of Israel—referred to as the '48 territories by Palestinians—the Jordanian-controlled West Bank that included East Jerusalem, and the Egyptian-controlled Gaza Strip (Gregory 2004). The estimated 700,000 Palestinians who had been forced to flee their homes during the fighting became refugees in the newly created Occupied Territories and in the surrounding countries of Lebanon, Syria, Iraq, Jordan, and Egypt (Morris 2003).

Much fuller accounts of the nakba than I can offer here can be found in the references cited above. One consequence that is particularly important for understanding the present geography of debt was the growth of the Ramallah conurbation. Taraki (2008b, 66) argues that "apart from Gaza City (and to some extent Jerusalem), Ramallah is the Palestinian city most affected by the war of 1948 and its aftermath." Prior to 1948, Ramallah was a village. Its only distinction from other villages in the Jerusalem area was the first (of what would become two) Friends School set up by Quaker missionaries in 1889 (Ramallah Friends School 2017). Nearby Al Bireh was known as a waypoint on the pilgrim trail from Jerusalem to Nablus (Taraki 2013). The two villages grew during the British Mandate period as residents working in the Mandate's bureaucracy and remittances from émigrés funded a building boom (Taraki 2008a, 29–30).

However, it was the nakba that transformed Ramallah–Al Bireh into the city it is today, as thousands of refugees fled there. Some of the new arrivals were middle class, fleeing from Mandatory Palestine's coastal cities, particularly Jaffa. They moved in with family members already living there or rented apartments, and the wealthiest moved into their own summer residences (see Shehadeh 2012). In the months and years that followed, many set up businesses in Ramallah and were responsible for the settlement's growth as a commercial center. There were also many refugees from rural villages in the coastal plain between Jaffa and Jerusalem, who were poorer and lacked social connections with existing residents. They were briefly allowed to stay in the grounds of the Friends School and on land just outside the original town centers, where the current Qaddora Refugee Camp remains to this day. Most were then moved to the purpose-built refugee camps of Qalandia and Al Am'ari located to the south of Al Bireh, and to Jalazone and Deir 'Ammar, located to the north of Ramallah (UNRWA 2015). These camps were administered by the United Nations Relief and Works Administration for Palestine Refugees in the Near East (UNRWA), created in 1949 to manage the 700,000 Palestinians forcibly displaced at the outset of the nakba. No longer able to practice agriculture, many of these poorer refugees became wage laborers.

From 1948 until 1967, Ramallah, like the rest of the West Bank, was under Jordanian control. During this period, neglect was prominent. "Like Israel's, Jordan's policy was to discourage any economic development within the West Bank and any genuine form of political participation. Jordanian policy was to cultivate the traditional Palestinian leadership as a co-opted elite in order to mediate between the Jordanian regime and the local Palestinian population" (Zureik 1977, 14). While coveting the territory for a greater Jordan, the Jordanian monarchy was cognizant of the threat of Palestinian nationalism and did not want to empower indigenous leadership. Palestinian nationalism became increasingly formalized during this period, most notably with the establishment of the Palestine Liberation Organization (PLO) in Cairo in 1964. The PLO, an umbrella organization for Palestinian resistance groups, remains the official representative of the Palestinian people (Said 1992).

The Palestinian Arab banking sector was also heavily affected by the nakba. Many bank branches were closed during the fighting in 1948 and 1949. The largest bank (by capital) currently operating in the Occupied Territories, the Arab Bank, was established in 1930 (Mitter 2014). It was forced to close its branches in Jaffa and Haifa during the first months of the nakba. The bank's headquarters were moved from Jerusalem to Amman during the same period, where they remain to this day. The Haifa branch subsequently reopened in

Beirut and then Amman, and the Jaffa branch reopened in Nablus and then Ramallah (Arab Bank 2017). Banks that remained in the '48 territories were forced to freeze the accounts of all their Arab customers in June 1948, and then the following year to transfer this money to the newly created Custodian of Absentee Property, part of the state of Israel (Mitter 2014, 105–7).

1967–1993

In 1967, Israel invaded and captured East Jerusalem, the West Bank, and the Gaza Strip (Gregory 2004). As a result, the West Bank experienced another influx of refugees, albeit smaller in number than in 1948–49. One of the most significant impacts of the 1967 war for the newly Occupied Territories was the Israeli settler-colonization that followed, which radically reshaped space, politics, economy, and society in Palestine. Four Israeli colonies had been constructed by the end of the following year. The number of Israeli colonies and settler-colonists has continued to grow since, and B'Tselem (2017) estimates that by the end of 2015 there were 248 colonies, housing 588,000 settler-colonists in the Palestinian Territories occupied in 1967. As the UN has continually reaffirmed, all of these Israeli colonies in the Occupied Palestinian Territories, including East Jerusalem, are illegal under international law (UN 2016). As Eyal Weizman (2007) demonstrates, the state-supported construction of settlement colonies has fragmented Palestinian territory in order to undermine any future claims to political sovereignty. Sari Hanafi (2013) calls this process spaciocide, the deliberate targeting of land in order to remove the Palestinian population living on it. Settlement colony construction includes an elaborate infrastructure of roads, checkpoints, and utilities, or what Jeff Halper (2009) terms the "Matrix of Control," which enables Israeli rule over the Palestinian population through sovereign, disciplinary, and biopolitical forms of power.

The Ramallah conurbation provides a good case study of the spatial consequences of settler-colonialism. The first Israeli settlement colony in the Ramallah governorate, Ofra, was built in 1975 to the north of Al Bireh on land belonging to the villagers of 'Ein Yabrud and Silwad (B'Tselem 2008). Beit El appeared to the north of Al Bireh in 1977, followed by Bet Horon (southwest, 1977), Giv'on HaHadasha (1980) to the south of Beitunia, Psagot (east, 1981), Givat Ze'ev (south, 1983), Dolev (northwest, 1983), Nahliel (northwest, 1984), Kochav Ya'akov (southeast, 1985), and Talmon (northwest, 1989). These illegal settlement colonies now house 42,623 settler colonists (B'Tselem 2017). They are also spatial facts on the ground. As map 2.1 shows, collectively their

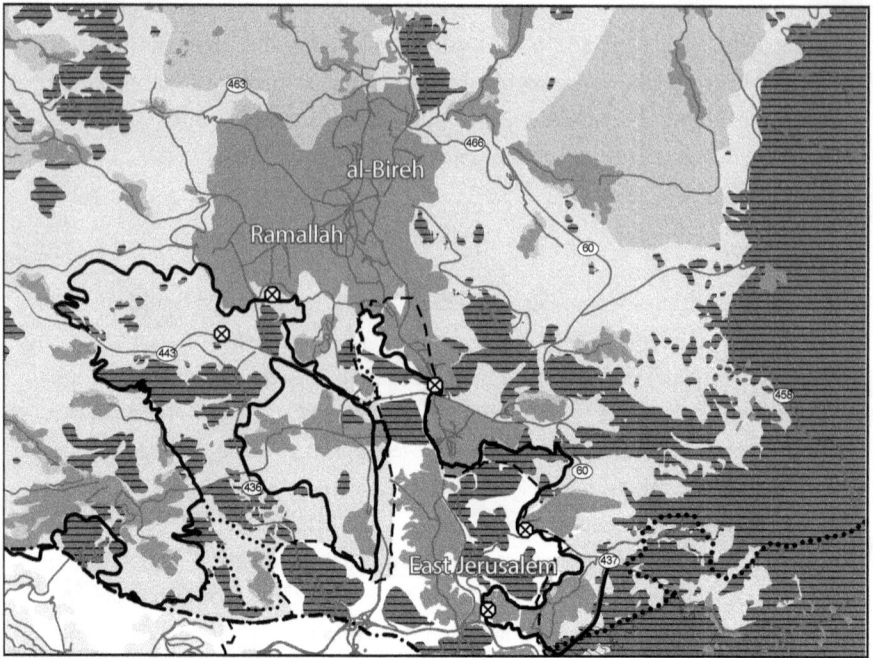

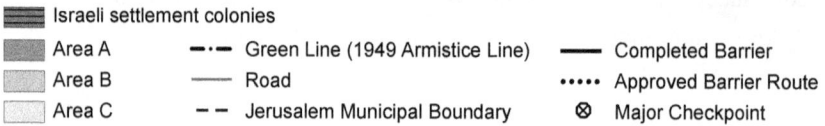

Israeli settlement colonies

Area A	—·— Green Line (1949 Armistice Line)	—— Completed Barrier
Area B	—— Road	••••• Approved Barrier Route
Area C	– – Jerusalem Municipal Boundary	⊗ Major Checkpoint

MAP 2.1 Settlement colonies in the Ramallah governorate. *Source: Adapted from B'Tselem 2014.*

construction has created a territorial ring around the Ramallah urban area, preventing its horizontal spread (Harker 2014). These settlement colonies constitute one part of a broader policy of colonization designed to prevent Palestinian urban expansion (Weizman 2007) while stealing agricultural land.

Across the Occupied Territories, the Israeli theft and control of Palestinian land through settlement colonization has been enabled by military force and governance. The Israeli Military Governorate was created in 1967 to rule the Palestinian population in all areas conquered that year except East Jerusalem, which was annexed and placed within the Jerusalem Municipality. In 1981, the Military Governorate was replaced by the Civil Administration, which despite its name is part of the Israeli Ministry of Defense. During this period, all Palestinian political activities in the Occupied Territories were violently repressed by Israel. Particular measures, such as agricultural loan schemes and training programs (Gordon 2008), were introduced as part of a broader program that sought to mitigate the negative economic effects of colonial occupation (and thus create a docile population) without ending or radically changing the political structure of that occupation. Such measures can be interpreted as the first attempt to create an economic peace. This colonial fantasy relied on Palestinians being not only politically docile, but also economically dependent and subservient. Through the Military Governorate and the Civil Administration, Israel heavily influenced economic life in the Occupied Territories, creating an overall relationship characterized by scholars as dependency (Zureik 1977), pauperization (Sayigh 1986), and de-development (S. Roy 1999). These concepts point not only to the impact of Israel on Palestinian life in the Occupied Territories but also to the asymmetric reintegration of the territory of Mandatory Palestine that had been severed in 1948.

Yusif Sayigh (1986, 47) argues that dependency is most obvious in relation to trade. After 1967, Israel was not only the dominant trading partner with the Palestinian economy, but also the major beneficiary of inequitable exchange. This was in part accomplished through the "open bridges" policy adopted by Israel in the 1970s: "a one-way system allowing only some Palestinian exports to Arab markets with severe restrictions on imports from those markets. Under direct Israeli military rule, the Palestinian areas became a 'partner' with Israel in a de facto, one-sided customs union—Israeli products had free access to the markets of the occupied Palestinian territory, while Palestinian products were subject to a wide range of quantity and regulatory restrictions" (UNCTAD 2012, 10–11; see also UNCTAD 1989a). By 1986, 85 percent of Palestinian exports of goods and services went to Israel, while 80 percent of imports to the Occupied Territory originated in Israel (UNCTAD 1989a, 38).

The ability for Palestinians to buy Israeli imports was in part enabled by similarly asymmetric flows of labor. While Israel created loan schemes and training programs that made Palestinian agriculture productive (Gordon 2008, 63–65, 72), leading to an increase in agricultural production in the 1970s (UNCTAD 1989a, 12), these schemes also ensured that this sector would not be competitive with Israel's own agricultural sector. These loans also extended to certain kinds of industry (UNCTAD 1989b, 45), although the overall pattern of the Palestinian industrial sector was stagnation, with 90 percent of industrial enterprises employing fewer than eight people (UNCTAD 1989a, 17). Declining employment opportunities in agriculture and limited opportunities in industry encouraged Palestinians in the Occupied Territories to work in the labor-intensive sectors of the Israeli economy where pay was higher (UNCTAD 1989a, 1; S. Tamari 1981). According to UNCTAD (1989b, 29), "In 1970, the

21,000 Palestinians working in Israel constituted only 12 per cent of the labor force. The number and proportion peaked in 1984, with 90,300 Palestinians working in Israel, constituting some 37 per cent of the total Palestinian work force. By 1985, the figure had dropped to 89,200, though this still represented just under 37 per cent of the total." During this period, there were also high levels of Palestinian work-related migration to the Gulf. Migrants earned relatively good salaries as engineers and teachers, and many sent part or all of their earnings back to their families in the Occupied Territories (and also Jordan and Lebanon) (Abed 1991). UNCTAD (1989b, 31) reported that "net total Palestinian migration out of the territories is estimated at more than 760,000 during the period 1967–1984." While harder to estimate, total net transfers (e.g., remittances, aid) to the Occupied Territories "rose from US$240 million in 1978 to US$470 million by 1984" (UNCTAD 1989b, 107).

Like other industries in the Occupied Territories, the Palestinian financial sector was largely nonexistent between 1967 and 1993. Some of the first military orders passed in June and July 1967 banned Palestinian and Arab banks and gave monetary authority to the Bank of Israel (Gordon 2008, 72; Mitter 2014; UNCTAD 1989b, 33–35). After 1967, the only banks that operated in the newly Occupied Territories were Israeli. Their main function was to facilitate the payment of wages to Palestinians working for the Military Governorate and then the Civil Administration (UNCTAD 1989b, 38). Access to credit for both business and private use was extremely limited, with informal money changers providing a small but important role as intermediaries in a monetary system that now included the Israeli shekel, the Jordanian dinar, and the U.S. dollar (UNCTAD 1989b). Individual branches of the Bank of Palestine and the Cairo-Amman Bank (re)opened in the 1980s, although without the ability to offer many services (UNCTAD 1989a, 19).

In summary, the Palestinian economy after 1967 was characterized by a decline in agricultural labor and output, a lack of industrial growth, and a high reliance on external finance from transfers and wages earned in the Gulf and the '48 territories. Most private investment during this period was in residential construction. Sara Roy (1999) uses the term "de-development" to describe Palestinian economic activity after 1967. She argues that between 1967 and 1993, de-development encompassed (1) expropriation, through which key economic resources such as land and water were stolen or restrictions placed on their use; (2) integration and externalization, through which Palestinian economic growth became conditional on employment in Israel and other externally generated sources of income, which led to the de-skilling of the workforce, the decline of Palestinian productive capacity in agriculture and industry, and growing dependence on Israel for trade; and (3) deinstitutionalization—the prevention of the development of Palestinian institutional infrastructure, including financial and banking systems, local government structures, and appropriate educational and health institutions. De-development also had spatial consequences, since cities with strong industrial (Hebron) and trade (Nablus) centers began to decline. Conversely, Ramallah, as center of and for consumption, grew, particularly because after 1967 Jerusalem became increasingly separated from the rest of the West Bank (Taraki and Giacaman 2006).

After twenty years of de-development and political repression, the first Palestinian intifada (uprising) began in Gaza in 1987, and quickly spread throughout historic Palestine. The first intifada was a broad-based and largely nonviolent anticolonial uprising, involving strikes, boycott of the Israeli Civil Administration and Israeli goods, refusal to pay taxes, and protests (Said 1989). The first intifada was a sustained and widespread Palestinian response to the nakba and Occupation. Broad-based collective resistance sought to expose the violent realities of Israel's Occupation to the world's media, unify the Palestinian population in the Occupied Territories politically, and damage the Israeli economy (Bishara 1989). This final feat was possible because of the extent to which the Israeli market relied on Palestinians living in the Occupied Territories as a cheap source of labor and on the Territories themselves as a captive market for the sale of Israeli manufacturing and agricultural products (S. Roy 1999). The intifada also worked toward the conscious goal of Palestinian economic self-sufficiency, particularly with regard to food (UNCTAD 1989a, 89). The cost of the Israeli military response to the intifada added to these impacts (Gazit 1995).

The Palestinian economy was also hard hit by the first intifada, as strikes led to a rapid increase in unemployment, while the boycott of Israeli goods impacted trade within the Territories. These economic effects were accentuated by the Iraqi invasion of Kuwait in 1990, where 400,000 Palestinians were living at the time. The Iraqi invasion devastated the Kuwait economy, the livelihoods of Palestinians working there, and, in turn, the families they were supporting. PLO support for Iraqi leader Saddam Hussein meant that nearly all Palestinians were subsequently expelled from Kuwait after the Iraqi forces were defeated by the U.S.-led coalition. Abed (1991, 38) suggests that slightly more than half of the US$700 million flowing into the Occupied Territories during this period was lost.

The first intifada played a significant role in forcing Israel to start negotiating with Palestinian representatives, initially in Madrid in 1991. The Palestinian leaders in Madrid came from the Occupied Territories, because Israel would not negotiate with the PLO leaders in Tunis (Said 2001). The PLO leadership had also had its budget cut by 70 percent by 1993 (Haddad 2016, 41; for a discussion of how this money was distributed, see Shweiki 2014). Fearing a loss of influence and control, the PLO leadership in exile began a set of parallel negotiations. Despite vast asymmetries in power between the U.S.-supported Israeli delegation and a PLO delegation that knew very little about the situation on the ground in the Occupied Territories (Said 2001), the Oslo Accords were ratified in 1993. The Accords, named after the Norwegian capital city where they were created, were a series of diplomatic agreements between Israel and the PLO. Now largely referred to as Oslo within the Occupied Territories, they include agreements signed subsequently as part of the ongoing negotiations, such as the Protocol on Economic Relations signed in Paris in 1994. A crucial part of these negotiations was the role played by donors, particularly the United States, the EU, Japan, the UN, and the World Bank (Haddad 2016).

From the Palestinian perspective, the key to Oslo was the agreement to create a Palestinian state. In order to facilitate this transition to statehood, the Palestinian Authority (PA) was created. The PA was to acquire governance responsibilities during a five-year transitional period, at the end of which it would become the governing body of an independent Palestinian state. The territorial extent of this state was subject to future negotiations when the Accords were signed. As Edward Said (1993, 3) noted at the time, the agreements were "an instrument of Palestinian surrender," a Palestinian capitulation of "truly astonishing proportions." While the PA was created, the transition to an independent Palestine was not achieved. Under the banner of the peace process, Oslo actually entrenched and ensured the continuation of the Israeli Occupation, but in a new, "outsourced" manner (Said 2001). The World Bank became a "shadow government" to the PA, ignoring questions of political justice, and focusing instead on its externalities (Haddad 2016, 57–58, 63; see also Turner 2014). However, while Oslo was a failure in terms of its stated objective of creating an independent Palestine state, the Accords radically reshaped Palestinian life both within and beyond the Occupied Territories. While I focus on the former in what follows, it is important to recognize that the exclusion of Palestinians living outside the Occupied Territories from most discussions of Palestinian political and economic development has been one of the most damaging aspects of Oslo (Farsakh 2016).

One of the most significant changes Oslo instigated was to the geography of the Occupied Territories. After 1967, Israel had gone to great lengths to erase the Green Line and create a greater Israel between the River Jordan and the Mediterranean Sea. This facilitated the colonization of Palestinian land in the newly occupied territories and enabled Palestinians to work in the territory controlled by Israel after 1948. The Oslo Accords redrew this map, dividing the West Bank (minus East Jerusalem) and the Gaza Strip from Israel (which now incorporated East Jerusalem). The West Bank and Gaza were then subdivided into a convoluted patchwork of areas assigned one of three designations: A, B, and C. The PA was granted administrative and security control in areas designated A. In areas designated B, Israel maintained control of security, while the PA was granted administrative power. In areas designated C, which composed 60 percent of the territory, Israel maintained full security and administrative control (Gregory 2004). The patchwork nature of Areas A and B meant that Israel controlled access to all these areas, as well as all land, air, and sea borders around the Occupied Territories. As Weizman (2007) notes, Oslo's geography extended above the surface to the electromagnetic spectrum, and below the ground to include aquifers. Israel maintained control of these too. A checkpoint infrastructure in and around the West Bank and the Gaza Strip was developed to maintain these spatial divisions (Gregory 2004; Halper 2009). This checkpoint system enabled Israel to severely curtail Palestinians' freedom of movement within the Occupied Territories, particularly during the second intifada. Oslo thus transformed Palestinian cities into enclaves (Falah 2005; Taraki 2008a), which are often referred to as Bantustans to invoke explicit comparison with the Apartheid geography of South Africa (Zureik 1977; Farsakh 2005a; Abourahme 2009).

The checkpoint system also contributed to the significant reduction of Palestinians working in Israel. Israel restructured its economy to reduce its reliance on Palestinian labor, and thus its vulnerability to strikes and boycotts (Farsakh 2005b). "During the first three years of closure, the unemployment rate in the West Bank and Gaza Strip almost tripled, from 11 percent to 28 percent. Following the total closure of March-April 1996, 66 percent of the Palestinian labor force was either unemployed or severely underemployed" (S. Roy 1999, 69). From a Palestinian perspective, this meant a significant decline in income for many Palestinians who had previously worked in Israel. Net transfers to the Occupied Territories, which were over US$60 million in 1987, were halved by 1994, and were reduced further the following year (UNCTAD

1995, 10). Even those who got jobs in the West Bank and the Gaza Strip suffered a decline in wages, which were much lower in the Occupied Territories. While the newly created PA (including various security services) created a large number of jobs—65,000 between 1993 and 1997 (S. Roy 1999, 70)—these often went to returnees, PLO members in exile who moved to the Occupied Territories after 1993. The Palestinian private sector was poorly placed to absorb more workers after twenty-five years of de-development under the Israeli Occupation and Jordanian neglect before that. The Palestinian economy continued its transformation from production- to consumption-based. Between 1995 and 2008, the share of agriculture in GDP declined from 12 percent to 5 percent, the share of industry fell from 21 percent to 12 percent, and the combined share of the nontradable goods sector, services, and construction rose from 67 percent to 83 percent, with services accounting for all the increase (UNCTAD 2012, 4). Israel remained Palestine's most important market, accounting for 90 percent of trade (UNCTAD 2012, 72). Sara Roy (1999, 68) describes new forms of de-development emerging after Oslo: first, economic autarky, "a turning inward of economic behavior away from international market relations toward more traditional activities and production modes"; second, and relatedly, "economic enclavization," as trade between Israel and the Palestinian territories, and between the West Bank and the Gaza Strip, declined (S. Roy 1999, 68; see also Levine 2009).

Many of the new economic weaknesses after Oslo stem from agreements codified in the Protocol on Economic Relations (1994), or Paris Protocol, as it is now commonly known. Having already ceded control of external borders (land, air, and sea) to Israel during the initial Oslo Accords, in Paris the PA agreed to let Israel exercise effective control over imports and exports and collect customs on its behalf. UNCTAD (2014, III) estimates that fiscal leakage (or the amount of money lost by the PA) from this arrangement in 2011 exceeded US$310 million, or 18 percent of PA tax revenue (see also UNCTAD 2018, 4). Furthermore, the Paris Protocol granted both parties unrestricted access to the other's agricultural and industrial markets, an agreement that benefited the much stronger and more developed Israeli economy.

Another significant legacy of the Paris Protocol was the creation of the Palestinian Monetary Authority (PMA). Article IV of the Protocol defined the PMA's areas of responsibility as including regulation and implementation of monetary policy, as well as acting as financial adviser to the PA and as lender of last resort to banks in the Occupied Territories. In this same article, the new Israeli shekel was established as one of the official currencies in the areas to be controlled by the Palestinian Authority. The possibility of creating a new

Palestinian currency was deferred to the later discussions of the Joint Economic Committee. Therefore, when it was established by Presidential Decree 184 in 1994, the PMA was a central bank in waiting that had no currency of its own, and thus no ability to control interest or exchange rates. Consequently, the PMA's activities have been limited to forms of measurement and regulation. As the PMA (2016, 83) itself notes, "In view of the limited availability of monetary policy tools at the disposal of the PMA, the credit channel becomes the main channel of transmission of monetary policy to the economy."

After Oslo, Arab-owned banks were able to operate in the Occupied Territories again. Twelve of the sixteen banks currently located in Palestine commenced trading in 1994 or 1995 (PMA 2014b, iii). Although the arrival of the PA enabled banking to resume, the provision of credit/debt was slow to take off. Banks rarely lent money to most of the population due to the risk of non-repayment. Heightened risk stemmed from the ongoing Occupation and the poorly functioning nascent PA legal system, which made it hard to recoup defaults through the courts. Foreign banks in particular had little incentive to invest in Palestine, preferring to move capital to places where returns were more assured, such as Jordan and Israel. Perhaps more significantly, many Palestinians living in the Occupied Territories still to this day choose not to deposit money with banks.

While Oslo significantly shifted relations between Palestine and Israel, it also empowered other actors in new ways. One of the defining features of the post-Oslo economic landscape was the growth of aid, in terms of both volume and number of donors (Turner 2014, 33). The donor economy is dominated by particular actors, captured in Anne Le More's pithy summation: "The US decides, the World Bank leads, the EU pays, the UN feeds" (quoted in Turner 2014, 38). Mandy Turner (2014, 33) argues that "Western aid has played a major role in the political economy of the oPt [Occupied Palestinian Territories] in three ways. First, through the impact of donor-funded spending and involvement in the governance structures of the Palestinian Authority. Second, by helping to fragment the oPt geographically by working through the Oslo framework long past the five-year interim period. And, third, through the 'partners for peace' discursive framework which has been used to manipulate Palestinian elites." Toufic Haddad (2016, 2–6) characterized the period between 1993 and 2000 as focused on "peace-building" policies, strongly shaped by World Bank views that development and economic prosperity would retard war and conflict. During this period, the World Bank acquired a large measure of control over Palestinian economic development through its technical assistance program and the creation of policies guidelines (Haddad 2016, 84). This led to the promotion of free-market capitalism and private sector development, support for the PA to avoid economic collapse and preserve the peace process, and acceptance of Israeli red lines on economic, geostrategic, and civic powers (Haddad 2016, 91–94).

The donor economy positioned the PA as a subcontractor, with the power to create and disperse rents. By retaining monopolies, and therefore control, over all key goods imported into the Occupied Territories (Parry 2004; Dana 2015), the PA established patronage networks, through nepotism and corruption (Haddad 2016, 88–89; Dana 2015). Key to this network was PA president and PLO chairman Yasser Arafat. "Arafat literally was sitting at his desk in Gaza approving every single Palestinian application for a driving license and other utterly mundane administrative tasks. Stories of nepotism, corruption, and mafia-style threats swept through the local grapevines like wildfire, each additional story of intimidation of a business owner in one part of the country leaving no doubt as to what was happening everywhere" (Parry 2004, n.p.). The political centralization of the PA in the figure of Arafat was mirrored by its spatial centralization in the city of Ramallah. The nascent PA was not permitted to operate in East Jerusalem—the intended capital of a future Palestinian state—because of Israel's ambitions to ensure that the city remained an undivided Jewish capital (Mendel 2013). Therefore, after short periods in Gaza City and Jericho, the first two cities transferred to PA control, the PA moved to Ramallah in December 1995. Ramallah's proximity to Jerusalem and its location at the center of the West Bank made it suitable for what was envisioned at the time as a temporary capital. New PA ministries were located in existing buildings, many of which had been built for residential use (Saqfalhait 2015). While purpose-built buildings were replacing these original locations at the time of this research, every PA ministry headquarters remains in Ramallah except for one. The PA's centralization in Ramallah was accompanied by the growth of NGOs in the city, another spoke in the state-building wheel (Said 2001, 91, 101). In addition to the influx of international NGOs and development organizations, many local NGOs were created from existing Palestinian community organizations that had been active during the intifada (Hammami 1995, 2000; Dana 2013). The exposure of these community groups to international donor funding, and their subsequent professionalization, subsumed social and political activism in the Occupied Territories to the political-economic imperatives of global development (i.e., UN, United States, and EU) and capitalism. The much higher salaries paid by NGOs also skewed living costs in the city (Haddad 2016, 199).

The significance of the spatial, economic, and political changes created through the Oslo process quickly became apparent to Palestinians in the Occupied Territories and created the impetus for the second Palestinian intifada in 2000. Unlike the first intifada, the second intifada was a militarized uprising, largely carried out by young men (Hammami and Tamari 2001). However, all Palestinians in the Territories were affected. All major Palestinian cities were attacked and (re)invaded by the Israeli military in 2002 (Gregory 2004), causing widespread destruction of the built environment (Graham 2004) and the introduction and intensification of movement restrictions and curfews across the Occupied Territories (Gregory 2004; Hammami 2004; Weizman 2007; Halper 2009). The physical destruction of the Palestinian built environment, coupled with Israeli checkpoints, curfews, and military incursions that peaked between 2002 and 2004, caused the collapse of the Palestinian economy. "By 2006, Palestinian gross domestic product (GDP) per capita in real terms was 40 percent lower than in 1999, unemployment levels hovered at 20 to 38 percent, and poverty rates reached 47 percent in the West Bank and 82 percent in the Gaza Strip" (Farsakh 2016, 60). This collapse was geographically uneven. Northern cities such as Jenin, Tulkarem, and Qalqilya were the most severely impoverished, particularly after the construction of Israel's illegal Apartheid Wall (ICJ 2004), which prevents residents of these cities from accessing their land and working in the '48 territories. The situation in the southern West Bank was similarly dire, although the number of family businesses in Hebron made it (slightly) more self-sufficient (Raja Khalidi 2017). In the center of the West Bank, the construction of the Apartheid Wall devastated many villages in Ramallah's hinterland, further encroached upon and stole land in Al Bireh and Beitunia, and physically separated the conurbation of Ramallah from Jerusalem. However, the political centralization after Oslo meant that there was more paid work in Ramallah. The increasing difficulties of working in Jerusalem, the '48 territories, and other cities in the West Bank meant that there was heightened demand for those largely public sector jobs. And the relative lack of armed Palestinian resistance in Ramallah, compared to other cities such as Hebron and Jenin, meant that the overt presence of the Israeli Occupation in Ramallah diminished (but certainly did not disappear) quicker than in other cities, allowing institutions and businesses to function with comparatively greater ease (which is not to suggest that their operation was easy). Consequently, during the second intifada there was another significant but hard to quantify population transfer, as Palestinians from other towns and villages in the West Bank migrated to Ramallah for work.

Due to the movement restrictions, most of these internal migrants rented accommodation in the Ramallah conurbation and visited their families when they could. During my research, these most recent migrants to Ramallah were often referred to as *ahli shamel* (people of the north), or even *thailandiyeen* (people from Thailand). This latter term refers to the Thai migrant workers who came to Israel after Oslo to replace Palestinian laborers who had previously worked in the '48 territories. The comparison is made because, like Thai workers in Israel, migrants to Ramallah are often thought to work for lower wages, undercutting the earning power of the conurbation's existing residents. While many of the overt forms of colonial occupation—widespread movement restrictions, closures, arbitrary arrests, and military incursions—gradually transformed to become less obvious (but certainly did not cease) between 2005 and 2015, many migrants who moved both during and after the second intifada continued to live in Ramallah. Many married male migrants bought apartments and moved their families to Ramallah after working there for six months to a year. Other migrants met their spouses in Ramallah.

The increase in migration to Ramallah was sustained because of the political-economic changes that occurred in the aftermath of the second intifada. Haddad (2016, 2) characterizes the post-2000 period as one dominated by state-building policies. Donor aid was increasingly directed toward relief and emergency assistance during the second intifada (UNCTAD 2012, 37). There was also a notable rise in conditionality, focusing on transparency and sound fiscal policy, which previously had been lacking (Haddad 2016, 182). Israeli military violence was the other factor that created significant changes. In 2004, after being imprisoned underground in his Ramallah headquarters for two years by the Israeli siege, PLO chairman and PA president Yasser Arafat died. Mahmoud Abbas, a longtime deputy, succeeded Arafat the following year. However, the cult of personality that had largely protected Arafat from popular disaffection with the Fatah-led PA did not extend to Abbas. In January 2006, the political arm of the Islamic resistance movement Hamas won the majority of seats in the Palestinian Legislative Council (PLC), the Palestinian parliament in waiting. Hamas was not part of the PLO and opposed both Oslo and PA corruption. (They stood as the Change and Reform Party on the 2006 ballot.) Their rejection of Oslo and their commitment to armed resistance meant that the international community opposed the newly democratically elected representatives of the Palestinian people. Donor funding from Western states to the PA froze almost as soon as Hamas took control of the PLC. This economic siege prevented the Hamas-led PA from functioning, and in 2007 Abbas's forces staged a coup, which succeeded in the West Bank but failed in the Gaza Strip, where support for Hamas was more extensive. This led to two governments, a Fatah-led one in the West Bank and a Hamas-led one in the Gaza Strip. Abbas dissolved the cabinet and appointed Salam Fayyad as the new emergency prime minister (MERIP 2014).

2008–2017

Fayyad, affiliated with neither Fatah nor Hamas, had served as finance minister between 2002 and 2007. Prior to that he had received a PhD in economics from the University of Texas in 1986, worked at the World Bank in Washington from 1987 to 1995, and was the International Monetary Fund representative to Palestine from 1996 to 2001 (BBC 2007). He assumed the role of prime minister through presidential fiat, and his appointment was never confirmed by the PLC. The widespread destruction during the second intifada created a stage for Fayyad to propose a series of rapid and far-reaching economic policies in the West Bank. These proposals have come to be known as Fayyadism (Friedman 2009; Raja Khalidi and Samour 2011).

Fayyadism at its broadest level names a political program that sought to establish a Palestinian state as a fait accompli, by creating the institutional and legal framework necessary for such a state. This process was laid out most clearly in *Palestine: Ending the Occupation, Establishing the State* (PA 2009), the program for the thirteenth Palestinian government. The stated goals in this program of improving governance, social cohesion, the economy, and infrastructure are underpinned by commitments to public security and the rule of law, building accountable institutions, effective service delivery, and practicing good governance. However, as Raja Khalidi and Sobhi Samour (2011) argue, what this has meant in practice is the creation of more bureaucracy, the promotion of the private sector, and the further expansion of PA security services loyal to Abbas. All of this was funded by a significant spike in international donor aid to the PA in the West Bank, and vigorous attempts to encourage foreign investment. By 2013, donors were giving double the amount of aid they had provided during the 1990s (Haddad 2016, 227), although subsequently donor support has significantly declined. "In 2017, [PA] budget support from donors dropped by 10.5 per cent from the 2016 level. Total international support was US$720 million, only one third of the US$2 billion in 2008" (UNCTAD 2018, 3).

The dynamics of Palestinian political and economic governance in the West Bank since 1993 are often cited as neoliberal (Raja Khalidi and Samour

2011; Hanieh 2013; Haddad 2016). Clearly, Fayyad's published policies constitute a critical reflection on governmental practice that is closely aligned with widely traveled traditions of (neo)liberal thought (Collier 2011). However, the implementation of the written plan was far from straightforward. On the one hand, fiscal austerity has reduced the PA budget deficit from 27 percent of GDP in 2006 to 8 percent in 2016 and 2017 (UNCTAD 2018, 2). On the other hand, if the PLO and the PA under Arafat could be characterized as both autocratic and populist (Haddad 2016, 161), then many of the practices that developed during Arafat's long reign continued. For instance, while Fayyad was rhetorically opposed to social transfers, prisoner payments increased during his leadership (Issacharoff 2012). This occurred in part because Fayyad lacked support within the PA's bureaucracy, which was still largely administered by Fatah loyalists. The Palestinian population at large had also, by the late 2000s, become accustomed to various social transfers from the PA. The policy transformations envisioned by Fayyad also failed to take hold because of the Israeli Occupation. While certain infrastructure projects were permitted, Israel maintained restrictions on the movement of goods and people, particularly in and out of the West Bank. This, in turn, limited foreign investment. As Farsakh (2016, 64) illustrates, numerous World Bank and IMF publications have criticized the economic effects of the Israeli Occupation on the Palestinian economy, even if they stop short of indicting the Occupation itself.

The growth of debt after 2008 is often used as a key piece of evidence that demonstrates the arrival or spread of neoliberalism and/or Fayyadism in the West Bank (Raja Khalidi and Samour 2011; Haddad 2016; Ross 2017). Many residents also attribute the increase in debt to Fayyad and his policies.

ABU OMAR This is the policy of banks, which started lending to the people after Salam Fayyad was appointed as the Prime Minister. One year ago, official statistics indicated that over 80 percent of people had borrowed from banks.

DAREEN And even more.

ABU OMAR Yes, I guess now it's more than 90–95 percent. The increasing numbers of borrowers is because of the bank facilities. (Interview with Abu Omar, 12 September 2013)

However, a more precise understanding is necessary. It was changes in the Palestinian banking sector, coupled with the long-term impoverishment of the population, that led to the growth of debt. These changes were not directly connected with the political reforms Fayyad tried to implement. While certain personalities cross both the banking and political sectors in Palestine, and recent changes in banking regulation and practice align with some of the aims and methods of Fayyadism, they do not stem directly from them. Rather they resonate with each other (Connolly 2005). This is in large part because of the power of donors—particularly the World Bank—to shape ideas about development, and in particular the promotion of specific forms of finance as crucial for state building (Haddad 2016, 239).

The PMA has played a crucial role in transforming banking in Palestine, and there are two processes through which the PMA enabled the growth of debt/credit in Palestine. The first was the creation of a credit information system, a project that began in 2007 and was launched in 2010 (PMA 2011). The database collects and provides information on whether someone has loans, "whether he/she has unpaid due instalments, and . . . the customer's history in dealing with the banking system" (PMA 2014b, 72). This information is not only displayed, but also used to calculate a risk (of default) score for anyone who wants to borrow money. Since April 2014, sufficient historical data has been acquired to use the credit registry for issuing mortgages (interview with Riyad Abu Shehadeh, 25 May 2014). The bespoke system for evaluating risk was built by Creditinfo Schufa (PMA 2012a), and the information required was initially collected from banks and other financial institutions. However, since 2013, numerous private sector companies have gained access to the system, including telecommunication firms, vehicle rental companies, the Union of Palestinian Real Estate Developers, and the Student Loan Fund (PMA 2016, 64). The PMA is quick to celebrate the registry, proclaiming that with "the launch of this system, the PMA has occupied the second rank among world central banks in this area after the central bank of Malaysia" (PMA 2011, 41). Such international comparisons, which can be found throughout the PMA's published literature and public media presence, indicate a desire to speak to an international audience, who are also the source of particular ideas about how to organize an economy. The global networks of the World Bank and the IMF are particularly important for enabling the extensive circulation of such ideas (Haddad 2016). However, the Palestinian credit information system is possible only because of the unique identifiers each Palestinian living in the Occupied Territories is allocated by Israel as part of its Palestinian population database.

The second role the PMA played in the growth of debt in Palestine was through banking legislation. In 2009, the PMA limited the proportion of customer deposits banks could move outside Palestine (PMA 2010, n.p.). Banks, forced to keep more capital in Palestine, channeled this money into the sectors deemed to be lowest risk: housing and the service sector. Coupled with declining risk of selling credit after the introduction of the database, and the growth in demand for housing in Ramallah due to the latest influx of migrants, levels of private debt expanded rapidly.

The expansion of credit has also been enabled in part by the PMA's strategy of creating financial subjects who are included in the financial sector. As they note in their 2013 annual report, "The PMA has been keen to make banking services available across Palestine, while giving priority to rural and distant areas in order to facilitate trade and economic activity and allow access to all kinds of financial transactions to all citizens" (PMA 2014b, 68). A National Strategy for Financial Inclusion (PMA 2014b, 78–80) has been developed, based on the G20 Principles for Innovative Financial Inclusion. This is justified as a means of reducing inequality and alleviating poverty. The PMA has also run a series of banking awareness campaigns, which included the Second Annual Child and Youth Banking Week, promoting e-banking, increasing awareness about consumer rights, and a campaign "urging the public to restrict their financial and banking activities to PMA-supervised financial institutions" (PMA 2014b, 77). However, speaking in early 2015, Hashim Shawa, chairman of the Bank of Palestine, noted that "less than 60 percent of the population is banked" (Halligan 2015, n.p.). At the end of 2015, there were 274 bank branches, which represented a branch density of around 15,600 people per branch or office, well below the PMA's desired density of 10,000 people (PMA 2016, 65).

CONCLUSION

Rising levels of debt in contemporary Ramallah emerge from a long history of living through Israeli settler-colonialism. Settler-colonial violence has impoverished the Palestinian population over many decades and de-developed the Palestinian economy. The Oslo process in the 1990s shifted the nature of the Occupation in ways that led to the centralization of Palestinian political and economic life in Ramallah. While the physical geography of the Occupied Territories became both more closed and more fragmented, Oslo also opened Palestine to foreign donor governance. It is crucial to understand the current Israeli Occupation as extending to these donor relationships, and thus enfolding the United States, the UN, the World Bank, and the EU. However, the growth of debt in Palestine was not due to a broader political initiative but occurred because of a confluence of factors and practices. The relationship between closure and porosity also points to the need to think more about debt's geographies, which is where the next chapter begins

theorizing debt space

You must go to the bank. Because you won't meet anyone who can give you $40,000. No one can give you this amount of money. Your only choice is the bank. The solution is the bank, not the people.
—Interview with Nasser, 27 August 2013

"YOU MUST GO TO THE BANK"?

Nasser purchased a new apartment in Um al Sharayet in 2012. The apartment cost US$120,000, and he took a mortgage from a bank that he was repaying over a nineteen-year period. With a fixed annual percentage rate (APR) on the loan of just over 6 percent, his repayments are due to total US$202,200. Therefore, his claim about needing US$40,000 is a significant underestimate. His belief that only banks can provide such large amounts of money is much closer to the mark. The need for such large sums of money stems in part from rapidly increasing housing prices. New apartments in Um al Sharayet were selling for US$90,000–120,000 at the time of research. This represents a significant cost, even for a midlevel civil servant like Nasser, whose monthly income was 8,000 NIS (about US$2,000) in 2013. To appreciate the increase in the price of housing, we might compare Nasser's purchase with the US$37,000 Abu Samir committed in 2006 for a similar-sized apartment, albeit a basement suite in a part of Um al Sharayet considered less desirable. While Abu Samir, who worked in a service sector job, took home 3,600 NIS each month, his monthly housing payments did not include interest because he was paying the building owner directly, in monthly installments. Abu Samir's repayments were just under a third of his salary, while Nasser, who earned twice as much each month, was giving half of his salary to the bank.

These examples illustrate two ways in which the high levels of debt that have emerged in Ramallah since 2008 have been produced and are performed. This chapter examines these processes in detail to deepen the spatial conceptualization of debt outlined in the first chapter. This means thinking about debts as topological binds—between residents, banks, and building owners—as well as temporal relations. These topologies are entangled with other topologies, such as kinship ties, and with topographic spaces such as apartment buildings, to produce debt ecologies. The chapter then examines the specific ways in which debt topologies and ecologies have emerged since 2008, and how these debt spacings are being iterated and amplified in the present. Debt topologies are produced through practical acts, such as visiting the bank or visiting family and friends. They are entangled with other topological relations, particularly kinship and friendship, which can lead to the intensification, disconnection, substitution, and/or separation of different relations. Topological entanglements are also folded into topographic spaces. These topographies govern the possibility of debt, create demand for debt, and are spaces in which debt topologies are created. Debt topologies in turn produce topographies of residence, urban space, and mobility in Ramallah. In conclusion, I reflect on the generative nature of debt ecologies. They are relationally shaped, which is to say they reflect the relations with which they are entangled and shape those relations in turn. This insight challenges broader theoretical accounts of financialization that examine only how (debt) finance shapes broader worlds, without taking into account how those broader worlds shape finance in turn.

THEORIZING DEBT SPACE

Existing theorizations of debt often begin—either explicitly or implicitly— with its temporality. For instance, Gustav Peebles (2010, 226) suggests that "the crucial defining feature of credit/debt is its ability to link the present to the past and the future." Debt is present consumption bought with the promise of future labor (Mauss 1954; Bourdieu 1977; Derrida 1992). Credit is the opposite: a method of lending resources in the present and demanding (or hoping for) a return in the future (Peebles 2010). Once a credit/debt relation is established, it also conjoins a past moment with the future. This approach is exemplified in the IMF's definition of debt as "outstanding financial liabilities arising from past borrowing" (IMF 2017, n.p.). As Peebles (2010) shows, a temporal understanding of debt builds on a vast body of anthropological scholarship stretching back to Marcel Mauss's (1954) study of gift exchange. Other key interventions include Pierre Bourdieu's (1977) *Outline of a Theory of Practice*, which stresses the importance of timing for understanding the gift as an improvised practice rather than a rule-bound structure, and Jacques Derrida's (1992, 39) *Given Time: 1. Counterfeit Money*, which argues that time is "the guardrail against the madness of the gift," ensuring its reciprocation and thus circuits of giving. More recently, the subtitle of David Graeber's (2011) popular account, *Debt: The First 5,000 Years*, again stresses a temporal frame, while Lazzarato (2015, 70) tells us that "the question of time, of duration, is at the heart of debt. Not only labour time, or 'life time,' but also time as possibility, as future. Debt bridges the present and the future, it anticipates and pre-empts the future."

A temporal understanding of debt underpins much critical social scientific scholarship, including political-economic research that contextualizes growing levels of debt in relation to the restructuring of welfare states in Euro-America since the 1980s (Montgomerie 2013; Roberts and Soederberg 2014; Searle and Köppe 2015), scholarship examining the role played by debt in the 2008 so-called global financial crisis (Blyth 2013; Langley 2014; Lazzarato 2012, 2015; Mian and Sufi 2014), and studies of overindebtedness: impoverishment due to debt that includes material loss, downward social mobility, extreme dependency, shame, and/or humiliation (Guerin, Morvant-Roux, and Villarreal 2014, 2; Marron 2012). This literature also provides an important starting point for developing a spatial understanding of debt, because it does not ignore space as either a conceptual or an empirical concern. Following Peebles (2010), I want to suggest that existing work on debt has drawn on and advanced (at least) four geographical concepts: mobility, place, distribution, and boundaries. However, as I will show, space is largely treated as a passive surface or outcome of debt in these studies, rather than an active co-constituent.

First, debt shapes the movement of bodies through space. Nancy Munn (1986) argues that becoming a creditor initially appears to enable a more expansive range of movement, while constraining the mobility of debtors. However, in her study in Gawa, Papua New Guinea, this spatial (and temporal) extension is enabled by an expectation of reciprocity in another time and place, where roles are reversed (creating what she terms a dialectical system). Gawans are only able to extend their "names" through hosting others because they will visit and become indebted to those people in turn. In other contexts, such reciprocal systems do not exist, and the movement of debtors becomes heavily constrained, the most extreme examples being the debtors' prison (Peebles 2012) and the incarcerated slave (Graeber 2011).

Second, debt plays a key role in making place through the construction of consistent transactional pathways and networks, such as those associated with remittances, international development programs, debt bondage, and saving schemes that link financial markets with middle-class suburbs (Mauss 1954; T. Mitchell 2002; Elyachar 2005; Shipton 2007; Langley 2008; Datta and Aznar 2019). For instance, Graeber (2011, 150) argues that the slave trade triangle between Europe, Africa, and the Americas was "a gigantic network of credit arrangements." An increasing number of places have been created through the purchase of objects—particularly homes—with credit/debt (Maurer 2006; Langley 2008; Montgomerie 2013; Searle and Köppe 2015). Joe Deville's (2015) UK-based study demonstrates how debt can transform not only the materiality but also the emotional experience of place. Credit-collection practices, primarily letters and phone calls in the UK context, transform the debtor's home into a place of anxiety and conflict (see also Davies, Montgomerie, and Wallin 2015).

Third, a number of authors have explicitly examined the spatial distribution (Walks 2013) and growing global influence of debt (Cooper 2008; Lazzarato 2012, 2015). Walks (2013) uses a range of statistical datasets to maps levels of indebtedness across and within Canadian cities (see also D. Simone and Walks 2019). His studies show that debt-related risk is associated with high and rising real estate values, particularly within Canada's larger cities. Smaller cities are more dominated by unsecured forms of consumer debt. A multiscale analysis also shows how new communities at the urban fringe generally have the highest levels of household debt, as the need to commute via automobile exacerbates indebtedness at the local scale (Walks 2013, 180). By contrast, Lazzarato (2012, 30) draws on Marxist and poststructuralist theory to explore the power relations constituted by the creditor-debtor relationship that entail specific forms of production and control of subjectivity or what he terms the "indebted man" (sic). He argues that because of the massive increases in sovereign debt, "indebted man may end up becoming the most widespread economic-existential condition in the world" (Lazzarato 2012, 122), occupying "the totality of public space" (Lazzarato 2012, 38). While in places his argument implicates the entire world, at other points Lazzarato specifies that the transformations he is describing affect "Western societies" (Lazzarato 2012, 35).

Fourth, debt relations create boundaries such as the spatial limits of regulatory bodies (state and nonstate) or common bonds of trust (Peebles 2012; Flaherty and Banks 2013; Stasavage 2015). Peebles's (2012) study of whitewashing and leg-bailing in the UK provides an exemplary illustration. Leg-bailing refers to the nineteenth-century practice of leaving for a foreign jurisdiction in order to evade debts at "home" (Peebles 2012, 430). This practice led to the growth of debtors' prisons, a spatial technology designed to counteract the threat of debtors absconding by fixing their bodies in a specific jurisdictional space. "Whitewashing," or legal debt forgiveness, developed as an alternative spatial-legal technology "for repatriating people back from the exile of the prison, or alternatively, enticing them to stay inside the nation and abandon the temptations of leg-bail and foreign exile" (Peebles 2012, 433). Peebles shows how debt relations, and particularly the problem of ensuring repayment, created the spaces of the debtors' prison and debtors' court, which in turn reproduced the legal boundaries of the nation-state.

Read collectively, these studies demonstrate that space is an important category for thinking about debt. Different spaces are created and shaped by debt, as are the bodies and practices that co-constitute places. However, conceptually, space is largely treated as an outcome or effect of debt. Rarely is space considered as actively co-constituting debt. Peebles's (2012) research on leg-bailing and whitewashing is one of the few exceptions. He clearly shows that nation-state boundaries determine where debt contracts and repayment can be legally enforced. Another example of research that examines the active role space plays is David Stasavage's (2015) study of the historical emergence of public credit/debt in European city-states. He argues that "on one level it was the intensive form of political representation within city-states that was the key to their success in gaining access to credit. However, this form of political representation was itself dependent on two underlying factors: compact geography and merchant dominance" (Stasavage 2015, 528). One of the key factors for the growth of debt in European city-states was their relatively small size. This meant that they were able to maintain representative assemblies—a crucial mechanism for ensuring that governments or rulers serviced their debts—without the high transport and communications costs faced by larger territories. Like that of Peebles (2012), Stasavage's research offers an account of space's power to actively co-constitute and transform debt. Stasavage is also careful not to fetishize space. There are other factors—the dominance of merchants in his account—that co-constitute debt too.

In addition to research that explicitly examines the active role of space, it is possible to read existing studies for further evidence of space's role in co-constituting debt relations, even if such studies do not foreground the work space is doing. For instance, Graeber's (2011) history of debt could be read as arguing that the *spaces* of modern nation-states are key for facilitating the growth of financial forms of debt. Jan Flaherty and Sarah Banks's (2013) study of debt in poor households in Teesside, UK, shows that it is the intimate and familiar social spaces of the home and neighborhood that shape choices about whether and how families become indebted. Building on these studies,

I want to develop a more precise conceptual vocabulary for thinking about the geography of debt.

DEBT AS TOPOLOGY

The people are taking loans from the banks, so they are dominated by the banks. They can't live a free life. They have to work and to pay off their debts.
—Interview with Abu Tariq, 15 September 2013

Debts are promises to pay in the future. But they are also binds that connect debtors with other people and institutions that have become their creditors. Being bound to an institution like a bank is clearly not a physical connection. Banks do not incarcerate residents (at least not in Palestine). Rather, the sense of capture Abu Tariq evokes in the quote above is more like an invisible bit of string that ties indebted residents to people and institutions that have lent them money. By invisible, I mean to suggest that these binds are real, but immaterial; the invisible bit of string can stretch quite far, and its extensiveness depends on who exactly is bound to whom. For instance, while a debt to a bank can only be enforced within the jurisdictional space of the Occupied Palestinian Territories (something I explore in the next section), a debt to a family member may endure wherever the two parties are in the world (although it may be harder to enforce repayment the farther apart those family members are). These spatial binds are topologies.

There is now an extensive literature on the concept of topology (e.g., J. Allen 2011; Lury, Parisi, and Terranova, 2012; Secor 2013; Harker 2014, 2017; McFarlane 2016; Lata and Minca 2016), to the point where Lauren Martin and Anna Secor (2014, 420) note that "topology . . . is everywhere." As they go on to suggest, topology offers "a way of thinking about relationality, space, and movement beyond metrics, mapping, and calculation" (Martin and Secor 2014, 420). Elsewhere Secor (2013, 431) clarifies: "Topology focuses on the qualitative properties of space (as opposed to the geometric). Topologically speaking, a space is not defined by the distances between points that characterize it when it is in a fixed state, but rather by the characteristics that it maintains in the process of distortion and transformation (bending, stretching, squeezing, but not breaking). Topology deals with surfaces and their properties, their boundedness, orientability, decomposition, and connectivity—that is, sets of properties that retain their relationships under processes of transformation." Thus "topology directs us to consider relationality itself and to question how relations are formed and then endure despite

Chapter Three

conditions of continual change" (Martin and Secor 2014, 431). John Allen (2011, 284) suggests something similar when he describes topology as a particular kind of relational space in which "the gap between 'here' and 'there' is measured less by miles or kilometers and more by the social relationships, exchanges and interactions involved."

What distinguishes debt from other topologies is that the binds created are made through promises quantified using money (Graeber 2011). This claim does not seek to replace temporal understandings of debt (as a present-future relation). Rather, it seeks to augment them, so that debt is conceived as a fully spatial-temporal relation. Munn's (1986, 10) insistence on space-time in her discussion of the creation of value is useful here: "A given type of act or practice forms a spatiotemporal process, a particular *mode* of spacetime. Defined abstractly, the specifically spatiotemporal features of this process consist of relations, such as those of distance, location (including geographical domains of space), and directionality; duration or continuance, succession, timing (including temporal coordination and relative speed of activities)." However, rather than an object that bodies and practices extend, in this book I want to think about space-times as active performances that shape practices and bodies in turn (Massey 2005; Thrift 2006).

DEBT ECOLOGIES

People in Ramallah are indebted to family members, friends, flatmates, banks, municipalities, their landlords, employers, and colleagues. These multiple debt relations do not simply sit alongside each other but become entangled. If debt topologies are like an invisible piece of string, multiple debt topologies are like a cat's cradle, the game in which a piece of string becomes twisted in increasingly complex figurations. On the one hand, each strand retains its specificity. For instance, while direct access to wages ensures the strength and endurance of debt topologies tying people to banks, social closeness enables and maintains debt topologies between relatives or good friends. On the other hand, the interaction between different topological relations can transform those relations, creating stronger connections, disconnections, substitutions, and separations, as I discuss later. These spatial entanglements also bring debt topologies into proximity with other relations.

As a topology, debt does not possess a tangible materiality in the same way that many topological figures are materially impossible in topographic space (Lury, Parisi, and Terranova 2012). However, topologies are co-constituted and become embedded within topographic landscapes (including bodies).

As Martin and Secor (2014) note, topologies and topographies are mutually generative. In this book, I deploy the concept of debt ecologies to think about topological and topographical entanglements. The concept of debt ecologies draws on a substantial body of work that advances relational geographies of money and finance (see for example Leyshon and Thrift 1997; Langley 2008; French, Leyshon, and Thrift 2009; Pike and Pollard 2010), and particularly Andrew Leyshon and colleagues' concept of financial ecologies (Leyshon, Burton, et al. 2004; French, Leyshon, and Wainwright 2011; Lai 2016; Langley and Leyshon 2017). Financial ecologies are "arrangements that emerge and that are more or less reproduceable [*sic*] over time. These processes unfold across space and evolve in relation to geographical difference so that distinctive ecologies of financial knowledge, practices and subjectivities emerge in different places. An ecological approach is not an alternative to a network approach, but constitutive of it, in that the topology of networks is uneven in their connectivity and material outcomes. Thus, some places are better connected to networks than others, while networks differ in their length and durability" (French, Leyshon, and Wainwright 2011, 812).

Financial ecologies are set against approaches in which "geography can all too often be subordinated to the status of mere empirical surface upon which processes of financialization are enacted and inscribed, or abstract, spatial container of socio-economic relations" (French, Leyshon, and Wainwright 2011, 808). The term "ecology" foregrounds the dynamic, constitutive force of space, which may nevertheless lead to durable spatial arrangements (Lai 2016). However, while Shaun French, Andrew Leyshon, and Thomas Wainwright (2011) suggest that financial ecologies add up to a broader financial system (see also Lai 2016), I eschew this more structuralist imaginary in which a single system sits hierarchically above local ecologies. Instead I conceptualize ecologies as entangled, ongoing practical achievements that are both more or less spatially extensive and temporally durable (and thus potentially constitutive of local, urban, national, and transnational spaces). What French, Leyshon, and Wainwright (2011) term the financial system may be thought about conceptually as a complex and very extensive ecology. The fact that ecologies are practical achievements also means that they are—in part—shaped by forms of intentional behavior, and thus political. However, this does not mean that such forms of intentionality determine, or even easily map on to, the resultant ecologies.

The move from financial ecologies to debt ecologies emphasizes that debts are never just financial. As this book continually illustrates, debt topologies among banks, individuals, and families are entangled with other kinds of debt, nonfinancialized forms of obligation, mutuality, and sharing (James 2015; Shipton 2007; Gudeman 2016), and colonial occupation as lived experience (Abourahme 2009; Taraki 2008b). Debt ecologies illustrate how a wide array of social relations co-constitutes the diverse economies present in the world (Gibson-Graham 2014; Lee 2006).

MAKING AND MAINTAINING DEBT TOPOLOGIES
IN RAMALLAH

Debt topologies have been able to expand in Ramallah due to a range of geopolitical and economic factors, primarily different aspects of the Israeli Occupation (including the PA), which have collectively impoverished the majority of people living in Palestine. The concentration of such topologies in Ramallah can be traced to the Oslo Accords, and their reworking of Palestinian political, economic, and social geographies. Debt has become an increasingly popular solution for coping with impoverishment in part because of a range of technical and legislative changes, which have facilitated the growth of banking post-Oslo. However, while these changes create conditions conducive for the growth of credit/debt, debt topologies themselves must be actively made and maintained in the present. This section of the chapter examines the ways in which this happens in Um al Sharayet.

The most common way in which debt topologies are made is through visits to the bank branch. Abu Ghassan, whom we met at the beginning of the book, suggested that the primary reason banks in Palestine wanted to attract customers was to sell them credit. "They just want to attract you to take loans from them . . . They advise you but they try to attract you to take the loan" (interview with Abu Ghassan, 2 June 2013). Residents also reported bank employees visiting them at their place of work and calling them at home to encourage them to take on debt. Such visits mirrored social visits where requests for loans from family members and friends were made. There are also a series of technologies, such as advertising, that encourage and entice families to purchase housing, cars, and consumer goods on credit (see figure 3.1).

Deville (2015) uses the concept of "lure for feeling" to describe the means through which debtors are enticed and cajoled into maintaining an affective connection with their unpaid debts. In a Palestinian context, advertising might be thought about as a lure for feeling that is designed to generate a connection between people and the promise of a "good life" (Berlant 2011). This good life has increasingly been defined in terms of consumerism rather than national liberation (see figures 3.2 and 3.3; Taraki 2008b), and resonates

3.1 Advertisement for
the National Bank credit
card, Ramallah, 2014.
Source: Author.

3.2 Billboard advertising Rawabi housing development, Al Tira, 2014. *Source: Author.*

3.3 Advertisement for consumer goods, Al Bireh, 2014. *Source: Author.*

with post-Oslo attempts to revivify the fantasy of an economic peace (Haddad 2016; Arafeh 2017). As such, this promise needs to be understood in relation to the long-term, ongoing experience of living under Israeli Occupation, and the failure of the Oslo Accords to end it. The way in which people are invited to connect to this good life is through bank debt.

Once established, debt topologies need to be practically maintained too. Moral discourse about honoring one's debts and various technologies of securing debtors' income are key to accomplishing this in Ramallah. In the case of debts to banks, once a debt relation has been established, it is maintained through an automatic repayment system. As part of the debt contract, borrowers are required to allow banks to transfer an amount that can be up to 50 percent of their monthly salary to the bank as soon as that salary is deposited in their account. Debtors who do not have a regular salaried job must name a guarantor who does in order for the debt relation to be established (interview with Rami, 6 August 2015). What is effectively garnishment is a condition of becoming indebted to a bank in Palestine. The ties binding people to their debts are also maintained through the national credit registry (cf. Deville

2015). While there was no evidence of residents self-governing to maintain their credit rating during my research (cf. Lazzarato 2012; Kear 2016), the potential for the credit registry to become a disciplinary mechanism remains.

Debt topologies with family members and friends are maintained by reminders to pay and moral discourse about honoring one's obligations. Frequently these moral discourses (about what is the right thing to do) are articulated as self-imposed social pressures, such as Abu Tariq's claim that "although my brother will forgive me if I don't pay him back, I can't just let him suffer" (interview with Abu Tariq, 31 August 2013). Self-imposed pressures stem from a broader set of understandings about expected forms of behavior, as Shadi explains: "In the social rules, it's considered failing, it's depressing for the person" (interview with Shadi, 26 August 2013). However, in other cases, external pressure is used. Waleed lent money to a colleague who wanted to make Hajj (the Islamic pilgrimage to Mecca) and assured him it was not *haram* (religiously forbidden) if he repaid the debt when he returned. Despite the religious imperative to avoid being a debtor, his colleague did not repay Waleed. Therefore, Waleed used daily reminders to maintain the connection, although even this method is not necessarily effective for enforcing payment. In cases where participants were indebted to individuals who were neither kin nor friends, threats could be used to ensure that debts were honored. Abu Samir, whose hire-purchase arrangement for his flat was discussed at the start of this chapter, told us, "If I don't pay two payments the owner will take the apartment and it will be considered rented [only]. The owner then will give me back my money within two years" (interview with Abu Samir, 1 September 2013).

These moral discourses and practices exist amid a broader discursive sphere where renting property is considered highly insecure, but becoming indebted is judged by many people, particularly older residents, to be wrong. As Abu Samir's mother-in-law put it, "It's better to cook the meal without salt than to borrow it from others" (interview with Abu Samir, 1 May 2013). While residents of Um al Sharayet are acutely aware of the difficulties presented by the high cost of living, many are not necessarily sympathetic toward debtors. In this way, debt itself becomes a form of what Ariel Wilkis (2017) terms moral capital, sustaining, altering, and/or undermining moral hierarchies.

TOPOLOGICAL ENTANGLEMENTS

Debt topologies are entangled with other topological relations. The most common entanglements were with social relationships, particularly kinship ties. For instance, Ziad's brothers loaned him money so he could pay his university tuition and get married. However, entanglements of debt and kinship could take various forms. Ziad suggests that his financial debt affirmed and intensified the social bonds with his brothers.

ZIAD When I told my brothers about this debt, they all supported me . . .

DAREEN So, you depended on the social relationships to solve your financial obligations?

ZIAD Yes, I trusted them. They can't leave me alone. (Interview with Ziad, 26 September 2013)

Other entanglements pull subjects in different directions. Mohammad works in the service sector. Enforced loan repayments to his bank mean that his remaining salary is not enough to meet his monthly expenses. In order to cope he borrows money from friends, but this can create social conflict with them. "I have to pay the [bank] loan and because of that I have to take money from my friends. In addition, problems might occur before I take the money, when I ask my friend to give me money and he says no. That creates a problem between us" (interview with Mohammad, 25 August 2013). While Ziad describes an entanglement in which a debt topology strengthens his bond with his brothers, in Mohammad's case the debt relation weakens his friendship. Mohammad provided another example of the ways in which different topologies can be antagonistically related: "I am talking about personal loan guarantors, and when the person who takes the loan doesn't pay the bank, it will be taken from the guarantor's salary, and the problems will begin between them" (interview with Mohammad, 25 August 2013).

In Ramallah, bank debt is able to exert power over other social relations because it is so tightly sutured to people through the compulsory transfer agreement. In other words, the topological connection is maintained through the specific temporality of the (legal) agreement to become indebted. This agreement, which allows the bank to deduct monthly repayments as soon as someone's salary is deposited, negates the possibility of people refusing to pay. In other words, it negates a particular kind of future (Lazzarato 2012, 2015). The technical apparatus underpinning the bank's electronic ledgers ensures that people cannot intervene in the transfer of their salary from their employer to the bank. Here space and time are not separate but intertwined. The bank maintains a close topological proximity to its debtors through interventions that are temporally almost instantaneous.

However, there are other space-times of debt in Ramallah, which lead to other kinds of entanglement. One relation may be substituted for another. Ali borrowed money from his friend to get married so he would not have to borrow from his father. He suggested that this not only strengthened his friendship, but also allowed him to establish his independence from his father: "I did not want anyone in my family to tell me that I need to pay him back his money! I wanted to avoid family conflicts. I was very young, and they expected me not to succeed in my marriage. I wanted to prove to them that I will not fail and that things will be okay" (interview with Ali, 28 August 2013). In this case, the substitution of one bind for another was a means of loosening Ali's bond with his father. Borrowing money from someone he worked with, rather than from the family he lived with, was mirrored by Ali's move out of his family home to his own apartment when he got married. As with Ziad above, Ali's relations with his friends strengthened as a result of this debt. However, Ali continues to have a good relationship with his father. Fadi, who is an employee, told another story of substitution in which an existing social tie took the place of a debt topology with a bank: "My sister helped me with 70,000 NIS for repairing the house and for the wedding. Also, I tried to borrow from the bank, but they refused . . . So I took money from my sister again" (interview with Fadi, 17 April 2013). Finally, there were also various instances where residents sought to keep debt topologies separate from other relations. "We don't borrow from friends or relatives. It's better not to borrow from them to avoid conflicts" (interview with Im Tariq, 11 June 2013). As Im Tariq notes, separation is often practiced because residents are fully aware of the effect debt ties may have on other relations. These examples of intensification, disconnection, substitution, and separation illustrate the dis/entanglement of relations that are simultaneously economic, social, temporal, and spatial.

TOPOLOGICAL AND TOPOGRAPHIC ENTANGLEMENTS

Debt topologies are also entangled with topographic relations. There are at least three types of topographic spaces that co-constitute and transform debt topologies: topographies that govern the possibility of debt; those that create demand for debt; and topographic spaces in which debt topologies are created. The possibility of becoming indebted to a bank in Palestine is governed in part by the jurisdictional boundaries of the PA, particularly through practices of law and policing (cf. Harvey 1982). Both these practices instantiate and maintain territorial boundaries that demarcate where contracts are enforceable and who will enforce them (Graeber 2011; Lazzarato 2015). These boundaries are largely determined by the Israeli Occupation, particularly through the division of territory and jurisdiction in the Oslo Accords and the construction of the Apartheid Wall from 2003 onward. Since Oslo granted the Palestinian Authority civil jurisdiction in areas A and B, these are the only areas where banks based in Palestine will make mortgage loans. The risk of property destruction in Area C, which is under complete Israeli control, is too great.[1] Furthermore, even within areas A and B, banks will only offer mortgage loans when the property is registered with the Taabo, the land registration agency. The topographic spaces created by Oslo also demarcate the area in which the PMA can regulate (e.g., through enforceable banking laws) and ensure the smooth functioning of the debt economy (e.g., through its credit registry).

Other debt topologies are not governed by these topographies in quite the same way. Familial, community, and work relations determine whether and how debt topologies are created, maintained, and ended between individuals and families. For instance, Im Ghassan borrowed 1,000 JD from her brother in Jordan, something she would not be able to do from a Jordanian bank. This loan was taken to solve her family's "financial crisis," caused by high interest repayments on another loan her husband took from a bank in Palestine. Im Ghassan also told us that while she borrowed money from her brother, her husband's relatives who live in the West Bank do not lend them money (interview with Im Ghassan, 31 August 2013). Even though they share the same topographic space as her husband's family (although this depends on whether Israeli checkpoints that restrict movement in the West Bank are operating), this does not govern the production of debt topologies as it might for bank loans.

Commodities (i.e., topographic objects) such as housing, cars, and household items create the demand or (in the case of housing) need for debt in Ramallah. "Today an apartment costs 100, 120, 150,000 dollars. And the middle classes just have 20,000 dollars. And the poor just have their salaries" (interview with Abu Mahmoud, 28 August 2013). "Apartment prices are very expensive, more than 250,000 dollars. No one can give me such a large amount of money, so the bank is the only source for getting money" (interview with Dina, 24 August 2013). "It is only for the house. I oppose taking loans for marginal needs. I needed to buy a house and I got this house. I can't take loans for other things" (interview with Abu Samir, 1 September 2013). As noted earlier, the demand for housing in Ramallah is itself shaped by more

1 In 2015 the PMA incentivized bank lending to Palestinians living in East Jerusalem by discounting those loans from the bank's capital requirements (Abu Jazar 2015). East Jerusalem was separated from the rest of the West Bank during the Oslo Accords. Although inhabited by Palestinians and claimed as the site of a future Palestinian capital, it is fully controlled by Israel.

extensive colonial practices that have robbed Palestinians of their land and confined them in increasingly smaller enclaves. Another consequence of the frustrated aspirations for a national homeland is the development of a particular kind of urban ethos in Ramallah. Taraki (2008b) argues that the emerging landscape of the city embodies and reflects a desire for a "modern" lifestyle (see also Abourahme 2009), something that will be explored in more depth in the next chapter. Sometimes this modernity has the character of a necessity or a demand too. "You see, ten years ago, social obligations weren't that big. Today if . . . one of my relatives gets married, it will cost me . . . 1–2,000 NIS, besides what I have to buy for my family. When I go to my village, I have to buy clothes for 5,000 NIS, for the wedding and Eid. Ten years ago, people were not like today, where they observe what you wear" (interview with Mohammad, 25 August 2013).

Third, topographic spaces are sites in which debt topologies are formed. Bank branches, workplaces, and homes are all sites where residents of Um al Sharayet have become indebted. After traveling through checkpoints to get to a wedding hall during the second intifada, Abu Omar decided to move from his village to Ramallah, which led to him becoming indebted. "We were invited to a wedding party held in Ramallah, and we endured a lot of the checkpoints. Reaching the city was very complicated, and when we arrived, we were very late and totally exhausted . . . We started thinking of returning to [village name omitted] the moment we arrived! I thought the solution was that we have to move to Ramallah as soon as possible. We took the decision then and there" (interview with Abu Omar, 30 May 2013). After moving to Ramallah, Abu Omar subsequently borrowed money from his two sons-in-law to build a house in his village. Hence, he did not literally become indebted at a checkpoint or in a wedding hall; rather, his process of becoming indebted enfolds both of these spaces and his family's experiences of them. His story illustrates the diversity of topographic spaces in which people can potentially become indebted.

If various topographies govern the possibility of and create demand for debt, as well as becoming sites in which debt topologies are established, then debt topologies also constitute and produce particular topographic spaces in turn. In the Ramallah conurbation, topographies of residence, urban space, and mobility are increasingly being produced through debt topologies.

Debt makes owner-occupation possible for many residents of Ramallah, and debt is also used to fill those homes with televisions, digital devices, power tools, kitchen appliances, and various other commodities. As such, debt has become a key means for enabling some residents to live modern lives (Taraki 2008b). For migrants who have moved from other parts of the West Bank, the modern is most clearly articulated in relation to village of origin. "In the village there is one culture. One village. There is no cultural diversity. In Ramallah there is cultural diversity" (interview with Mohammad, 30 April 2013). "When I come back home, my mum keeps telling me stories about people's lives and activities, and that X did that, and Y wants to do this. In Ramallah, you don't see these things. People don't interfere in your personal life. I can do and say whatever I want . . . Life in a city is better than living in a village. The services are better for sure. Education, medical treatment, entertainment: all of these things are better" (interview with Dina, 5 May 2013).

While research participants rarely used the term "modernity," Ramallah is widely understood as a distinctive space because of its cultural heterogeneity, the relatively superior provision of services and infrastructure, and greater personal freedoms. These characteristics of the urban environment are all partially enabled by topologies of debt, which enable migrants to buy otherwise unaffordable housing in Ramallah and furnish their homes with what are considered the appropriate or necessary accoutrements.

Debt topologies also affect topographic mobilities. Some residents of Um al Sharayet suggest that they are not able to visit their families as often as they would like because of reduced income tied to debt servicing. For instance, Nasser, who has a large mortgage for his apartment and smaller debts to friends, visits his hometown very infrequently now. This has affected his children's mobility, which in turn has transformed their social connections with their extended family.

On Saturday, I visited Tubas, my town, in order to see my brothers, my mother and my sisters. I spent one day there, but my sons didn't go with me. This plays a critical role in educating them that the obligations will be less for them. Not for me, for them. Because they are thinking in a different way, the new generation. They think that the obligations of life are becoming too hard. It's difficult. For this reason, they are not taking care of these obligations, as before. For this reason, the obligations will become less, for them. But for me, no. I think it's still the same. (Interview with Nasser, 10 September 2013)

CONCLUSION

This chapter has emphasized the active role space plays in co-constituting debt, building on the argument made in chapter 1. The constitutive force of debt space in the Occupied West Bank includes not only things like territorial banking regulations, laws, and policing (Christophers 2013; Dodd 2014), but also the lived intensities of home, family, neighborhood, and migrant mobilities. This chapter has shown empirically how debt topologies are entangled with other topological and topographic spaces to create debt ecologies. Exploring these entanglements in detail illustrates how debt ecologies are not simply financial, but also geopolitical, economic, and cultural. Accounts of indebtedness in Um al Sharayet demonstrate how debt ecologies are dynamic and generative spatial arrangements, as the interaction of different topologies and topographies transforms those relations. In conclusion, I want to discuss the generative force of debt ecologies at greater length.

Debt topologies are a specific means of dis/connection, which in turn shapes topographic space. Much has been written about the topographic fragmentation of space in the Occupied Territories, with comparisons being made to the Apartheid regime in South Africa through use of the term "Bantustan" (Gregory 2004; Falah 2005; Farsakh 2005a; Taraki 2008a; Halper 2009). Palestinians frequently refer to the Ramallah conurbation itself as a bubble (Rabie 2013). This term describes the topographies of inequality that have developed between different spatial enclaves within the Occupied Territories, which have led to Ramallah becoming wealthier and more isolated from other cities (Taraki 2008a; Abourahme 2009). Debt relations reveal attendant topologies of inequality, particularly in terms of unequal connections between different places (Rabie 2013). Many indebted residents of Um al Sharayet are migrants who have moved from other parts of the West Bank to live in Ramallah, while maintaining strong connections with their families elsewhere. Stories like Nasser's at the end of the previous section provide evidence that some of these family relationships are waning. Such forms of disconnection are different from, but intertwined with, the topographies that make Ramallah a Bantustan and/or a bubble. For instance, spatial barriers like checkpoints that prevent physical movement become entangled with limited finances and waning social relationships with family and friends. However, many residents' commitment to maintaining their family relations and their desire for green space (of which there is very little in Ramallah) actively work against the topographic limits to their mobility. Ramallah's reputation as an affluent city, something that debt has partially enabled, is another topology that connects migrant families such as Waleed's with relatives in other places. "Of course, they think I have a lot of money. That's the first thing. Because it's not easy to buy a $100,000 apartment to live in, when the average salary for an employee is $1,000 or less . . . So, the first thing they think is that you have a lot of money. So, they start to borrow money" (interview with Waleed, 5 May 2013).

Debt ecologies are generative, transforming the relations that co-constitute them. The growth of debt in Ramallah has clearly enabled financialization, understood as "the growing power of money and finance in contemporary processes of economic, political and social change" (French, Leyshon, and Wainwright 2011, 814) and the creation of financial subjects (Kear 2016; Langley 2008). The necessity of borrowing to afford housing in Ramallah, and the extensive efforts of the PMA to ensure that more Palestinians have bank accounts, are two ways in which financial subjects are being created in this context. Mohammad's account of debt-related problems with friends and guarantors is an example of how the growing power of money can often be damaging or destructive. However, it is important to recognize that while these examples illustrate the power of debt ecologies to shape other types of social, economic, and political change, this is a contingent rather than necessary outcome. As Fadi's loan from his sister and Im Tariq's refusal to borrow from friends and relatives show, debt ecologies are also reworked and/or refused by other obligations, commitments, and desires.

Many existing accounts of financialization and the transformational power of debt (e.g., Lazzarato 2012, 2015; Ross 2017) ignore the practices through which debt ecologies are both made and entangled. This not only simplifies what is actually a more complex state of affairs but is also politically disabling. Already existing alternatives to debt and moments of refusal are excellent starting points for those concerned about the growing power of finance. However, such moments never appear in accounts that narrate the spread of finance as though it were an economic tsunami (cf. Ong 2007). There is also a geographical dimension to this problem. Working through and from Ramallah illustrates how debt ecologies are entangled with specific (geo)political, social, and cultural practices. This is much harder to achieve in analyses of debt that remain tied to so-called global financial centers and their environs. Even concepts such as variegated financialization (Pike and Pollard 2010; French, Leyshon, and Wainwright 2011; Lai 2016), which account for how "distinct socio-spatial settings, industry structures and regulatory contexts shape how individuals and households are incorporated unevenly into global financial networks" (Lai 2016, 29), are inadequate. In this theoretical frame, global financial networks still sit above the fray, providing a context of contexts. Instead, financialization must be thought about as something that only ever occurs in relation to various other processes, and thus not something that can capture entire empirical contexts and their complex entanglements of practices. This in turn means that global financial networks are not a coherent system governing and engaging with other practices (even if in different ways), but rather diverse spatialities whose coherence is an ongoing practical achievement—not so much a world, but rather one powerful act of worlding among many (Ananya Roy and Ong 2011). This understanding resonates with the definition of debt ecologies as entangled practical achievements that are both more or less durable in time and differently extensive spatially. This argument is pushed further in the next chapter, by expanding the understanding of the city as a debt ecology.

thinking debt through the city

"EVERYTHING COMES FROM OUTSIDE RAMALLAH"

The people from the North and the people from '48 are benefiting much more than the people of Ramallah itself.
—Interview with Ola, 17 August 2013

In Ramallah you're living on a rock. Believe me, it's a rock; a rock that doesn't have anything in it. As a city, it's just buildings . . . Everything comes from outside Ramallah. If all the other cities refused to give Ramallah food, everyone would die of hunger.
—Interview with Waleed, 5 May 2013

The previous chapter began to foreground the distinctive role Ramallah plays in the spatiality of debt in Palestine. This was also a topic that residents discussed frequently. In some cases, residents positioned the city itself as either a creditor, as Ola does above, or a debtor, as Waleed does. What unites such accounts is a conception of obligation that is much broader than bank credit/debt. Both of these narratives emerge from the geographies in which residents of Um al Sharayet are entangled. These geographies enfold their everyday lives, the Israeli state as the primary colonial force shaping Palestinian life and land, the would-be nation-state of the Palestinian Authority (PA), and international donors. This chapter expands the geographic scope of the book's main argument by focusing on the relations between debt, obligation, and urban space. This is accomplished by building on the grounded theory approach discussed in the introduction that theorizes from and through the everyday life of debtors (cf. James 2015; Deville 2015). The chapter develops two interrelated arguments with regard to cities and debt.

First, in many existing studies linking cities and debt, debt is understood in purely financial terms. Drawing on anthropological work that examines how financial debts are tied up with other forms of obligation (Schuster 2014; James 2015; Kar 2018), this chapter broadens conceptualizations of debt beyond finance. A range of debts and obligations intersect and encompass the urban. The chapter argues that focusing only on financial debt (through municipal financing or mortgage markets for instance) risks missing this expanded geography. Building on residents' representations of the city, I argue that Ramallah is obligated to other time-spaces for its money, culture, and urban imaginaries. Ramallah can be said to owe other space-times, even if money, culture, and imaginaries are flows rather than easily locatable objects. They move, and in relation to the city can be thought about through forms of centrifugal (away from a center) and centripetal (toward a center) motion. In Ramallah, centripetal movements of money, culture, and imaginaries exceed centrifugal movements. Residents' discussions of imaginative geographies also draw attention to their performative power (Gregory 2004). In other words, the relations embodied in flows of money, culture, and imagination are productive, playing a key role in co-constituting the contemporary city through unequal relationships with other places within and beyond Palestine.

If everyday understandings of the relationship between debt and cities broaden our understanding of debt's spatiality, the second contribution of this chapter is to explore how this conceptual frame impacts how we think about urban space. Urban governments play an important role in shaping cities, as do mortgage markets and housing prices. However, to reduce the urban to municipal governance, mortgage markets, or the aggregation of households evacuates cities of much of what makes them lively and interesting (Amin and Thrift 2002; A. Simone 2016). Urbanism, as Louis Wirth (1938) famously put it, is a way of life. This way of life is diffuse, emerging through residents' practices, objects, gestures, bodies, and feelings, as much as it does through policy, law, policing, and markets (A. Simone 2014). Furthermore, as Wirth himself stressed, an urban way of life is not limited to the terrain of cities (i.e., municipal boundaries). Cities are assemblages that concentrate flows originating in other places, while impacting areas and populations elsewhere in all sorts of ways (Lefebvre 2003; McFarlane 2011a, 2011b). This chapter pushes such understandings of the urban by thinking about highly uneven and asymmetric urban relations as debts and obligations. As noted, for many of the people who participated in this research, Ramallah takes more than it gives, or borrows more than it repays. It relies on external investments of money and ideas, while being constituted by people from other places. The city's growth comes at the expense of other parts of Palestine. Consequently, I develop the case for thinking about urban space as a series of asymmetric obligations. This approach builds on existing conceptualizations of the city as an assemblage (McFarlane 2011a, 2011b; Weszkalnys 2013), by demonstrating how this theoretical tool kit is well placed to examine urban inequality (contrary to arguments made by some of its critics). In the research context, this frame augments urban imaginaries of Ramallah as a bubble, Bantustan, and/or enclave (Farsakh 2005a; Taraki 2008a; Abourahme 2009) with an account of the relational geographies through which the city is both enriched and rendered vulnerable to its multiple outsides. Assemblage also offers a better understanding of the differently extensive debt topologies that create specific urban debt ecologies such as Ramallah.

DEBT AND URBAN SPACE

There are various extant approaches to understanding the spatiality of debt through the city. Stasavage's (2015) historical work foregrounds the role city-states played in enabling the emergence of public credit in medieval Europe. As noted in chapter 3, he argues that it was precisely the compact size of cities, and the political dominance of a merchant oligarchy within them, that ensured that city-states could enforce debt servicing and prevent default. When territorial monarchies in France and Spain first developed public credit, they did so by adopting the system developed in autonomous city-states. In contrast, the creation of sovereign debt through the establishment of a central bank in England was initially an exception, while still relying on the relatively small territorial extent of that particular nation-state.

While nation-state governments and central banks now control sovereign debt, the creation and circulation of credit/debt relations by cities have continued through to the present day. In the United States, for instance, municipal bond markets have become increasingly visible after a series of bankruptcies, most notably that of Detroit in 2013 (Peck 2012). The roots of these defaults can be found in the 1980s when nonlocal institutional investors replaced commercial banks and households as the primary purchasers of municipal bonds (Hackworth 2007, 28). Such bonds became attractive to (and often aggressively pursued by) institutional investors because historically cities have low default rates and are effectively underwritten by the central state (Bow 2016). The rise of institutional investors exposed cities to the power of ratings agencies and the forms of fiscal governance they demand (Hackworth 2007). Default frequency rose after 2008 as both property tax receipts and federal funding declined (Peck 2012), and the number of cities going bankrupt reached a historic peak in 2013 (Moody's 2017, 7). This has had severe implications for urban life, as bankrupt municipalities and those deemed at risk of bankruptcy have been forced to adopt punishing austerity measures that have resulted in cuts to public services and public sector employment (Peck 2012, 635–37). Jamie Peck suggests that in post–2008 crisis America, only a "fortunate minority of cities" have access to the credit markets and are able to "fashion their own financial arrangements, independently of Washington and the state capitals" (Peck 2012, 629).

In the UK, city governments have also come under scrutiny because of their debts. Councils have borrowed increasingly large sums of money from banks in the form of LOBO (Lender Option, Borrower Option) loans, despite legal prohibitions that prevent local governments from entering into swaps or derivatives contracts (Debt Resistance UK 2017). Many councils have recently made cuts to public services to ensure that they can continue making repayments on these complex debt contracts (Bow 2016). Activist organization Debt Resistance UK (2017) argues that local councils are forced to become increasingly indebted because austerity policies have directly reduced their budgets and their access to the national government's Public Works Loan Board. However, the specific forms of debt taken have also contributed to reducing their budgets, as tax receipts are swallowed up in servicing high interest repayments.

In addition to city governments, property construction and mortgage markets are another important means through which urban geographies of debt are produced. David Harvey (2008) has long argued that debt financing has been a crucial mechanism for enabling capitalist urban (re)development since Haussmann's rebuilding of Paris in the nineteenth century. Urbanization in turn has played an important role in sustaining capitalism by absorbing the surplus product that capitalists produce in their search for profits. Since the 1970s, housing as a form of capital investment has significantly increased, leading to rapid inflation of prices and the need for more people to take larger mortgages. This transformation has had distinctly gendered and racialized dimensions. The expansion of mortgage markets in many Western countries was partially achieved through the extension of credit/debt to women and ethnic minorities (Allon 2014). Studies of redlining—the prevention of largely inner-city residents from accessing formal forms of credit/debt based on the ethnic and class composition of those places (see Aalbers 2009 for overview)—demonstrate how mortgage debt has reflected and reiterated the geographies of racial exclusion that shaped U.S. cities during the previous century. Subprime loans continued these practices with a twist, by developing new forms of more expensive mortgage debt targeted at previously disenfran-chised borrowers (Wyly et al. 2009; Allon 2014). Capitalist urban (re)devel-opment has co-constituted credit/debt in turn. Paul Langley (2008) argues that suburban housing and lifestyles in Anglo America have been key for the growth of more extensive financial markets since the 1970s. In addition to the use of mortgage payments to create debt-based financial products such as derivatives, suburban residents have been shaped into financial subjects by disciplinary mechanisms such as credit scoring (see also Kear 2016).

Alan Walks (2013) uses statistical data to argue that city size is an impor-tant determinant of the types of debt that dominate in different places. His re-search in Canada shows that higher housing prices in larger (so-called global) cities lead to more mortgage debt, while consumer debt is more prominent in smaller cities. His research also traces significant variations between neigh-borhoods within cities, with racialized immigrants often bearing higher debt burdens in Canada's global cities (D. Simone and Walks 2019), while neigh-borhoods on the outskirts have higher household debt burdens because of the costs of automobility.

There are also studies that use qualitative data to connect debt and urban space through lived experience. Kavita Datta and Camille Aznar (2019) argue that London as a global city enables immigrants to escape from (unpaid) debts elsewhere but also forces them into new debt relations. Migrants (re) create and utilize credit/debt institutions in London, such as rotating savings and credit associations (ROSCAS), when they cannot access formal banking services. These are not simply transported to London but shaped by, and em-bedded within, the translocal spaces of the city and experiences of financial exclusion there. Sohini Kar's (2018) research on microfinance in the informal settlements of Kolkata illustrates how a relative abundance of space within densely inhabited neighborhoods can become one means of accessing credit: "Women with larger houses receive loans not because they have larger in-comes, but because they provide the space to do so" (Kar 2018, 117). The provi-sion of space is folded into the gendered power relations of domestic life and labor, as women's ability to host microfinance group meetings in their homes is determined by their husband's need to prepare for work and their children's need to study. This competition for space has the potential to transform both familial relations and social relations outside the home: "Women are no lon-ger just neighbors, but responsible for each others' creditworthiness by pro-viding space and time to attend the meetings" (Kar 2018, 118). The (thick) social ties that emerge in such densely inhabited neighborhoods also shape debt in other ways. Microfinance companies transfer their officers between borrower groups every three to six months to limit their social relations with borrowers and any unofficial transactions that may result (Kar 2018, 96–97; see also Schuster 2014).

The insights offered by the existing literature provide a useful starting point for thinking through debt and urban space. Different forms of credit/debt spanning municipal finance, mortgage markets, and forms of consumer credit are contingently related to different kinds of urban space (e.g., inner city vs. suburban) at different points in time. Building on this understanding, the next section begins by tracing the ways in which money circulates through, and becomes embedded in, Ramallah in the form of ongoing debt relations. However, as residents of Um al Sharayet make clear, these ties are often entangled in other obligatory relations.

MONEY

Ninety percent of Ramallah is mortgaged to the banks.
—Interview with Ahmad, 12 August 2013

Ahmad is a public sector employee who moved to Ramallah during the second intifada. His hyperbolic suggestion that 90 percent of the city is mortgaged to banks is not statistically accurate. However, his sentiment illustrates how residents perceive the built environment in Ramallah, particularly housing, as increasingly bought on credit. As elsewhere in the world, financial forms of debt have enabled both the construction of residential and office buildings and, in the form of mortgages, the purchase of apartments and houses. Across the Occupied Territories, money borrowed for "real estate and construction" increased sixfold between 2008 and 2016 (PMA 2017a). Loans used to buy cars and vehicles show a similar rate of increase—almost 500 percent—in the same period. As noted in chapter 1, almost two-thirds of all recorded debt contracts with banks were registered in Ramallah by 2016 (see figure 1.1). In Palestine, debt is not simply an urban phenomenon, but one largely located in Ramallah. The manifestation of this debt in topographic space, most visibly through the growth of apartment buildings and increased traffic congestion, is something the city's residents register in their daily lives. "People will get new cars and new houses but in reality they don't own them. Many people now have new cars but are they rich? Of course, they are not rich, but they live like rich people. They have new cars and new houses. For instance, in [my village] there are no old cars like in the 1980s. They are all new. Most of the people bought them through bank loans" (interview with Ali, 28 August 2013).

The transformation of the built environment in Ramallah mirrors to a certain extent the changes Harvey (2008) describes, as property becomes the key means through which capital ensures its continued circulation. Banks in Palestine began to extend increasingly large amounts of credit when they were forced to limit the percentage of deposits they could move abroad by the PMA. The growth of financial debt has also changed the material landscape of the city in less easily discernible ways. For instance, medical facilities are sustained, in part, through credit money. Residents such as Khaled and Abu Ghassan both took loans for medical emergencies. The proliferation of private schools in Ramallah has, in part, been supported by credit money. A number of participants' school-age children were sent to private schools, where aspirations for a better life through education are paid for with debt (cf. James 2015). These examples also begin to point to the importance of family relations as conduits through which credit money flows. While numerous ethnographic studies have explicated the entanglement of financial credit/debt relations with other obligatory relations (e.g., Han 2012; Bear 2015; James 2015), these insights have yet to inform urban studies of debt. Understanding obligatory practices and ties is important because the resultant geographies, particularly those that emerge through family and kinship ties, have shaped Ramallah as much as financial forms of debt.

Remittances

As noted in chapter 1, the neighborhood of Um al Sharayet is constituted by refugees who have moved out of camps and families who have migrated to Ramallah for work. A common stereotype about these migrants is that they work in Ramallah but spend their income elsewhere. "All my neighbors from the North buy their basic needs from other cities, and some of my colleagues who are from the North buy their needs from their cities before they come to work" (interview with Abu Omar, 31 August 2013).

> OLA They work here and buy their consumer goods and all their needs from their towns at much cheaper prices . . . The people from the North and the people from '48 are benefiting much more than the people of Ramallah itself.
>
> IM ALA I told you, they work in one city and spend their money in another city. (Interview with Ola and Im Ala, 17 August 2013)

Abu Omar and Ola and Im Ala are themselves migrants who were born in other parts of Palestine. They all regularly visit their families, who live elsewhere. However, despite not describing their own practices, they suggest that other migrants do behave in the manner described above. This urban geographical imagination envisions Ramallah as a source from which migrants strategically extract wealth (in the form of wages). This is then spent in other parts of the West Bank where prices are (said to be) cheaper. The (semi)-regular trips migrants make to their original homes are understood as an embodied form of capital flight, which impoverishes the city of Ramallah and its people. The city is implicitly positioned as a creditor to these other places, particularly towns and villages in the north of the West Bank, which are indebted to Ramallah for their incomes.

There was certainly some evidence to support this geographical imagination. The Ramallah municipality estimates that 30,000 people leave Ramallah at the beginning of each weekend to travel north (interview with Moussa Haddid, 12 May 2014). One example is Dina, a single woman working in a public sector job and sharing an apartment with four other single women, who visited or "returned to" her village in Tulkarem every weekend. She was the sole income provider for her mother and younger sister who were living there, save for a small amount of income her family generated from small-scale farming (interview with Dina, 5 May 2013). Dina gave her mother US$300 every month, and sometimes bought vegetables and meat in Ramallah for her mother and sister before visiting (interview with Dina, 21 May 2013). She was the sole income provider because her father had died, her mother did not perform paid work, and her unmarried sister was in school full-time. Dina's remittances were enabled by the relatively good salary she earned working in a job that was only available in Ramallah. This spatial transfer of money in turn enabled her to continue living in Ramallah: "I feel I'm responsible for my family. I support them financially in particular, and because of that they don't try to persuade me to move back" (interview with Dina, 5 May 2013). Not everyone who works in Ramallah is as well paid as Dina. Her flatmate Huda worked two jobs when she first moved to Ramallah. This meant she could give her mother, who lived in the Bethlehem governorate, 700 NIS each month. However, when Huda began working one job only (in the private sector), she could no longer support her parents regularly, and gave them money only when they asked for it.

Dina's support for her family was also premised on her gender and her unmarried status. Hiba, who also lived with Dina and Huda, provided a monthly income for her mother, who was living in a village near Jenin. Although some of her siblings had jobs, Hiba was the sole provider because she was female and unmarried.

DAREEN You have two sisters in the house, so they have to pay.

HIBA They don't care! . . . Both are married. One lives abroad, and the other lives in Ramallah. Sometimes they said we will support and give 500 NIS each month, but they didn't follow through. Hopeless! (Interview with Hiba, 21 May 2013)

While our research involved far fewer unmarried males who worked in Ramallah, one participant who fit this category, Ahmad, also provided regular support for his family, who lived in the Jenin area. While quantitative research is needed to make representative claims on this topic, qualitative research reveals nuances in relation to marital status and gender, and how they affect the movement of money. These are important to note because they begin to show how the geographies of obligations that infuse Ramallah are asymmetric. The potential impact of being married or single on flows of money in and out of Ramallah becomes clearer when the accounts of married couples are included. Migrant participants who were married and had children transferred money to other places irregularly. Instead, they tended to support relatives elsewhere through irregular cash gifts, purchasing specific commodities on their behalf and paying off bills and emergency medical expenses. In one case, Abu Tamer told us he did his shopping outside Ramallah (as per the stereotype about migrants), but this was more expensive than shopping in Ramallah. This practice was one of familial care rather than economic rationality. "Usually when we go to [my village], we buy everything we need from my aunt's supermarket there. My aunt is a single woman and she owns a supermarket. So, I buy everything from her place to try and help her" (interview with Abu Tamer, 24 June 2013).

The relative paucity of money transfers made by married couples with children complicates the narrative of Ramallah as creditor. Unlike Abu Tamer, all other research participants who had migrated to Um al Sharayet told us they shopped in Ramallah for food and consumer goods. Furthermore, land or other property in Ramallah is often purchased with money earned elsewhere, usually by family members working abroad. Many residents, including Ali, Abu Usama, Waleed, and Abu Mahmoud, told us versions of the following story: "My brother was working in Saudi Arabia and he sent money. All of them sent money. They were working in Saudi Arabia and the situation was good. His share was the other apartment and the downstairs because he sent a lot of money" (interview with Ibrahim, 1 May 2013). Remittances flow into Ramallah and become embedded there in the material spaces of housing. As noted in chapter 2, relatives working in the Gulf were a key source of income for many families in the Occupied Territories during the 1970s and 1980s.

Many long-standing residents of Um al Sharayet were able to buy land and/ or construct housing with such money. Family ties in the United States have enabled a more limited number of residents to do the same.

Family members working elsewhere provided financial support in other ways. In some cases, migrants received minor but crucial help when they moved to Ramallah. Dina's mother, for instance, bought her clothing and bed linens when she first moved. Relatives also gave money when they visited and could be called upon in times of emergency. Nasser, a married participant with adolescent children, relies on his brother in Saudi Arabia. "I just have my brother in Saudi Arabia, and sometimes I ask him to send me money. This happens every two or three years. Not every year, not every month. It only happens if I have a situation and I need more money. I'll call him for this reason and ask him to send money to me" (interview with Nasser, 20 June 2013). Many of these transfers were said to be gifts rather than debts, and thus were not repaid financially. Instead, gifts create harder to quantify nonmonetary obligations about expected forms of behavior (Mauss 1954). In particular, gifting practices are a key means through which obligatory circuits are established and maintained (Mauss 1954; Munn 1986). The gifts residents of Um al Sharayet received demonstrate migrants' ongoing intimate connection with family members living elsewhere. Migrant residents also reported taking gifts with them when visiting their families. The frequency of these visits varied significantly. While Dina visited her family every week, Abu and Im Omar were unable to visit their extended families because they live in Gaza. However, once residents were married, in nearly every case they did not lend money to relatives, and they reported visiting more infrequently. Instead, like Nasser above, they tended to be borrowers. As far as money was concerned, their obligatory relations were decidedly asymmetrical.

To briefly summarize and return to the conceptual frame of the chapter, flows of money embodied in family relations are captured in discourses about Ramallah as creditor. However, such narratives are nuanced by closer examination of migrants' practices, which often reveal the opposite to also be true. In the daily lives of Um al Sharayet's migrant residents, more money enters Ramallah than leaves. Ramallah is not simply a creditor, but also, simultaneously, a debtor. Positioning Ramallah in this way draws on an understanding of urban space as a series of centripetal and centrifugal forces, absorbing and spitting things out. Henri Lefebvre describes this geography through the concept of implosion-explosion: "The tremendous concentration (of people, activities, wealth, goods, objects, instruments, means, and thought) of urban reality and the immense explosion, the projection of numerous, disjunct fragments (peripheries, suburbs, vacation homes, satellite towns) into space" (Lefebvre 2003,

14). Such ideas have been given greater detail and precision through the concept of assemblage. Colin McFarlane (2011a, 2011b) uses assemblage to think about cities as dynamic spaces in which different practices come together (or not) to co-constitute urban life. As Ben Anderson et al. (2012, 184) argue, "The form of assemblages is not determined by some external social, biological or physical force, but is rather contingently determined by the capacities of the parts that make up an assemblage." Such an approach helps us think about cities beyond their municipal and topographic boundaries. Instead, assemblage points to the dynamic and extrovert way in which urban life is constituted by and through series of movements and encounters between people, objects, money, and ideas. What happens within each urban assemblage is (contingently) determined by the interaction of elements that come together in that specific space-time (Massey 2005). McFarlane (2011a, 2011b) is clear that this approach to urban studies is committed to exploring the highly uneven power relationships that emerge within cities, and between cities and their outsides. However, the concept of assemblage has been read as glossing over urban inequalities and injustices (see Brenner, Madden, and Wachsmuth 2011). Such a reading is inaccurate and ungenerous. Nevertheless, it may be possible to give greater prominence to the inequalities at the heart of urban assemblages. I do so here by thinking Ramallah as asymmetrically obligated. This in turn requires an expanded scope with regard to the temporal and spatial movements of money.

Investments

As in the past, Ramallah relies on money generated in villages in the Ramallah governorate, other places in the Occupied Territories and the '48 territories, and other countries (see chapter 2). One way in which residents understand such reliance is by positioning Ramallah as indebted. This geographical imagination needs to be understood within ongoing practices of colonial occupation and broader patterns of de-development discussed in the previous chapters. Therefore, this section examines Ramallah's metaphorical debit column in more detail.

Perhaps the earliest source of outside investment in the Ramallah conurbation came from the original residents of Ramallah and Al Bireh who migrated to America. The term "original resident" refers to families who owned the land in the villages prior to 1948. Taraki (2013) suggests that many male villagers traveled to America at the turn of the twentieth century to work, and then returned to Palestine once they had earned their fortune. Later migrants, who traveled to the United States after 1948, tended not to return. Some of these international migrants have been responsible for constructing the apartment buildings and wedding halls found in Um al Sharayet. The Al Bireh Society (2017) and the American Federation of Ramallah Palestine (2017), diaspora associations based in the United States, also provide a coordinated form of charitable giving to both the municipalities and their residents through targeted schemes that focus on medical, educational, and cultural programs.

Families in Jerusalem and the '48 territories have also invested in Ramallah. Businesses were opened in Ramallah because their owners could not do so in nearby Jerusalem. Palestinians living in the '48 territories visit to benefit from cheaper prices in Ramallah.

> Why do people from outside Ramallah come here to the parks and restaurants? Why don't they go to Jerusalem? Look at Al Aqsa on the second day of Eid. You will see it is empty. Everyone goes to Ramallah and '48 only. The Ramallah people go outside Ramallah, and the strangers come here. Even Jews come to Ramallah, the village of Ramallah . . . People from Jerusalem come here every day to study at the Birzeit University, and to work. People from Jerusalem have shops here in Ramallah. Even though they have many shops in Jerusalem city center, because of the harassment they open shops in Ramallah. (Interview with Ibrahim, 22 August 2013)

The imagined impact of so-called outsiders is so significant that some participants suggested that Ramallah's growing service sector is only for such people, and not for the city's residents themselves. "The people of Ramallah don't go to restaurants. The people from other cities go to restaurants when they visit the city. It is better to eat at home rather in restaurants" (interview with Abu Omar, 31 August 2013). Palestinians who live in the city but work elsewhere also bring money into the city. While the number of Palestinians working in Israel has significantly declined since the Oslo Accords, particularly during the second intifada (see Farsakh 2005b), 48,000 permits to work in Israel were issued in 2013 when research for this project was conducted (Harel 2013). This number was predicted to rise to 87,000 by the end of 2017 (Kashti 2017). Such workers continue to earn higher wages than those working in the West Bank. While this data is not spatially disaggregated, anecdotal evidence suggests that at least some of these permit holders live in Ramallah, and thus they embody another conduit through which money enters the city.

Since the mid-1990s, many sources of external investment have rapidly diminished. In addition to the decline of better-paid work in Israel (Farsakh 2005b), there are also fewer opportunities to work in the Gulf states. This is due not only to the legacy of Arafat's support for Saddam Hussein during the 1991 invasion of Kuwait (see chapter 2), but also to the increasing preference in Gulf states for cheaper and politically disenfranchised migrant laborers from non–Arabic speaking countries (Ulrichsen 2015). Immigration to the United States also became significantly harder after the terror attacks on 11 September 2001. These changes are important because they align with the rise of another source of monetary income—the donor economy.

In 1994, foreign aid per capita to the Occupied Palestinian Territories was US$350 and fell during the Oslo years to just under US$200 in 1999. By 2009 it had increased to US$760 (Hever 2010). Given the high birthrate of the Palestinian population, this represents a huge increase in total aid during the first decade of the twenty-first century. However, per capita figures disguise the uneven distribution of this aid. Much of it is for PA salaries, and most PA jobs are in Ramallah. In 2013, the PA's total budgetary expenditure was US$3.25 billion. Of this, US$1.8 billion, or 51 percent, was spent on wages and salaries (PMA 2017c). Ramallah's recent and rapid growth is thus intimately tied to the growth of donor aid, which subsidizes incomes for the PA's own workforce, as well as the capital for the construction of the new ministry buildings since 2010. This reliance was vividly illustrated following Hamas's victory in the 2006 parliamentary elections and the subsequent economic siege, when international donors withdrew aid and brought the Palestinian Authority to a standstill. Many private donors also directly employ those working in Ramallah's large NGO sector (Dana 2013).

Conceptually, this aid is a gift (Mauss 1954), and thus another means of creating nonmonetary obligations about expected forms of behavior (Haddad 2016). As Shir Hever (2010) argues, aid not only subsidizes the Israeli Occupation, but also limits the type and scope of possible development projects. Aid conditionality means that the PA is not simply financially beholden to donors but obligated to behave—to govern—in particular ways. For example, a press release announcing the donation of €252.5 million of aid from the European Commission to the PA in 2016 included the demand that "Palestinian institutions must continue to grow stronger, become more transparent, more accountable and more democratic" (European Commission 2016, n.p.). Specific donors often support specific ministries and even specific units within those ministries. Many residents see donor influence extending not only to the policies of the PA, but to Ramallah's very existence, given the role of the PA in creating Ramallah as a center of employment. Consider Ahmad's indictment: "We left our land to work here for 2,000 NIS [a month]. I don't know if it is a conscious decision, or they simply don't know what they're planning or doing, because they evacuate people from all over the West Bank and crush them into Ramallah . . . If Israel decided to finish the Authority, everyone will

go home . . . This a political decision that depends on the donors and countries that want the Authority to stay" (interview with Ahmad, 12 August 2013).
The "they" in the second sentence is ambiguous, and could refer to PA decision makers, Israel as the sovereign power in Palestine, or international donors whose aid and influence shape the PA's very existence. In many ways,
Ahmad elides the PA with Israel and donor countries, illustrating how the
current Occupation is spread (albeit asymmetrically) across these different
actors. His suggestion that the employment the PA provides sustains Ramallah is amplified by Waleed's characterization of the city. "Believe me, water,
food, everything comes from outside Ramallah. If all the other cities refused
to give Ramallah food, everyone would die of hunger. There's nothing to support Ramallah, nothing here" (interview with Waleed, 5 May 2013). While it is
difficult to produce Ramallah's balance sheet in quantitative monetary terms,
residents of Um al Sharayet such as Ahmad and Waleed understand the city as
asymmetrically obligated to the point of dependency. The mobilities of family
resources and donor aid—resources generated by the labor of people living elsewhere—go a long way toward enabling urban inhabitation in Ramallah. While
money earned in Ramallah moves to other parts of the West Bank through
family relations, in all likelihood these outgoings are dwarfed by the foreign aid,
diasporic investments, and support given by residents of Jerusalem and the '48
territories and by residents' relatives in other parts of the West Bank, the Arab
world, and beyond. However, residents' accounts of Ramallah as debtor exceed
a financial frame. As the next section argues, Ramallah also owes other places,
in the West Bank and further afield, for what I have termed its culture. I use
this term to indicate ways of life or being that are specific to the city.

CULTURE

Ramallah–Al Bireh–Beitunia is a city largely constituted by refugees, migrants, and their family members. The conurbation has grown rapidly since
Oslo, partially because PA and NGO-sector jobs have drawn people there from
other parts of the West Bank. While urbanization is often understood as a process enabled by rural-to-urban mobilities (Wirth 1938), in Ramallah this type
of migration is responsible for the city's growth only at certain points in its
history (cf. S. Tamari 2008, 22–23). As Taraki (2008b) has argued, the influx of
refugees in 1948 from coastal cities—particularly Jaffa—was the most important cause of Ramallah's most significant population growth (see also Taraki
and Giacaman 2006). As part of this urban-to-urban migration, middle-class
refugees were, and still are, responsible for many of the businesses in the

Chapter Four

current city center. And poorer refugees who were peasant farmers prior to 1948 have provided much of the city's labor (see chapter 2). The impact of these involuntary migrants on Ramallah's urban transformation is not simply historical either. The refugee camps established after 1948, while initially located at some distance from the centers of Ramallah and Al Bireh, have now been surrounded by, but not politically integrated with, the urban fabric of the conurbation (Abourahme 2011; Woroniecka-Krzyzanowska 2017). Furthermore, the bodies and social relations of these refugees have increasingly exceeded the spaces of the camps through both work and residence. As previously noted, the neighborhood of Um al Sharayet was largely established in the late 1970s and early 1980s by refugees buying land and moving out of camps, particularly nearby Al Amari. In some cases, these longer-standing residents distinguish themselves from and harbor various prejudices against more recent work migrants, who have moved to Um al Sharayet from other parts of the West Bank since 2000. Abu Mahmoud, a retired worker who moved out of Al Amari Camp after buying land in Um al Sharayet many decades ago, provides one example. "We were working and everything was okay before. The newcomers benefited more, while for us it was bad. For us as contractors, our situation was good in the past, and we worked more. Those who came from outside Ramallah got more chances" (interview with Abu Mahmoud, 14 August 2013). While such views are not universally held, the key point is that while Ramallah might be considered a city of migrants, these migrants are not homogeneous. Long-standing residents do not identify as migrants, particularly those whose children were born in the city. "The new strangers who moved to Ramallah have families too, and many of these families moved to Ramallah. But they are families without a geographical basis [literally, ground]. They are from other cities and their social roots are not in Ramallah. My family moved to Ramallah many years ago, so our social roots formed in Ramallah. Ramallah's main families are Christian families, not Muslims, but because most of them have traveled to [the] USA, new families are forming the Ramallah society" (interview with Ola, 17 August 2013).

By contrast, other migrants refuse to identify with Ramallah, and maintain their identity as people from other places. What most residents do agree on is that Ramallah is a mixed society, with a distinctive urban culture. This urban imaginary resonates with assemblage theorizations discussed earlier, which understand cities as spaces of thrown-togetherness (Massey 2005; McFarlane 2011a, 2011b). Just as Anderson et al. (2012, 184) argue, "the form of assemblages is . . . contingently determined by the capacities of the parts that make up an assemblage," Ramallah's distinctiveness stems from the people who have moved to live there, and the habits and behaviors they bring with them. "Because the nature of life in Ramallah attracts people to it, the population has increased significantly. Ramallah is not exporting its lifestyle to other cities. It imports different lifestyles, cultures, and people into it. I guess it is a political and economic plan to import everything to Ramallah" (interview with Abu Omar, 3 October 2013). Abu Omar's account might be understood as contrary to Anderson et al. (2012) because it positions external forces as shaping Ramallah. However, a closer examination of the reconfiguration of the city, drawing on residents' understandings, suggests that it is the combination of different practices and beliefs within Ramallah that comes to define the city. There are two ways in particular through which this recombination has been named and understood: Ramallah as a city of "business" and Ramallah as a "free" city. Focusing on these characterizations deepens our understanding of Ramallah as an asymmetrically obligated city.

Ramallah as a City of Business

The people here have financial relationships only, and if there is no money they will go home. The only sort of relationships between people in Ramallah is business. And the people of Ramallah are two types: businessmen and consumers.
—Interview with Waleed, 21 August 2013

Inhabitants of Um al Sharayet commonly refer to Ramallah as a city of business. In part, this description captures the ways in which Occupation-inflected circulations of money and power have become concentrated in or captured by Ramallah. Such concentrations have made Ramallah wealthier than other cities in the Occupied Territories, particularly those that were historically larger and more prosperous, such as Nablus and Hebron (Taraki and Giacaman 2006). However, business describes more than just practices of trade and exchange. Julia Elyachar (2005, 165) notes in her study of markets in Cairo that "the agent of biznis . . . pursues individual gain at the expense of others." Like "biznis" in Cairo, the word "business" marks a contact and conflict zone between market relations and social obligations in Ramallah.

> YOUSEF The relationships with people outside the family are mainly based on common benefits like business.

> RAFIQ When the business relationship ends, the ties disappear! (Interview with Yousef and Rafiq, 6 June 2013)

"Everything is based on business and benefits, and I'm worried that our social life will be affected by business too" (interview with Im Ala, 17 August 2013).

Business relationships contrast with normal social relationships because of the weak, nonobligatory nature of the former. Residents characterized them as temporary rather than enduring, goal-orientated rather than means-orientated, and tied to individual financial benefit rather than to a more generalized social benefit. In some senses, they are almost nonrelationships (Harrison 2007), since the ties they embody are shallow. Furthermore, business relations are not simply something that happens at work but are said to pervade the city in its entirety. Basma, a young, single woman working in a service sector job, was particularly animated by the topic. "Usually when most people come to Ramallah, they try to internalize the city way of thinking and the way they behave and the way they appear. People here are mean, bad, and rude. In Jenin people take care of each other. In Ramallah relationships are based on business interests and financial benefit" (interview with Basma, 4 June 2013). "Business is not just a word that reflects investment and money. It goes beyond particular situations [literally, scenes]. It is the sum of power relationships in the city . . . Business is in everything. It is in all relationships and in the simple relationships too. Business affects not only financial deals" (interview with Basma, 14 August 2013). Residents like Basma feel a significant tension between business and other social relations. This unease is an index of the ways in which new economic and political practices are seen in opposition to, and as a threat to, normative social ties in this context. As Basma's reference to "the sum of power relationships" makes clear, business therefore names the post–second intifada transformations in the West Bank associated with Fayyad's prime ministerial reign and the PA's move away from resistance toward state building (Haddad 2016). Other residents framed these changes in terms of necessity, suggesting that the need to make money demands the cultivation of business relations that may be considered good. "Now relationships and public relations are common here . . . Things depend on relationships. If you open a business, it will depend on good relations, more than anything else. You know, if you have good relations with many people, you'll succeed more than people with mass media" (interview with Nasser, 6 June 2013).

While normative scriptings of associational life in Um al Sharayet reject business as a mode of relating, it is clear that adjustments are occurring. Eyad is a young, unmarried resident who has just begun paid work in construction and is still living with his parents. In his everyday life, business relations have become a form of practical competency through which he and other young people navigate the city (cf. A. Simone 2014). "I know half the guys in Ramallah, but I only have three or four friends" (interview with Eyad, 30 May 2013). The accounts of business relations offered by Basma, Nasser, and Eyad mirror theoretical accounts of the spread of finance, and debt in particular (Lazzarato 2012; Graeber 2011). Lazzarato's (2012, 38) argument that "debt breeds, subdues, manufactures, adapts, and shapes subjectivity" is exemplary of such arguments. It is clear that business relations are shaping forms of subjectivity in Ramallah, something that is explored in the next chapter. However, it is important to underscore that as in other contexts, business relations not only rework, but are themselves reworked by, existing social ties and practices (Elyachar 2005; A. Simone 2014). Business is not an economic tsunami destroying everything it encounters (Ong 2007). Instead, it has emerged from within, and as a result of, other relational practices that constitute the Ramallah urban assemblage. For instance, a number of participants pointed out the links between the growth of business and the post-Oslo political impasse. "If we can talk in politics, from my point of view there is a plan to make the country grow, or what they call economic peace, at the expense of the Palestinian case. To [make us] forget. There are people who benefited from that, like the businessmen, so it will last" (interview with Mohammed, 13 August 2013). Often discussions of businessmen explicitly or implicitly referred to returnees, Palestinians who were part of the PLO in Beirut and then Tunis, and returned as part of Oslo and the creation of the PA. Many returnees work in the PA. Their economic and political interests are seen to overlap, unsurprising given the monopolies the PA maintains (Dana 2015). Waleed in particular was adamant that "Ramallah does not belong to the people, but it is the property of some businessmen and there are just a few of them."

> [In] Ramallah, people are just interested in their position and money. Ramallah has no roots, has no base. While the people from al Bireh have a culture, they only care about themselves! Ramallah is controlled by a foreigner, loyal to a foreigner, with no lands, and no local products. [The purpose of] Ramallah is to dominate the indigenous people, by a foreigner. Ramallah is the main problem for all Palestinians.
>
> . . .
>
> Relationships are different between men and women, rich and poor, the owner and the employee. But with all of these differences people can have things in common. There are real chances to meet. But Ramallah is affecting all of this negatively! Decision makers try to create new kinds of relationships: money, profits, selfishness, individuality. All of this is not our real culture! New thoughts, new behavior. We should put an end to it. (Interview with Waleed, 2 May 2013)

Waleed suggests that the city of Ramallah has become almost entirely an object of Israeli settler-colonialism. Like Ahmad, who was quoted earlier in the chapter, his reference to "a foreigner, loyal to a foreigner" could refer to and enfold the PA elite, the Israeli Occupation, and international donors. Such elliptical references are necessary because of the growing repression of free speech, discussed in the next section. Therefore, residents' critiques of business and the PA often took on a more indirect form. During field research, Mohammed Assaf's victory in the pan-Arab television show *Arab Idol* in June 2013 provided one example of this. Assaf, a wedding singer from Gaza, became a genuinely popular "symbol of hope and unity in the West Bank and Gaza" after his victory (Sherwood 2013, n.p.). However, his success was widely seen as subsequently co-opted by politicians and businessmen. Residents interpreted this co-option as a microcosm of the city at large.

> The government's policy is orientated toward increasing the population and increasing consumption. The businessmen want to benefit financially. The media also plays a main role in transforming people's main priorities. Look at what they did to Assaf. They created a hero called Assaf and let people spend their money on encouraging his art. I'm not saying that Assaf is a bad person. No, he is a good singer. But we have to focus on other priorities. Abu Mazen encouraged him rather than [focusing on] other important things. Money talks. The majority is not corrupt. It is only a small class of people, who own money and the media that try to create Ramallah's new characteristics and [give it] a bad reputation. (Interview with Abu Tariq, 24 August 2013)

> ABU SAMIR In Ramallah, business is a basic aspect. Look what Muneeb al Masri did for Assaf. He supported him more than the poor.

> DAREEN Why?

> ABU SAMIR Because al Masri owns many companies and Assaf is a key for improving his business. He doesn't care about Assaf as a person or a singer. He only cares about the money that Assaf will add [literally, bring] to his wealth. Why are the PA leaders interested in Assaf? They are businessmen. The Palestinian leaders don't care. (Interview with Abu Samir, 17 August 2013)

It is notable in these stories that the evils of business are clearly localized in the city of Ramallah. Even though Muneeb al Masri famously lives in a very ostentatious palace overlooking Nablus, in Abu Samir's account his actions are linked to the West Bank's central city. Business creates an urban environment characterized by exploitation and inequality, in which concerns about making money override others, such as an anticolonial politics of liberation. This inequality is not simply economic, in terms of salaries and class formation, but material, pervading land and even religious practice. "People who live in Ramallah are only interested in business and gaining financial benefits. There is no empty land. Businessmen are buying all the lands in Ramallah to build on and invest" (interview with Abu Tamer, 9 September 2013). "It is weird that even the people who come to pray in the mosque in Ramallah talk about business inside the mosque" (interview with Ziad, 12 August 2013).

Such critiques can be linked to more extensive changes in Palestinian political economy in the West Bank since the end of the second intifada discussed in chapter 2 (Raja Khalidi and Samour 2011; Farsakh 2016; Haddad 2016). However, residents' use of the term "business" also repeatedly draws links between political-economic change and their everyday lives. Business registers political-economic changes at the level of daily practices and interactions, and in so doing points to spaces for some form of agency. If we are to understand Ramallah as an asymmetrically obligated assemblage, which residents themselves play some part in shaping, it is important to follow residents' lead in thinking through their everyday lives.

Ramallah as a Free City

"Free" is my mum's favorite word . . . Free is another word for going out a lot, mobility, staying out till midnight. In Ramallah people can go out, walk, have fun, even after midnight. Whilst in Tulkarem we see nobody walking in the streets after ten P.M. Dating is allowed here . . . It has a gendered dimension. Relatives are worried that their daughters will not feel safe in Ramallah. They keep telling them to watch out, to take care, and don't go out.
—Interview with Dina, 14 August 2013

If "business" names relations that are weak and only loosely binding, entangled with and enabled by post-Oslo political-economic developments in Ramallah, then "free" describes forms of subjective practice that are thought to be enabled by such loose/weak binds. Free is the social consequence of a city dominated by business. As with the use of the word "business," residents always used the English word "free." The meaning of free is thus clearly distinguishable from the Arabic words hura (free) and hurriyah (freedom), often used in opposition to Occupation and oppression. Instead, free denotes freedom from obligations and forms of collective governance and discipline, particularly those that are practiced through familial ties. The use of the English term also links imaginaries of life in Ramallah with other parts of the world. "It is true people of Ramallah are like foreigners. They can do whatever they want, and no one can prevent them from doing anything" (interview with Abu Tamer, 9 September 2013).

Like the term "business," "free" is not a neutral descriptive term, but is almost always used to denounce or criticize a lack of constraint and freedom from obligations. "No limits. To wear inappropriate clothes, and to dance in the Manara Square . . . It is to stay outside home until late at night. Not to wear a veil is free. Anything that is not related to our customs and traditions and culture is free. Modernity has something to do with this concept. In previous years, we had better traditions and culture" (interview with Hiba, 14 August 2013). For many residents of Um al Sharayet, and for their relatives living elsewhere, free becomes a sign of danger. This is particularly the case for women. "So my family just worry that in Ramallah life is 'free.' They keep telling me to take care and be careful" (interview with Huda, 14 August 2013). "It is a true discourse. Ramallah is a 'free' society. We have to take care of ourselves when we decide to move and live in this society. It is easy to be exposed to corruption here" (interview with Basma, 14 August 2013). These critiques, and the value judgments they contain, not only diagnose a problem, but also simultaneously reaffirm normative values around family and community solidarity as an alternative. However, free did not have negative connotations for all residents of Um al Sharayet.

DINA Things that are not allowed in Tulkarem are allowed in Ramallah and no one will stop you. No one will ask you about anything, "when," "where," or "what." We feel independent. No one has social authority over anyone else. Also we don't interfere in each other's lives and this is why it is easy to feel free in Ramallah. We don't know our neighbors and we don't have any social relationships.

DAREEN Is this a good thing?

DINA Yes. (Interview with Dina, 14 August 2013)

OLA Yes, personally, yes. I enjoy it . . . For me, it is to do whatever I want to without being watched or prohibited by others. Some people say "free" is to express their opinions without being banished by the law or the Authority.

DAREEN And which freedom is allowed and available in Ramallah?

OLA To do whatever you want to do. And this is not only allowed in Ramallah but in most of the main cities of the Arab world. People can wear, drink, and do whatever they want to do, but they can't speak! (Interview with Ola, 17 August 2013)

Ola articulates very clearly the difference between freedom from social obligations and constraints (free) and political freedom—such as the ability to speak freely (hurriyah). Building on the discussion of the good life in the previous chapter, Ola provides insight into how free can be understood to inhabit and replace the values and practices associated with hurriyah, specifically anticolonial struggle. As noted, many residents' critiques of the PA are phrased ambiguously or elliptically precisely because during the research period freedom of speech was severely curtailed by the PA (Beaumont 2017). It is also important to note that in both Dina's and Ola's case, gender clearly informs their experiences. The ways in which women are unequally bound by obligatory family ties mean that free can be an opportunity for them. Research stemming from other neighborhoods of Ramallah (Taraki 2008b; Abourahme 2009) indicates that class also plays a role in both understandings and practices of free. However, free is not just an assessment of individuals or certain groups (or classes) within the city, but also an evaluation of the city itself. Once again, this evaluation is largely negative.

> Free is a new term. It appeared when the PA was established in the year 1993 and the centralization of business emphasized this characteristic of Ramallah. People come from different places, and they have one aim, which is the job opportunity. And because they are from different places, they are different in their local cultures, traditions, and social customs. So different societies became one society, and this non-homogeneous society reflected a new sort of freedom that encourages the people to act freely. Without being committed to their social constraints, they act in a different way than they use to act in their small societies. (Interview with Ziad, 12 August 2013)

"If there is freedom, crime will increase. If you compare Ramallah and Hebron, there is less crime [in Hebron] because of the family threat. And in Jerusalem crime is even greater. Ramallah became more 'free' because people came from outside Palestine and changed it a little" (interview with Khaled, 25 August 2013). These quotations tell us two things about how Ramallah is inhabited and understood. First, they map different geographies of free. Some residents, like Ziad, understand free to result from social mixing within Ramallah. Khaled, however, suggests that it is people living elsewhere who cause problems and engage in free behaviors. It is not clear whether he is referring to Palestinians living elsewhere in Palestine or (non-Arab) foreigners living in Ramallah. Of course, given the number of migrants from elsewhere who live in and constitute Ramallah, outside and inside become hard to distinguish as they are folded together (Secor 2013). Second, free is contextualized within broader changes that occurred after, and as a result of, Oslo. Like Ziad above, many participants suggested that the PA has played an active role in promoting Ramallah as a free city, as part of attempts to create an economic peace. Free is therefore also a form of governance, as Ola notes above. Drawing on Ahmad's and Waleed's earlier quoted perspectives, we can understand the PA as part of the broader Israeli Occupation, which extends to international donors too (Haddad 2016). This governance assemblage has fomented the decline of social and economic constraints, while increasing religious and political restrictions. "Free is to do whatever you want but on one condition, which is to not be involved in politics and to not make religion play any role in social and political life" (interview with Abu Samir, 17 August 2013).

Like "business," the term "free" also characterizes the Ramallah urban assemblage. Residents' descriptions (and condemnations) of free practices provide an illustration of how post-Oslo political-economic transformations have been folded into the everyday life and culture of the city. Both business relations and free practices are seen as specific characteristics of Ramallah that have emerged because of the specific combination of people, practices, and forces. The outside is folded to become the inside (Secor 2013) as a threat or corrupting influence, both external and internal to the city. This threat or corruption, particularly with regard to values, is seen as responsible for the inequality that characterizes Ramallah. For migrants with strong attachments to places elsewhere, free practices and business relations highlight the growth of inequality within Ramallah, and between cities within the West Bank. Such connections become increasingly clear in broader imaginaries of the city.

URBAN IMAGINARIES

If Ramallah might be said to be obliged to other places for its population, and their capacities to work and generate a specific urban culture, then the same is true for the urban imaginaries that enliven the conurbation's development. For example, the strategic development plan for the Ramallah conurbation was created in 2007 by the German Agency for Technical Cooperation (GTZ, now part of the GIZ, the German Organization for International Collaboration), with financial support from Cities Alliance. The plan creates a smooth development narrative of the conurbation's future, ignoring the significant challenges—such as land titling issues—that make implementing such a future almost impossible. On the face of it this is a good example of how urban policies are shaped by powerful state and private sector actors with

4.1 Visualization of Ersal Center, Ramallah. *Source: http://www.ccjo.com/en/content/shopping-mall-al-ersal-development-center.*

extensive global reach (Ananya Roy and Ong 2011; Ward 2017). However, in practice, things are more complicated. One employee at Al Bireh municipality told us that the municipality uses the glossy brochure produced by GTZ to apply for further funding from international organizations. In becoming a tool for generating future income, it is far less important as a blueprint that shapes urban development (interview with Deema Junieh and Ala' al Deen, 4 May 2014).

Other practices and images of urban development often evoke other cities of the Arab world. This should not be surprising, since the architectural and engineering firms designing and transforming particular—often very spectacular—urban spaces in Ramallah are transnational in scope. One of the city's largest developments is the Ersal Center. It was being built during the research period by Arduna Real Estate Development Company, which is part-owned by the Jordanian firm the Land Real Estate Investment and Development Company. The development was designed by Jordanian-headquartered Consolidated Consultants–Jafar Tukan Architects, who have designed a number of buildings in Amman in addition to the Mahmoud Darwish Museum and the Yasser Arafat Memorial in Ramallah. The visualizations they have produced, and particularly the high-rise towers, have more in common with Amman and Beirut than Ramallah, where towers have been, until very recently, absent from the city's landscape. The images of women wearing sleeveless dresses and no headscarves (see figure 4.1), while undoubtedly resonating

Chapter Four

4.2 Photograph of Al Reehan. *Source: Courtesy of Hanna Baumann.*

with middle-class populations living in neighborhoods like Al Tira, go beyond many Um al Sharayet residents' actual experiences of Ramallah to visually describe and create what Taraki (2008b, 62) has termed "a new globalized
and modernist urban middle-class ethos." As the term suggests, this ethos is
the product of other places, as much as it is a characteristic of Ramallah.

While a "globalized ethos" is tied to Arab capitals and cities beyond the
Arab world, there are also instances where urban imaginaries take inspiration
from sources much closer to home. In the master plan for Al Reehan, a recently
completed residential project built on the northern outskirts of Ramallah (also
designed by Consolidated Consultants–Jafar Tukan Architects), the visual design bears more than a passing resemblance to Israeli settlement colonies, particularly the contouring of the roads to mirror the hilltop on which it was built
(see figure 4.2). The new town of Rawabi, built in the north of the Ramallah
governorate, is frequently described as a Palestinian settlement colony.

Urban imaginaries and design practices, which borrow a great deal from
other places, but engage little with the city's existing built form and architectural styles, have been cleverly satirized by artists Emily Jacir and Yazid
Anani. In their work *Al-Riyadh* (see figures 4.3 and 4.4), advertisements for

Thinking Debt through the City   85

4.3 *The Tower, Al Riyadh*, by Yazid Anani and Emily Jacir. *Source: Yazid Anani and Emily Jacir.*

4.4 *The Suburb, Al Riyadh*, by Yazid Anani and Emily Jacir. *Source: Yazid Anani and Emily Jacir.*

two fictional real estate projects were printed on billboards and displayed in the center of the city. In the two images, the tower and the suburb are visually juxtaposed with the existing urban landscape to raise questions about the appropriateness of nonvernacular architectural styles in Ramallah. Al Riyadh, the name of the fictitious company and also the capital city of Saudi Arabia, draws connections between urban development and the powerful role played by Gulf-based capital in the region: "Al-Riyadh Tower is a proposition to destroy the old vegetable market and replace it with a modern Dubai style tower, promoting a clean business environment and spaces for foreign trade exchange while replacing the intimacy, heritage, and memory of the place. The other billboard promotes a gated community emulating the proliferation of housing projects around Ramallah, with walled perimeters, surveillance cameras, and private security personnel; projects that threaten to wipe out the historic center of Ramallah and replace its architectural heritage with a housing project that looks similar to that of Israeli settlements" (V. Tamari and Anani 2010, n.p.). As the eagle in the bottom right-hand corner of the poster (similar to the PA coat of arms) and the final sentence of the quotation suggest, the artists also implicate the Palestinian Authority and the Israeli Occupation in this process. Their work can be read as criticizing the ways in which elite urban development practices and imaginaries are enfolded in visions of modernity that not only mimic (Taussig 1993; Weizman 2007) but embody the colonizer's vision of an economic peace. This public criticism of the PA was met with swift retribution. When the billboard depicting the tower was installed in the center of Ramallah, it was taken down immediately. The gated community billboard was destroyed with knives after two days of public display (Toukan 2014, 221).

Residents' Imaginaries

The circulation of urban imaginaries is not limited to development bodies, municipalities, large architectural firms, and artists (Weszkalnys 2013, 22). Residents of Um al Sharayet also frequently draw on representations of other places to understand Ramallah. Perhaps the most frequent citation is Amman. This is the most accessible foreign city for many Palestinians living in the West Bank, and many Palestinian families have become spread across the Palestine-Jordan border. Some research participants have lived in Amman and other parts of the Arab world, and thus have concrete points of reference for comparison.

WALEED People don't compare between entertainment venues in the main cities of the Arab world. They don't think it is a big deal. They are used to these places, while in Palestine we highlight these places and keep saying they are a part of Ramallah's characteristics.

NADIA In the cities of the Arab world, people consider these places as part of the natural evolution of major cities. While in Palestine people don't consider it a natural evolution of the city. (Interview with Waleed and Nadia, 21 August 2013)

"It is not only the case that Ramallah has many strangers who moved to live there. Most of the main cities all over the world, like Dubai, and the capitals of Arab states like Syria and Jordan, are all cities of strangers" (interview with Basma, 14 August 2013).

However, in most cases it is imaginations inspired by media representations, rather than lived experiences, that are used to understand urban life. In contrast to (negative) characterizations of Ramallah as a free city, geographical imaginations of other Arab cities often position what is happening in Ramallah as normal and, in some cases, better than similar developments elsewhere. "The irony is that the lifestyle in Ramallah is better than the lifestyle in other Arab cities" (interview with Abu Omar, 3 October 2013). Residents often suggested that life was better in Ramallah than in other Arab cities because social ties and religious norms were stronger. Such statements emerge from and underpin practices of endurance discussed later in the book. Furthermore, similar to the imaginaries fabricated by the brochure for the Ersal Center, residents also index urban life in Ramallah to cities beyond the Arab world. "The people from the North also like to come to Ramallah. They think it's New York City" (interview with Abu Omar, 31 August 2013). "I want to compare Ramallah to the USA. People consider America as the land of opportunity, and you can say that statement about Ramallah" (interview with Ali, 13 August 2013). Both of these statements build on understandings of Ramallah as free and a city of business. Abu Omar's statement positions Ramallah as not only foreign—in its values and practices—but also relatively cosmopolitan. Ramallah's modernity distinguishes it from other Palestinian cities in the North that are comparatively less modern. Ali's reference to opportunity (business), meanwhile, has a more positive tone, echoing his pride in his own relative economic independence from his family. As with the intra-Arab world comparison, such comparisons stem from mediated representations, residents' mobility, and connections to family members living in Europe and the Americas. And like the artistic response of Jacir and Anani, residents of Um al Sharayet employ practices of transnational comparison in order to critique Ramallah's development. The transnational urban imaginaries that are largely created by a professional elite, reiterated by some residents, and circulated through the city are held to account for falling short of describing urban life as it is actually experienced.

HUSSEIN The municipality tried to make Rukkab Street like the roads in Paris . . . In fact, Ramallah can't be similar to Paris. Ramallah is a small city compared to Paris.

CHRIS Why do people compare it with Paris?

HUSSEIN The municipality repaired the internal roads. They clamped down on all the banners, and they built roads with stones. They put up many lights too.

DAREEN Do you think Ramallah looks like Paris now?

HUSSEIN No, it is just the idea of imitating Paris. (Interview with Hussein, 29 September 2013)

The comparisons made by residents are thus ambivalent. Sometimes Ramallah is better than the city or cities it is compared to, particularly when references are made to foreign lifestyle (in implicit contrast to normative values and practices tied to obligatory relations). However, more often residents of Um al Sharayet suggest that Ramallah is worse than other places because of its political situation or poor infrastructure. The relationships between Ramallah and other cities, particularly in the West Bank, are also a subject of critique. Unsurprisingly for a population constituted by migrants, the growth of Ramallah is understood to be responsible for broader inequalities within the West Bank.

ALI The increase of population has a negative impact on the city and on the other cities all over Palestine, and this has made the economy of these areas weak compared with Ramallah. Ramallah became the main city and other cities have been . . .

DAREEN Marginalized.

ALI Exactly. The government should balance between all governorates. (Interview with Ali, 13 August 2013)

"The economic centralization made the economic cities like Hebron and Nablus collapse . . . We are for development, technology and growth, but in all Palestinian cities. And that is not what happened" (interview with Shadi, 12 August 2013). Such imaginaries chart a geography of inequality that extends beyond Ramallah to other Palestinian towns and cities.

Residents' urban imaginaries are also intensive, in the sense that they identify inequalities within Ramallah too. These inequalities, understood in relation to wealth and class, are spatialized in, and as, differences between the city's neighborhoods, understood as both built environment and groups of people.

ALI Some of the neighborhoods are more upscale in terms of construction and environment. The people living here are from the poor class, and the culture in this place is characterized by simplicity.

DAREEN A popular [shaebii] neighborhood?

ALI Yes, it is clear that the environment here is not perfect like in the other neighborhoods. (Interview with Ali, 24 September 2013)

"People consider Masyoun as A class. Rich people live in Al Masyoun. The people living here are poor, but they have better culture" (interview with Im Ala, 28 September 2013).

Someone who lives in Al Masyoun and pays 600,000 [NIS] is different from someone living here, and they have a different lifestyle. Also, it will be different between the people who work with the NGOs, and the people who live in cheap houses, costing [US$]20,000, like in the camp. It's different in culture. Let me say, Al Bireh people look to us as refugees and because they went abroad, they look at us as retarded. They think that they are more developed because they have seen life abroad. Personally, I think they have a bad time there and work in bad jobs. (Interview with Yazan, 25 September 2013)

In these accounts, residents suggest that Um al Sharayet is poorer than other neighborhoods in Ramallah, with worse infrastructure, and that residents live different lifestyles. However, other participants argued that the differences between areas within the broader city are not substantive.

CHRIS Are the culture and lifestyle and the people in Um al Sharayet different from other parts of the city?

AHMAD No, they're the same standard [literally, level]. Those who live in al Ersal are employees and it's also the same in Al Tira. And we all came from different places, from Jenin, Nablus, Hebron. So most people live in the same place, like Um al Sharayet. Then when they get married, and because of loans, they buy apartments in other places like Al Ersal and Al Tira, which they think is better. But it's the same standard and the same culture. (Interview with Ahmad, 1 October 2013)

CHRIS Do you think the people, the culture, and the lifestyle of Um al Sharayet are different from other neighborhoods in Ramallah?

ABU GHASSAN The people are not different. You can find two brothers living in different neighborhoods of Ramallah. It depends on their financial situation.

DAREEN Do you think Al Tira is better than Um al Sharayet?

ABU GHASSAN It is more expensive and more beautiful.

DAREEN It is cleaner than here.

ABU GHASSAN Sure it is.

CHRIS So what about the people?

ABU GHASSAN The people are the same. (Interview with Abu Ghassan, 26 September 2013)

These accounts offer a rich and complex imaginative geography of Ramallah from the context of Um al Sharayet, which works through both interurban and intra-urban comparison. As in other parts of the world, other cities and neighborhoods are invoked to trace a geography of urban inequality that is simultaneously intensive and extensive. In Ramallah, these comparisons draw attention to a decidedly uneven and unequal urban assemblage. Not only is the city indebted to other places, but the city itself is a heterogeneous landscape. This is fully in keeping with the conceptual framework outlined by McFarlane (2011a, 2011b), which acknowledges that the thrown-togetherness (Massey 2005) that constitutes each specific city is often a messy mix of unequal and asymmetric relations and practices.

CONCLUSION

Thinking debt as an urban spacing requires an understanding of how debt topologies are not simply enfolded in the topographic spaces of cities, but also entangled with other obligatory relations. This chapter has traced how debt space can be understood in Um al Sharayet through reference to money, donor finance, and other obligations, such as family and kinship ties. This broader approach enabled an understanding of Ramallah as an asymmetrically obligated city, which owes other space-times for its money, culture, and urban imaginaries, while being an internally heterogeneous space. This enriched understanding of debt and cities was made possible by staying close to residents' accounts of the city.

This chapter contributes to the broader argument of the book in two ways. First, the examination of Ramallah as an asymmetrically obligated city provides a detailed empirical illustration of Ramallah as a debt ecology. Here, the concept of ecology moves beyond the specific financial circumstances of residents to the collective enfolding of topologies of debt and other obligations that constitute the city at large, including remittances, investments, donations, ideas, and cultural practices. This chapter has been at pains to illustrate that such entanglements are characterized by unevenness and inequality. This approach builds on assemblage approaches to urban theory, with its focus on cities as dynamic orderings (McFarlane 2011a, 2011b; Weszkalnys 2013; A. Simone 2014). By illustrating the differential relations of composition that constitute Ramallah, this chapter has not only foregrounded the dynamism of these entanglements—something that is often talked up in discussions of assemblage—but also examined the emergence of inequality, in the guise of "business" and "free" practices and relations. Such insights demonstrate the utility of assemblage approaches for studying urban inequality (cf. Brenner, Madden, and Wachsmuth 2011).

Thinking about Ramallah as an asymmetrically obligated assemblage also reinforces the argument developed in the previous chapters that differentially extensive relations create specific debt ecologies. The empirical data discussed in this chapter shows the complex ways in which different topological relations and topographic spaces are folded together within, and as, Ramallah. Foreign donors and globally mobile ways of thinking about debt are only part of the story. Residents' familial geographies and critical assessments are also important. In bringing these complex entanglements to the fore, this chapter builds on recent theorizations of Ramallah as a bubble, Bantustan, and/ or enclave (Farsakh 2005a; Taraki 2008a; Abourahme 2009). Such accounts capture the spatial, political, and economic distinctiveness of the West Bank's central city. However, such conceptual frames downplay the relational geographies through which Ramallah is both enriched and rendered vulnerable to its multiple outsides. Thinking Ramallah as an assemblage of asymmetric obligations renders the city more porous than images of prison or enclave.

The second broader contribution of this chapter has been to illustrate how debts are one kind of obligation. This is an important argument because obligations are always entangled with one another. Any attempt to understand debt's geographies, in Ramallah or elsewhere, must necessarily pay attention to these entanglements, and thus other obligations that are not debts. In Um al Sharayet, it is entanglements of family and kinship obligations that are responsible for the transfer of resources, people, and cultures between different places. Crucially, these entanglements are shaped by asymmetries of power. Residents of Um al Sharayet have far less capacity to co-constitute the city than the PA elites, Israeli Occupation, and international donors they frequently critique. Nevertheless, residents' circulatory practices, and the spatial relations that emerge, do matter, both literally and figuratively. There are also asymmetries within family transfers that lead to inequalities. This argument is further fleshed out in the next chapter through a more sustained focus on subjectivity and debt space.

5   debt and obligatory subjectivity

In 2014, an advertisement for a Bank of Palestine saving scheme appeared in magazines and on billboards all around Ramallah (see figure 5.1). It depicts two adults and three children. The caption—"Together We Are a Family"—encourages the viewer to assume that this group constitutes a family. The viewer might also make this assumption because of the intimate postures (e.g., hand-holding, hand on shoulder), the physical resemblance, and the number of adults and children, which embodies the statistical average nuclear family size for the West Bank, which is just over five (PCBS 2018). Furthermore, this image represents an increasingly common aspiration for what in this context is considered a small family. However, a careful look at the advertisement reveals a sixth family member, because the speech bubble does not come from the group, but rather encapsulates them. They are captured by the speech of this other. While it is not unambiguously clear who this other is, we are clearly meant to think it is the Bank of Palestine itself. In other words, we are encouraged to think that this other is precisely not Other to the family subject. The "we" in "Together We Are a Family" incorporates mother, father, children, and bank.

This advertisement produces an imaginary that connects a good family life in Palestine with the bank. The bank is folded into and becomes part of the family. Although this advertisement

5.1 Advertisement for Bank of Palestine saving scheme, Al Bireh, 2014. *Source: Author.*

is for a savings scheme rather than a credit/debt product, there were many advertisements for credit cards, mortgages, and personal loans around Ramallah too (see figure 3.1). Such advertisements are one of the ways in which debt becomes folded into the everyday lives of Ramallah's residents. They are what Deville (2015) terms "lures for feeling." These advertisements also illustrate one of the ways in which spatial ecologies of debt and finance feed into and coproduce a particular kind of subject, in this case the small, nuclear family. However, while representations of a particular kind of good life draw energy from and performatively incite the practices and aspirations of many younger couples and parents (most visibly in neighborhoods like Al Tira), they struggle to describe the subjective experience of living with debt in Um al Sharayet. In particular, these advertisements do not account for the broader ecology of obligations through which indebted subjectivity is shaped.

Like the Bank of Palestine advertisement, existing social theories of indebted subjectivity often separate debt from other forms of obligation (despite a substantial body of anthropological scholarship that has shown otherwise; see, for example, James 2015; Bear 2015). Lazzarato (2012, 2015), for example, examines the capacity of debt to create individual subjects while also decomposing that subject into "dividual" pieces. While useful, his theoretical framework requires further development to account for both the complexity of debt and subjectivity and the heterogeneity of debt and indebtedness. In particular, Lazzarato's theoretical frame does not help to explain the ways in which debts become folded into other obligatory relations, particularly those that tie family and kin together. To address this lacuna, this chapter introduces the term "obligatory subjectivity," to name more-than-individual modes of being amid multiple social, economic, and political ties. This provides a platform for examining debt's role in producing subjects amid other obligatory ties and provides a basis for the discussion of endurance later in the book. The distribution, embodiment, and performance of debt relations through families is unequal, both socially and spatially. The second half of this chapter examines these uneven distributions in relation to the gendered practices of becoming, managing, and living with debt. Thinking about debt through the differences of gender and space returns us to the challenge of postcolonizing debt in the conclusion. Building on arguments developed in chapter 1, this chapter argues that obligatory subjectivity undermines the centrality and universalizing pretensions of extant Eurocentric debt theory.

DEBT AND SUBJECTIVITY

The Bank of Palestine posits an intimacy—to the point of identity—between family life and banking to promote its savings accounts (figure 5.1). Many residents of Um al Sharayet made a similar connection with regard to experiences of debt. "The bank takes 40 percent of my salary. That means $700. So that means that $1,050 remains, and I have the bills. So, $800 remains and I have to pay $300 to the [credit] card so $500 remains. So how can I pay for the schools and everything else? I rescheduled the loan. *All my life is pledged to the bank*" (interview with Mohammad, 25 August 2013; my emphasis). "A friend of mine took a big loan in order to get married, buy a house and buy a car . . . I told him if he was not able to repay the loan that he took to marry, the bank will take his wife back" (interview with Abu Omar, 12 September 2013). "The loan is like one of the family members. It eats and drinks with me, and it sleeps and wakes up with us. It is like a nightmare!" (interview with Im Ghassan, 31 August 2013). These descriptions position banks as sets of topological relations encompassing buildings, employees, advertising, symbols, and circulations of money that become folded into another set of relations that constitute family (Johnson 2006; Harker 2012). Through what are often highly durable ties, such as the automatic repayment system, debt becomes "like one of the family members," as Im Ghassan puts it. This binding and blending does not extend directly to topographic landscapes. Bank employees do not set foot in a family's home (although they may call on the phone). In the case of Islamic mortgages,[1] the bank that purchases the property will never use it for a branch office. However, topologies of debt became grounded in the topographic landscape as borrowed money enabled the particular forms of urban inhabitation that were practiced by families, including being able to buy an apartment, send children to private schools, and purchase commodities including cars, televisions, power tools, and mobile phones. Building on understandings that include all manner of nonhuman things as part of the family (Nethercote and Horne 2016), it is clear that debt and banking practices are not just entwined with, but coproduce, family life. In some instances, the intimacy between family and bank, embodied in a debt relation, enabled the biological existence of families in their particular form, as borrowed money was used to pay hospital fees and other medical costs, and thus pay for the sustenance of life itself (Cooper 2008). Such insights align with the work of Lazzarato (2012, 2015), and particularly his argument that debt is the "subjective engine of modern-day economy" (Lazzarato 2012, 25).

Lazzarato (2012, 31) argues that the financialized credit-debt relation has become the dominant form of biopolitics, producing individuals who are free to act, so long as their way of life is compatible with repaying their debts. In this way debt governs through the future, directing the behavior of debtors toward (ensuring) repayment and neutralizing the possibility for novel forms of politics (Lazzarato 2015, 23, 49). Lazzarato (2015, 108–9, 119) argues that debt is an apparatus of financial and state power, which operates primarily through a temporal relation. He uses the term "debt economy" to name the broader arrangement that holds a multiplicity of social, political, and economic mechanisms together (Lazzarato 2012, 106). This arrangement has an operational rather than a systemic unity, which is to say it gives rise to temporary and partial compositions that ensure the proliferation of debt (Lazzarato 2012, 106). Consequently, the unity and internal power relations of the debt

---

1 An Islamic mortgage is a housing loan that complies with Sharia law, which prohibits interest. While there are various methods for doing this, it is most often accomplished through an Ijara wa Iqtina mortgage, where the financial institution will purchase a percentage of the property, hold it in trust, and lease the housing to the buyer, followed by the eventual sale at the end of the lease term.

economy are part of a political process that is continually being composed and cannot be assumed a priori. This understanding is useful for framing the emergence of the debt economy in Ramallah outlined in chapter 2, and particularly the "operational unity" of Fayyad's political reform program, the development of the Palestinian Monetary Authority (PMA), and the eviscerated political-economic landscape of post–second intifada Palestine.

Lazzarato's work is also useful because it details how debt, as an apparatus of power, works on and within the lives of people. The debt economy is characterized by a growing exploitation of subjectivity—both extensively, in that it covers all sectors of society, and intensively, in that it encompasses the relationship to the self (Lazzarato 2012, 52). This occurs in two complementary ways. The first includes processes of what he terms "social subjection," which "operates molar control on the subject through the mobilization of his conscience, memory and representations" (Lazzarato 2012, 146). Social subjection functions according to norms, rules, and law (Lazzarato 2012, 150), such as the widespread expectation that one will pay one's debts. Subjection thus simultaneously produces and shapes the conduct of individuals and particular types of collectivity, such as nationalism. For Lazzarato, creating individuals—people disconnected from broader solidarities and the political resources that stem from collective struggles—is a key political objective of the debt economy: "the neutralization of collective attitudes (mutualization, solidarity, cooperation, rights for all, etc.) and the memory of collective struggles, action, and organization" (Lazzarato 2012, 114).

Second, operating alongside processes of social subjection, "'machinic subjugation' has a molecular, infrapersonal and pre-individual hold on subjectivity that does not pass through reflexive consciousness and its representations, nor through the 'self'" (Lazzarato 2012, 146). This socio-technical transformation or dissolution of subjectivity "involves only protocols, techniques, procedures, instructions, and asignifying semiotics requiring reaction rather than action" (Lazzarato 2012, 150). Lazzarato's key example of subjugation is the automated teller machine (ATM), with its demands to enter your code, choose your amount, and take your money (Lazzarato 2012, 147–48). Such processes transform the human into a function of a socio-technical machine created by the banking network.

Subjection and subjugation work alongside each other. Subjection demands and produces a particular kind of self, while subjugation dismantles this self. The result is "indebted man." This is not a person per se, but rather a social process or condition in which repayment never finishes and people remain indebted for life (Lazzarato 2012, 77). Public (i.e., state) debt (Lazzarato 2012,

122), taxation (Lazzarato 2015, 41), and a morality based on a dyad of trust and guilt (Lazzarato 2012, 30) make everyone indebted men, to the point where Lazzarato claims that "indebted man may end up becoming the most wide-spread economic-existential condition in the world" (Lazzarato 2012, 122).

Lazzarato's argument usefully moves beyond narrow, economic renderings of debt to think through the production of subjectivity. He provides a precise conceptual tool kit for thinking through the mechanics of this biopolitical production. For instance, his concept of social subjection resonates closely with residents' critiques of Ramallah as a city of business and a free city, dis-cussed in the previous chapter. His work on machinic subjugation is useful for unsettling the anthropocentric basis of much debt theory. However, his thesis is limited, not least because of its gendered and generalizing nature. While Lazzarato (2012, 32) notes that even if widespread, debt is a specific rather than a universal power relation, this specificity is severely underplayed. Alberto Toscano (2014, n.p.) suggests that the sociology underpinning in-debted man, such as the account of welfare to workfare transition and the centrality of the social, is "much more specific to France than Lazzarato lets on." Furthermore, one problem with identifying a single figure of subjectivity is that the debt economy "ranges across variegated social formations, geogra-phies and class positions" (Toscano 2014, n.p.). This line of argument is use-fully expanded by Tiziana Terranova (2014), who takes aim at the masculine, universal, and univocal "man" of indebted man. "The abstraction of debt as the most universal social relationship, overdetermining economic processes, based on a few Western male philosophers, without acknowledgment of femi-nist or postcolonial theories and histories of debt—without, that is, explicitly accounting for the heterogeneous formation and development of debt—risks being seen not as a useful abstraction but as a generalising, simplified thesis easily subjected to critique and dismissed" (Terranova 2014, n.p.).

Terranova recasts debt as "a dispositif that manages to capture the produc-tive powers of monadic cooperation by intervening on the capacity of such cooperation to produce not so much objects or subjects, but worlds to live in" (Terranova 2014, n.p.). This shift in emphasis, from subject to world, invites further conversation between Lazzarato's theoretical frame and feminist and postcolonial analysis.

> In *The Making of the Indebted Man*, the subject of indebtedness appears in this book to be a man, and thereby presents an inconsistency in relation to his analysis of debt as generalised condition. One might respond to this by drawing attention to the sexual and gendered character of debtor-creditor

relationship and how it intervenes in processes of reproduction (where debt incurred as a couple, for example in the form of mortgages or loans, produces stronger bonds than those of a marriage certificate), or by pointing at the ways in which debt has affected the lives of women in Africa, Asia and Latin America. But this would merely add a new subset to the theory of indebtedness, while leaving the real question unattended: can Lazzarato's neomonadology itself be queered, sexed and raced while still remaining non-anthropocentric, in such a way as to oppose its tendency to be translated into a general image of subjectivity? (Terranova 2014, n.p.)

This chapter builds on these critiques by examining the family, rather than the individual, as an indebted subject. The family demarcates the limits of Lazzarato's claims around debt, individualization, and subjectivity. These are limits that he briefly notes in passing: "Debtors are alone, individually responsible to the banking system; they can count on no solidarity except, on occasion, that of their families, which in turn risk going into debt" (Lazzarato 2015, 70). Focusing on the intersection between debt and families calls into question the power ascribed to de/individualization through processes of subjection and subjugation. People in Ramallah are not as individual as Lazzarato's frame assumes, but nor does this mean they act as a political collective. As I demonstrate, the individual-collective dyad alone is unsuitable for understanding subjectivity in Palestine.

INDEBTEDNESS AS FAMILIAL

Actually, purchase contracts with landlords do not differ in essence from the sale and purchase contracts undertaken by the bank. Both impose interest on the buyers. Landlords get $20,000 as a first, initial payment, and get a monthly amount. And if the buyer can't pay, the landlord will get his apartment back.
—Interview with Waleed, 4 September 2013

If I want to take from my family, I will be embarrassed. The bank will take interest and I don't like that at all, even if I will have nothing.
—Interview with Ibrahim, 28 August 2013

Ibrahim's comparison sees debt topologies with family and bank as broadly similar (i.e., negative), but different in terms of their precise effects. Waleed's analysis suggests that owing money to a building owner is the same as owing money to a bank for a mortgage loan. Both gesture to the ways in which financial debt topologies are entangled with other debts and obligations, many of which are embodied in friendship and kin relations. These include practices such as marriage, building or buying a home, and mourning someone's death. There are also connections with more extensive geopolitical and economic changes in the Occupied Territories. As Shadi explains, current entanglements of family and bank debt emerge from specific geographies and histories.

> There were strong relations in Palestinian families and in the [19]70s there were few banks. There was no [Palestinian] Authority and the Occupation was responsible for employment, so the Israeli and Civil Administration staff could take loans, and there were two Israeli banks here. So the alternative was to take a loan from your family. Also, our culture is to ask my brother before my neighbors, and I'll ask my father before my brother. But today because there are lots of banks, we prefer to take loans from the bank rather than disrupting our families. These financial institutions open alternatives for people to get loans. In the 70s and 80s, the alternatives were limited. (Interview with Shadi, 26 August 2013)

Practices of borrowing from family and friends have a historical political dimension, since Israeli banks did not lend to most Palestinians in the era prior to the Oslo Accords (see chapter 2). In the present day, as Nasser notes below, banks have not only become an alternative option, but often the only source of money for residents who want to borrow large amounts. This is because the cost of property and/or land now far exceeds most Palestinian families' incomes. "You can take from your friends, but not big amounts. You can take $1,000, $500, $200, not more than this. It is different. Only a small amount. Not like the bank. No one can give you a loan like the bank. They can only give you something in an emergency. $500, $200, $100, $1,000" (interview with Nasser, 27 August 2013). While increasing numbers of Palestinians are taking loans from banks, these debts are entangled, spatially and temporally, with family and kinship. It is precisely this entanglement that the Bank of Palestine recognizes and seeks to profit from through its advertising. Debt topologies become distributed through families and other social relations. Such entanglements and distributions require an expanded conceptualization of personhood in relation to debt, which I term "obligatory subjectivity."

OBLIGATORY SUBJECTIVITY

"It is not easy to avoid social events. I don't have any choice. There are many aspects obliging me to go. It is not only religion, but it is traditions, relatives and friends. I don't live in an isolated society. It is not easy at all" (interview with Ali, 28 August 2013). "I can't avoid occasions for other friends who are very close. I would borrow money to go if I didn't have enough money to go" (interview with Abu Samir, 1 September 2013). "It's like a duty. We have to go and give [literally, pay] a financial gift" (interview with Hussein, 14 May 2013). In chapter 1, obligations were defined as practices and relations that are understood by people to be mandatory, without the quality of absolute necessity or compulsion. Debts and social ties in Ramallah are obligations precisely because in both cases honoring them is perceived as mandatory. This notion of obligation can inform understandings of agency, capacity, and capacitation in relation to debt and subjectivity. An act that is mandatory and yet must be actively affirmed produces a form of agency that is caught between active and passive tenses. In such situations, lives are heavily influenced and crafted by other subjects and practices, times, and places, and the line between being an active and a passive subject can often be hard to discern. As Ali, Abu Samir, and Hussein suggest, many practices are thought about as duties to be fulfilled, regardless of whether the subject chooses to or not. There are parallels here with Lazzarato's (2012) concept of the indebted man, which is an involuntary condition (in that we are made indebted through public debt and taxation) and yet one that specific subjects actively inhabit.

The concept of obligatory subjectivity seeks to name personhood as it is distributed through obligatory relations, including debt. It is a means of thinking through a form or mode of subjectivity, not a subject in toto, in which agency hovers between active and passive tenses. In making this claim, I build on Saba Mahmood's (2012, 149) argument that "the distinction between the subject's real desires and obligatory social conventions—a distinction at the centre of liberal, and at times progressive, thought—cannot be assumed, precisely because socially prescribed forms of behaviour constitute the conditions for the emergence of the self as such and are integral to its realisation." Obligatory subjectivity is not a way of contextualizing individuals within a social structure, but rather an attempt to think through a more-than-individual form of being and acting (see Mahmood 2012, 152). Elizabeth Povinelli's (2011, 33) discussion of immanent obligation, "a no-man's-land between choice and determination," recognizes the affirmative dimensions of obligatory relations, and their world-making potential, even amid scenes of exhaustion.

By "immanent obligation" I am referring to a form of relationality that one finds oneself drawn to and finds oneself nurturing, or caring for in the midst of critical reflexivity. This being "drawn to" or "repelled" is often initially a very fragile connection, a sense of an immanent connectivity. Choices are then made to enrich and intensify these connections. But even these choices need to be understood as retrospective—the subject choosing is herself continually deferred by choice. In other words, she is and is beginning to be different in the vicinity of this choice; she is belated to herself, arriving too late to be any use to adjudication. I might be able to describe why I am drawn to a particular space and I may try to nurture this obligation or to break away from it, but still I have very little that can be described as "choice" in the original orientation. (Povinelli 2011, 33)

In her work, Povinelli uses immanent obligation to articulate an ethics of care that spans both the nonhuman and the all-too-human relations between liberal settler-colonist nation-states, indigenous peoples, and land. As Povinelli notes, our "original orientation"—what we might nurture and care for—is always a product of existing relations, rather than an attribute or action of a volitional subject. In so doing, she provides a language not only for describing the awkward agentic space between active and passive tenses, but also for thinking relationality beyond liberalism's individual and collective subjects. I use the concept of obligatory subjectivity rather than immanent obligation to maintain a conceptual focus on the subject, rather than just relationality. I do this because obligatory relations always take place in specific geographical and historical contexts, and thus amid forms of biopolitical subjectification, such as the debt economy Lazzarato describes (see also Povinelli 2011, 99, 145). For example, in Ramallah debt topologies are usually established between banks and individual men. However, while this process produces individuals with regard to the law, in everyday life the debt relation joins a bank to entire families. And as we will see later in the chapter, debt topologies are unevenly distributed across and embodied within those families. To develop this argument with more empirical depth, the next section examines precisely how debt becomes folded into the family in Ramallah.

NEGOTIATING OBLIGATORY SUBJECTIVITY

The reference Shadi makes earlier in this chapter to not disrupting or troubling your family was commonly invoked when residents of Um al Sharayet justified going to banks for loans. "Yes, people think it is easier to deal with the bank rather than with a friend! They don't want to feel embarrassed if they are not able to pay back the money to their friends" (interview with Abu Tamer, 9 September 2013).

IM TARIQ We don't borrow from friends or relatives. It's better not to borrow from them to avoid conflicts.

DAREEN Do they ask you to pay them back in a short time?

IM TARIQ No, it is not like that. We just don't want to feel that we rely on others. (Interview with Im Tariq, 11 June 2013)

ALI I took the decision to get married when I was very young, and this was not easy for me. But I thought, I need to prove my ability to have a new family without getting any financial help from my father . . . I decided to arrange everything myself. In fact, my father would have supported me [literally, didn't reject me] with money, but it was my own decision to do it without getting any help from anyone in my family.

DAREEN So, the reason for not getting help from the relatives was?

ALI It was that I do not want anyone in my family to tell me that I need to pay back his money! I wanted to avoid family conflicts. I was very young and they expected me not to succeed in my marriage. I wanted to prove to them that I will not fail and that things will be okay . . . My uncles expected me to fail. I told my father I will not borrow money from him and that I will not get married until I get all the money I need from my work. (Interview with Ali, 28 August 2013)

Decisions to not borrow money from family or friends were closely connected with actual or potential conflict, anxieties about reliance, and feelings of embarrassment and/or shame. Forms of what I termed separation in chapter 3 become a means of ensuring relationships (in this case with family) remain untouched by debt and thus avoid taking on particular qualities. Ecologies of debt are simultaneously shaped by rationalities (such as conflict avoidance) and emotions (such as embarrassment) beyond the economic imperatives that co-constitute debt topologies. These align with and are distributed through obligations to family and friends, which play an important role in shaping life in Um al Sharayet, and thus the relationship between subjectivity and debt. For instance, residents often describe owing money to a bank as a substitution of one obligatory relation for another. "I don't want to feel embarrassed if I am not able to pay back my friend's money. Dealing with your bank loans is easier rather than borrowing from relatives because the bank is an official institution and deals with people without the shyness or feeling embarrassed. The bank has a schedule of payments" (interview with Abu Tariq, 31 August 2013). Abu Tariq owned a small business and borrowed money to fund its expansion. The substitution—often a calculative decision—he describes is based on an understanding of the specific ways in which debt topologies with banks differ from those with family and friends. For Abu Tariq, being tied to a bank comes without the emotional attachments associated with other social relations. Similarly, Waleed prefers to borrow money from a financial institution because it is separated or disconnected from the other spaces of his everyday life. However, the specific capacity of banks to be independent of family and friends was also cast in a more negative light by some residents.

YOUSEF Those people are involved in the bank loans for the rest of their lives. I guess these people didn't find a friend to give them the money they needed.

DAREEN Ah. They didn't find a social bank to get money from.

YOUSEF They have no other financial resources or options. (Interview with Yousef, 3 September 2013)

While positioned as distinct, debt topologies with banks are nevertheless continually thought about through, and in relation to, broader ecologies of obligation. For instance, while Waleed notes that bank debts are accompanied by the threat of legal proceedings—another characteristic that is specific to them—this condition is evaluated in relation to and judged better than an alternative relation, which he terms "social methods."

WALEED The irony is that dealing with the bank is much easier than with people. The bank is an official institution that uses legal procedures in cases where monthly installments are not paid. The bank will tell me that the case will transfer to the court. While the lender will not leave me alone. He will keep calling and calling, and he may use a trouble-shooter, and will threaten me if the conflict becomes a huge crisis.

DAREEN You don't have a problem if you get condemned?

WALEED It is the bank's right to take his mortgage. The person who lends will make it a big story, which involves the entire community. Legal methods are better than social methods. During the legal proceedings I can continue in my natural life. But if the community intervenes in my problem, I will not be able to continue living my life normally. (Interview with Waleed, 4 September 2013)

The trouble-shooters Waleed refers to are usually elderly men who resolve social conflicts in which they are known to both parties. While we encountered stories of them resolving social conflicts of various kinds, there was no evidence that they were resolving debt-related disputes at the time of our research. It is also worth noting that Waleed, whose strong critique of Ramallah as a city of business we encountered in the previous chapter, is advocating a business relationship over a social tie here.

While Waleed considers social methods to be one of the ways in which debts with banks are distinct from those with people, social methods are in fact used by banks too. The head of consumer credit at the Arab Bank gave the example of a customer who was missing payments and not answering his phone. The bank called the customer's father and asked the father to tell his son that the bank wished to speak to him, knowing the emotions of anger and shame that such an act would provoke. In this example, the bank avoids or at least lessens the likelihood of default by utilizing long-standing forms of social pressure grounded in patriarchal power within families (interview with Rami Al-Najjar, 6 August 2014). When the bank extends a loan—usually to a man, as I discuss later in the chapter—it also records his father's name and contact details.

Residents who preferred to borrow from families and friends rather than banks attributed a different set of capacities to bank debts. In some cases, these attributions inverted those discussed thus far. For instance, some residents suggested that borrowing from a bank, rather than from families and friends, causes social conflict. Abu Omar told us that one of his son's friendships had been severely affected after his son had acted as a guarantor for a friend who subsequently defaulted on a bank loan. Abu Omar's son was then forced to repay the debt. Similarly, Yazan explained that "if I take a large loan, and I can't pay it back, I will ask my dad and brothers [for help]. And he will say, why did you take the loan? So, this will create a social crisis with my family and friends" (interview with Yazan, 28 August 2013). Such accounts support the argument that the boundary between debt topologies with banks and other debts and obligations is porous and leaky. However, residents performatively articulate divisions. The distinctiveness of bank debt is described in terms of banks lacking a heart, and the lack of flexibility associated with other types of debt topologies. This specificity is most immediately registered in terms of interest payments. For instance, Abu Mahmoud, who is debt free and told us "debt makes you feel ashamed, and poor," advocates what Waleed termed "social methods." "If you rent your landlord can wait for a month or two. But the bank will take interest if he delays" (interview with Abu Mahmoud, 28 August 2013). "We don't have to pay interest to our relatives who lent us the money. We borrowed money from relatives and friends, and it was 50,000 JD . . . The money I took from my relatives is a debt. I have to pay it back. But I feel comfortable because I don't have to pay interest as with the bank and I can pay it back easily, without any pressure. My relatives don't ask me to pay back their money" (interview with Abu Omar, 2 June 2013). Flexibility was associated with the possibility of debt forgiveness, whether money was owed to a family member, friend, or other institutions aside from banks. "When I need money, I take it from my father and brothers. I repay my brothers but not my father" (interview with Yazan, 15 May 2013). "[A Christian lending organization] forgave my friend who borrowed a loan and was able to repay part of it but couldn't repay the entire amount" (interview with Rami, 8 September 2013).

OBLIGATED SUBJECTIVITY AS LIVED EXPERIENCE

The previous section has shown how different types of obligatory ties are interrelated, and the ways in which residents distinguish between them. This section examines the lived experience of those entanglements. The Bank of Palestine advertisement (figure 5.1) with its visual assertion of family togetherness, happiness, and prosperity does not adequately represent the lived experiences of obligatory subjectivity. Given the number of stories we heard in Um al Sharayet that denounced debt, Im Ghassan's summary of family indebtedness as "like a nightmare" may provide a better understanding. In chapter 1, I noted that Im Ghassan's brother in Jordan sent money to her every month to help pay off the bank loans her husband had taken. However, concerned that this had displaced their suffering onto her brother's family, Im Ghassan ended these transfers. "I had to stop his suffering. I don't want to take advantage of my brother. It is wrong to depend on this financial source. I guess it is the right decision although we are having financial crises all the time. My sons have to depend on themselves. They have to work, save money, and think about their future" (interview with Im Ghassan, 31 August 2013). We can learn a lot about the relationship between debt and obligatory subjectivity here. Im Ghassan's recourse to borrowing from her brother distributed the bank debt across her family, using money derived through a gift relationship to repay the bank loan. This action could be interpreted as highlighting the potential of bank debt to weaken or even break her relationship with her brother, although Im Ghassan never suggested that this happened, just that he suffered financially. It certainly demonstrates how family finances are able to sustain bank repayments. Her alternative solution—her sons depending on themselves—redistributed the burden of repaying bank debt among different family members. This casts Im Ghassan's sons as individuals who are made responsible for their own lives, echoing Lazzarato's theoretical frame. However, the indebted subject after this redistribution remained the family (not individual members), albeit the composition of the family members exposed to bank debt and its effects changed. Her comment that debt becomes "like one of the family members" (interview with Im Ghassan, 31 August 2013) also suggests that it is financial debts that have been transformed by this change, becoming more like family. However, it is crucial that we understand family here as a highly unequal and heterogeneous subject itself.

Just as the banking sector in Palestine has changed over time, so too have family relationships (see Harker 2012). In particular, rural-to-urban migration (S. Tamari 2008), the ability to earn an independent income (S. Tamari 2008), and the repeated emasculation and undermining of older generations by colonial violence (see Jean-Klein 2000, 2003; Muhanna-Matar 2013) have led to the decline in some forms of patriarchal power in Palestine. This in turn has fed into some of the urban changes discussed in the previous chapter, such as Ramallah's reputation as free and a city of business. Nevertheless, inequalities within families, particularly with regard to the gender dynamics, endure and shape forms of obligatory subjectivity that include debt. Much has been written about the ways Palestinian women are (made) responsible for the maintenance of the home and family, while largely excluded from political and economic life (e.g., Jad 1990, 2011; Jean-Klein 2000; Shalhoub-Kevorkian 2000; Shalhoub-Kevorkian and Wing 2015). Here, the focus is on how the gender inequalities that characterize obligatory subjectivity in Um al Sharayet infuse recent practices of living with debt. The analysis foregrounds three particular practices: becoming indebted, managing debt, and wearing debt. These practices illustrate the lived experiences of forms of obligatory subjectivity that encompass debt. Analyzing them shows that women are not excluded from debt ecologies, but rather incorporated in ways that largely restrict their work to managing and wearing debt.

Becoming Indebted

Money management in Um al Sharayet, as in many other parts of Palestine, can be broadly defined as masculine and patriarchal. In the large majority of families we met in Um al Sharayet, men were the sole income earners and women were not paid for work. One of the older participants, Abu Mahmoud, told us he explicitly banned his daughters and daughters-in-law from undertaking paid employment. The gendering of paid work in Um al Sharayet conforms to broader patterns in Palestine, where only 19 percent of women were in paid employment in 2015 (PCBS 2017). Once they marry, most women's access to money is through their husband or male relatives (i.e., father, brothers, sons; cf. Zelizer 2013 on pin money). In such situations, many participants reported that men made decisions about large expenditures, while some women were responsible for smaller purchases, such as groceries. In other cases, men made smaller purchases too. This pattern extends to decisions about becoming indebted. While some participants told us that such decisions were made together, the gendered nature of power relations within families and husband-wife relationships suggests that in such cases female partners and children were not equal decision makers. Some participants freely acknowledge the gendered division of labor with regard to becoming indebted, with decisions being taken by older men.

Banking practices play a role in governing who can become indebted too. Banks require access to a regular salary (either the borrower's or a guarantor's) as a condition of issuing credit. The broader gendered division of labor in Palestine thus ensures that the practice of becoming indebted is largely male. This also means that becoming indebted through company loan schemes and salary advances was also largely a male practice. Female participants who became indebted borrowed money from friends, flatmates, or neighbors. Becoming indebted in such cases was almost always for small amounts of money and/or foodstuffs, and in some cases loans from neighbors were better understood as gifts (Mauss 1954; Strathern 1988).

Fadi and Bana, a married couple with young children, provide an interesting example of many of the factors discussed above, while departing somewhat from more general patterns. Fadi, who works as a public sector employee, explicitly told us he deals with all financial matters and decisions for his family. When we were conducting interviews in 2013, Bana was working full time, in a better-paying private sector job than her husband. She nevertheless ceded control of family finances to Fadi, unlike most other female participants in paid employment, who retained sole access to their salaries. "I have the two ATM cards, mine and my wife's. I withdraw both of the salaries. I put them in another account. I deposit dollars and we spend shekels. Then if we need, we spend dollars. In the past we didn't save all the money because I have a loan for health care and I also took a loan for my brother's wedding. Also, we have health insurance, which we pay in checks" (interview with Fadi, 19 June 2013). Fadi used both sources of income to deal with both daily and large expenses. In the past, this included debt repayment. Since their joint income was relatively high, and they own their house, unlike many participants Fadi was able to save money. At the time he allocated this money to his son, his wife, and his brother. "I am the only one who is responsible for money.

I have three saving accounts: one for my kid. I put 200 [U.S.] dollars in it each month. One for my wife, which I put 100–150 [U.S. dollars] in each month. And one for me, with less money. Our total income is 12,000 shekels [NIS]. 300–400 [U.S.] dollars for my brother and we travel a lot, so we spent a lot" (interview with Fadi, 19 June 2013). This gendering of financial practices extends to decisions about becoming indebted. "We decided to buy a car, but I took the loan in her name and registered the car in my name" (interview with Fadi, 19 June 2013). While both Fadi and Bana have salaried jobs, Bana's higher salary enables her to borrow more, since banks in the Occupied Territories can only claim up to 50 percent of a borrower's monthly income for repayments. Consequently, Bana's salary was tied to, and used to repay, the car loan. Ownership and use of the car were retained by Fadi. Furthermore, although Fadi used the first-person plural when discussing the decision to become indebted, it was clear that he was mainly responsible for this decision.

Space also plays an important role in intersections of gender and obligatory subjectivity. The loan Fadi and Bana took for a car must be understood in relation to their status as homeowners, and the labor of Fadi's father, uncles, and grandmother, who bought the land and built the house in which they live. They were able to do this by migrating to the Gulf to work in the 1970s and 1980s. For many participants who moved to Um al Sharayet more recently, and did not own their house (outright), the space of the home played an important role in the formation of gendered debt relations in other ways. Social norms about masculinity include owning a home prior to, and as a condition of, marriage. In Ramallah, debt has increasingly begun to intersect this long-standing relationship between normative masculinity and space. Debt makes homeownership possible for those with adequate salaries, while the strong preference for homeownership directs many to become indebted. Hence it is not simply that debt has become a new means through which men (i.e., socially recognized forms of male adulthood) are made, but home spaces play an important role in co-constituting this increasingly prevalent relation. This is evident in bank advertisements for credit cards and loans, such as the one discussed at the beginning of this chapter, which prominently feature the heteronormative nuclear family. This articulation of gender-debt-space can manifest in other ways. The increasing cost of housing in Ramallah has meant that some newlyweds rent rather than buy. Two families in our study had married sons, their wives, and infant children living with them during the period of our research, because these sons could not afford to rent their own apartment. These living arrangements in turn created financial pressures that were folded into debts both families owed.

Ramallah, as a distinctive type of urban political space, is also an important co-constituent of gendered practices of becoming indebted, and the resultant obligatory subjects that emerge. The previous chapters outlined how geopolitical and social processes have created the city as something of an exception in contrast to other Palestinian cities (Taraki 2008b; Abourahme 2009). This argument can be extended to female practices of becoming indebted. Unmarried, unrelated women, such as Dina, Huda, Basma, and Hiba, were able to rent a flat together because Ramallah is "free." These practices are commonly held to be not possible in other cities in the Occupied Territories. Living and renting together then fed into practices of borrowing money from one another, including informal loans for rent payments.

Each of the articulations of gender-debt-space discussed thus far demonstrates the co-constitutive role of space in becoming indebted. These cases contrast with accounts of indebted subjectivity that ignore not only the role of gender, but also space. For instance, Lazzarato's (2012, 147–48) subjectless description of using an ATM does not withstand the ethnographic test of theory, as comparison with James's (2015, 113–15) account of ATM use in rural South Africa shows. There, people's relationship with and use of ATMs are quite different because they are indebted to *mashonisas* (loan sharks), who confiscate their bank cards to ensure their own repayment. As elaborated in the next subsection, the importance of a spatial perspective extends to practices of managing debt(s).

Managing Debts

While becoming indebted is strongly tied to paid labor, and therefore reflects the gendered nature of participation in the paid labor force in Palestine, the work of living with debt is closely tied to unpaid labor. In both cases the space of the home is important. Managing debt refers to the (gendered) practices through which people live with and through indebtedness. While bank debts are automatically repaid upon deposit of the account holder's salary, nonbank debts, such as hire-purchase agreements with landlords and debts to employers, are also often prioritized when residents receive their salary. Therefore, in both cases the management of debt is often performed through forms of daily expenditure not directly tied to debt servicing. In other words, residents experience debt largely through managing a greatly reduced income after debt repayments have been taken. These management practices are often the responsibility of women and mirror the work of "shock absorption" women elsewhere carry out with regard to social welfare provision in times of financial hardship (Allon 2014, 13). As the following accounts indicate, the specific techniques employed to manage debt included buying cheaper goods, delaying expenses, and not making some purchases. "When there is a big expense, we try not to spend too much money on other daily expenses, and we tell the kids not to demand many things" (interview with Im Tariq, 11 June 2013). "I do not try to buy what is not important, and I don't buy what I can't pay for. I just try to accept the situation and the fact that I don't have money to buy it. I can wait until I get money to buy what I need. I always try to store basic things" (interview with Im Rami, 24 August 2013). "I try to convince myself that I don't need them. I pretend not to see the expensive goods!" (interview with Im Ghassan, 2 June 2013). Male participants also told us that they ask their wives and children to expect reduced and/or delayed expenditure (interview with Nasser, 20 June 2013). Such practices could be considered de facto forms of rollover. The term "rollover" describes the ways in which people pay off one debt by taking another one, thus in effect rolling over the debt from one creditor to another (Guerin, Morvant-Roux, and Villarreal 2014). However, in Ramallah the cost of repaying debts incurred for large expenses, such as housing mortgages, car loans, and expensive (domestic) commodities, is rolled over onto smaller but more regular everyday expenses. This connection is made explicit by Abu Omar. "I can't feel happy if I spend money for entertainment instead of paying off the debt. I just need to buy the basic things" (interview with Abu Omar, 2 June 2013). These practices of rollover are also spatial, as the burden of repayment moves from sites of paid employment that are largely the domain of men to the home and local shops where many women perform unpaid work.

Debt management practices clearly illustrate how debts, through forms of social redistribution, become folded into families beyond the (male) individual who became indebted. Studies of microfinance have noted how such schemes redistribute the burden of repayment from the individual to a social collective through the joint liability peer group (Rankin 2001; Schuster 2014). Lamia Karim (2008) argues that lenders in Bangladesh leverage family relationships to make repayment an issue of moral standing and female honor. In Ramallah, social redistributions work through existing intimate ties, and involve practices of sharing income within families. For instance, in the case of Abu and Im Ghassan, one of their sons contributed a portion of his income to the family budget. His paid labor was used to manage the debts his parents (and particularly his father) had taken on. One of these debts was incurred when another of their sons was involved in a car accident and required costly surgery. Children also participate in the work of managing debt by modifying their expectations about what can and cannot be afforded. Consequently, just as Fiona Allon (2014, 23) argues that "all kinds of difference then—racial, social, sexual and class—have the potential to be grasped as sites of optimization within financial markets," in Ramallah generation operates alongside the difference of gender to shape the management of debt.

The redistribution of debt management also occurs when unpaid social work, such as attending family social events and honoring social obligations, is sacrificed in order to pay back money to banks. Abu Omar's reference to "entertainment" above, while ambiguous, may well refer to visiting family. All residents discursively affirmed the importance of maintaining social relations. For the majority of Um al Sharayet's residents who are migrants, this means trips that are long and expensive, since their families live in other cities and villages in the West Bank, and there are often Israeli-imposed movement restrictions (Halper 2009; Harker 2009a). Such practices of visiting illustrate how obligatory subjects are shaped by relations that span multiple places. However, the topological proximity of the debt relation, particularly that with banks in which repayment is automatically deducted from salaries, means that some migrant residents manage debt by confining their mobility and limiting their circulation in/through topographic space, something explored in more detail in the next chapter (see also Harker 2017, 612–13).

There are other ways in which space plays an important role in gendered experiences of obligatory subjectivity through managing debts. In particular, the home, understood as a site of feminine interiority, is important.

DAREEN Who is the bank of this family?

ABU OMAR The Minister of Foreign Affairs! And we have the Minister of Internal Affairs.

DAREEN Who is the Minister of the Foreign Affairs?

ABU OMAR Me.

DAREEN And your wife?

ABU OMAR The Minister of Internal Affairs. (Interview with Abu Omar, 2 June 2013)

Abu Omar not only exemplifies a gendered normative understanding of the spatiality of everyday life in Palestine, but also draws our attention to how the home is a key site for female labor managing debt. Particularly for the many women who are not in paid employment, the home is the primary space through which family and consumption are organized and negotiated. The amount of time spent at home may be even greater in Um al Sharayet than in other places, since many migrants do not have thick social relationships with their neighbors and therefore make fewer social visits than they might do in their villages of origin. The interiority in, and of, the home maps onto gendered practices of seeing and understanding debt. "Poor people may have apartments and cars, but they don't have enough money. They are hungry. Banks cause this poverty. They encourage people to take loans. In fact, when people take loans, they lose everything they have" (interview with Abu Ghassan, 15 September 2013). "The loan is like one of the family members. It eats and drinks with me, and it sleeps and wakes up with us. It is like a nightmare!" (interview with Im Ghassan, 31 August 2013). While Abu and Im Ghassan, a married couple, experience ostensibly the same economic circumstances, their descriptions of managing debt are notably different. Abu Ghassan describes the indebted family as seen—or not seen—by someone outside the home, while Im Ghassan describes debt as an intimate part of the family home and experience. This external/internal binary echoes Abu Omar's language of "Minister of Foreign Affairs" and "Minister of Internal Affairs" quoted above. Such a spatial division reflects both the gendered division of labor in the Palestinian economy and the intimate spatiality of home through which women in Um al Sharayet manage debt. Im Ghassan also draws attention to the emotional, embodied labor of obligatory subjectivity.

"Wearing" Debt

Reflecting arguments about the need to understand indebtedness as an everyday process embedded in household dynamics (Deville and Seigworth 2015; Montgomerie and Tepe-Belfrage 2017), Seigworth (2016) argues that relationships with credit and debt are as much (and perhaps more) about touch and gesture than belief and guilt. He uses the term "wearing" to refer to the ways that debts are woven into lives "as new kinds of everyday *textures* to be engaged with and quite often worn" (Seigworth 2016, 24). While he is interested in new wearable technologies and interfaces through which capitalist debt circulates, his concept is useful for describing the embodied, emotional labor of living with debt that Im Ghassan describes above. Debt is not simply managed in an economic sense but worn by many residents of Um al Sharayet. It textures everyday life as a fully embodied experience. "I always try to keep calm. It's just the debt that makes me feel nervous. The friction happens when others ask me to pay them back their money!" (interview with Ziad, 19 June 2013). "I have to pay the [bank] loan and because of that I have to take money from my friends. In addition, problems might occur before I take the money, when I ask my friend to give me money and he says no. That creates a problem between us" (interview with Mohammad, 25 August 2013). "I got very anxious. I started to get mad about everything. My relationship with my wife was affected too" (interview with Abu Omar, 12 September 2013). As these examples illustrate, living with debt in Ramallah produces anxiety, tension, and conflict, which is worn through social relationships with colleagues, friends, and family members (cf. Stanley, Deville, and Montgomerie 2016). It is clear that gender inflects the way debt is worn, unevenly distributing the weight of what Greg Seigworth (2016) terms a debt garment. In addition to the stress and anxiety described by male participants above, a number of married female participants described how they were required to carry out additional emotional labor, by remaining calm and dealing with their husband's anger and frustration.

> IM TARIQ Usually, my husband spends all the money he puts in his pocket, and I save it. I blame him for spending too much, and particularly when he spends too much money on his relatives! And because he gets mad when I blame him for that, I decided to keep silent! I don't want this to cause conflicts within the family.
>
> . . .
>
> CHRIS Do the financial problems or crises points, when money gets tight, cause friction or tension inside the family?
>
> IM TARIQ Sure! When we borrow loans from the bank in particular. My husband feels stressed all the time. We don't feel relaxed when we take a loan, because we have debts to pay for the university and for the school. (Interview with Im Tariq, 11 June 2013)

As with techniques of managing debt, wearing debt is unevenly distributed across generations as well as genders.

> HUSSEIN If my father does not get a good income he gets very mad.
>
> DAREEN So, the whole family will be worried because of him?
>
> HUSSEIN When my dad gets mad, there will be explosions! (Interview with Hussein, 11 June 2013)

The space of the home plays a crucial role in shaping the gendered manner in which debts are worn. In many of the descriptions that follow, participants describe the space of the house or apartment itself as wearing debt. "I am tense most of the time I'm at home, as is my wife. But it's not a big argument, just tension" (interview with Mohammad, 9 June 2013).

CHRIS Does the financial situation cause problems within the household, and how do you cope with these tensions? . . .

IM GHASSAN So much tension that you can't imagine it! We can't feel comfortable when we don't have enough money. We can't have quiet conversations. I wish I could work again! My sons and [name of third-eldest son] in particular don't want me to work outside. (Interview with Im Ghassan, 2 June 2013)

IM OMAR When he first gets in the house, I know that he is facing a problem. I can see it in his face.

ABU OMAR They can understand this from my face. I don't fight with them, and I try to discuss the problem with them, like to advise them not to spend too much this month. (Interview with Abu and Im Omar, 2 June 2013)

The interiority of the home, and the privacy this affords, co-constitute the wearing of debt. Debt is woven into the textures of home as a lived experience. While the privacy of interiority hides the burden of wearing debt, in a broader context where normative discourses disparage indebtedness, it may simultaneously concentrate the anxiety of living with debt. Since many homes are inhabited by married couples and multigenerational families, this space also plays a key role in distributing the extent to which different people wear debt within families, and the different ways in which it is worn.

LIVING WITH(OUT) BANK DEBTS

As noted earlier, experiences of obligatory subjectivity also include the work families do to separate, exclude, or keep debt at a distance from other obligations. This section examines these practices. Many residents' practical navigation of the debt ecologies in which they were entangled included efforts to distance debt ties—particularly with banks—by drawing on forms of mutuality rooted in the ongoing practice of kinship, and money being gifted rather than loaned. "We, as brothers, help each other. When one decides to marry, we will all support him. Then he will . . . help the others when they get married. Our strategy is if you help me now, I'll help you tomorrow" (interview with Ziad, 7 May 2013). "I don't have any commitments, just to my sister, and she doesn't consider it a loan. But if God allows, I'll repay her" (interview with Fadi, 28 August 2013). "I'm very lucky. I work with my father, and the money I got from him is not a loan. It is like financial help" (interview with Hussein, 27 August 2013). Stephen Gudeman (2016, 12) defines mutuality as "connecting to others." Through such connections Um al Sharayet's residents avoid becoming indebted to banks and distance such debts from the broader ecologies of obligation in which they are entangled. Moral sentiments around kinship provide a justification for downplaying what Waleed refers to as financial obligations.

ABU OMAR We must sometimes sacrifice money for social duties. Money is not everything in life!

DAREEN Right.

ABU OMAR I can't lose my social relations, my relatives and friends in order to get money from work. (Interview with Abu Omar, 3 October 2013)

The social obligations don't stop. I think of them all day and night. I can postpone a financial obligation, and this will not affect my social life, but I can't postpone the social obligation, which is connected to financial obligations at the same time . . . Social commitment requires providing more things than money, such as psychological support, moral and cultural development. And because social commitment is linked to the culture of the community, it is the most difficult to meet because it requires a true representation of the identity of this community. I can stop thinking about the bills, but I just can't stop thinking about social obligation because it reflects my daily life. The family demands I don't stop. The wider family's obligations are harder to meet than the nuclear family's. Social obligations are the basic obligations, and financial obligations are just a means to facilitate social life. (Interview with Waleed, 4 September 2013)

Efforts to distance debt seek to create alternatives. These alternatives illustrate how space for rational and ethical reflection emerges amid obligatory subjectivity. Alternatives are grounded in different value systems, which are constantly in competition with each other. When asked, many residents affirmed the moral/ethical value of some obligatory ties, particularly with family, over their obligations to repay debts. This disregard for debt (and affirmation of family) is very different from the politics of collective debt refusal Lazzarato (2012) imagines as the means of resistance to indebted man (see also Davey 2019). However, in practice many residents of Um al Sharayet repaid debt obligations at the expense of fulfilling other obligatory ties. Often this occurred because bank debts were more tightly bound to subjects than other obligations, through the mandatory deduction of salary deposits. The discursive affirmation of social obligations but prioritization of repaying bank debts foregrounds the discussions of slow violence and endurance that follow in the next two chapters.

CONCLUSION: FAMILY, GENDER, AND POSTCOLONIZING DEBT

In this chapter I have argued that existing accounts of indebted subjectivity must be augmented by fuller consideration of the other obligations through which forms of personhood emerge. I have deployed the concept of obligatory subjectivity to foreground the entanglement of debt and other obligations, arguing that this form of subjectivity is unevenly co-constituted and inhabited, both socially and spatially. The complex ecologies of obligation mapped throughout this chapter are key for understanding the spatiality of debt in Palestine. Such entanglements intervene in and mediate the gaps between obligatory subjects and (local) financial institutions, states, and international financial institutions (Leyshon, Burton, et al. 2004; Flaherty and Banks 2013), complicating the biopolitics of debt that Lazzarato's theory assumes is at work. To state this is to reiterate the arguments for a postcolonial understanding of debt and obligation developed in chapter 1. I want to return to and develop these arguments further here, by drawing on anthropological scholarship of obligated subjectivity.

In her book *The Gender of the Gift*, Marilyn Strathern (1988, xii) argues that "to ask about the gender of the gift . . . is to ask about the situation of gift exchange in relation to the form that domination takes in these societies. It is also to ask about the 'gender' of analytical concepts, the worlds that particular assumptions sustain." Strathern's (1988) argument explores different understandings of personhood and practices of domination in Melanesia. She suggests that gift giving is a gendered activity, regardless of whether women are involved. Her work provides further evidence of the entangled relations between gender, obligation, and debt, which I have extended to include space in this chapter. However, Strathern also stresses that gender is a metaphor or fiction that is used to understand worlds. It is a conceptual category grounded in Western scholarship, where "Western" is deployed by Strathern (1988, 341–43) as a deliberately vague geographical reference to argue for explicitly situated knowledges, while noting the difficulties of locating oneself transparently (cf. Rose 1997). Consequently, the use of concepts such as gender, gift, and commodity to make comparisons must be understood as "an explicit Western device for the organization of experience and knowledge" (Strathern 1988, 31). Another way of framing this argument is that theories have specific geographies. As noted in chapter 1, much has been written about geographies of theory in the wake of European colonialisms (SJTP 2003; Robinson 2006; Ananya Roy 2009; Pollard et al. 2009; SJTP 2014). This body of literature demonstrates how colonialisms have long shaped the epistemic and political grounds on which knowledge is constructed in ways that reaffirm and reiterate Eurocentric privilege (Chakrabarty 2000). The production of scholarly knowledge also occurs alongside and through colonial legacies of socioeconomic inequality that differentially distribute the rewards of doing theory and/or policy-relevant work among different regions, institutions, and scholars (Oldfield and Parnell 2014, 2–3).

In relation to conceptualizations of debt, Parker Shipton (2007, x) argues that while "lending over long distances . . . weaves webs of obligation between places that hitherto had few common ties . . . that does not mean that everyone, everywhere, understands borrowing and lending in the same way." Strathern and Shipton push us to think more carefully about how geography co-constitutes debt theoretically. This chapter has shown how Ramallah, a space shaped extensively by settler-colonialism, unsettles singular accounts of debt that are often attached to the high-velocity circulations of capital in financial centers. While such circulations stretch well beyond these centers, they are not all-encompassing, nor do they operate in the abstract. By focusing on only those circulations, we miss the ways in which they become entangled, folded, absorbed, or expunged from particular ecologies of practice, co-constituting action and being co-constituted differently in turn. In other words, existing theorizations of debt do not account for its entanglement in practices of social obligation and (colonial) violence. Strathern's (1988) work is useful here because it explicitly draws attention to the ways in which postcolonial critique intersects with and proceeds through the difference of gender. For instance, the practices of social-spatial rollover and "wearing" debt in Ramallah are different from the "feminisation of finance" Allon (2014) examines in the global North, where women become debtors, and mortgages underwrite derivative markets. Theorizing through the gendered, colonial geographies of debt in Ramallah opens up and pluralizes understandings of debt everywhere by demanding more detail about these other circulations. In other words, the experiences of families in Um al Sharayet demand a theoretical account of bank debts as one of a number of different ways in which people can be indebted, and debts as one of many obligations. This renders existing theorizations of debt, like Lazzarato's (2012, 2015), more parochial. This critique is productive, since it forces scholars to think more carefully about the specificity of their theoretical apparatus, in terms of its movement and translation. Doing post-colonial critique through its intersections with gender-as-difference (Strathern 1988) also holds existing theoretical apparatuses to account for the ways in which they write out multiple forms of difference. Perhaps the most obvious axis of difference when writing from Palestine is settler-colonial violence. The precise relationship between debt and violence requires considerably more exploration. This is the task of the next chapter.

debt, violence, and financial crisis ordinariness

"POOR PEOPLE . . . DON'T HAVE ENOUGH MONEY"?

■ The previous chapter examined how proliferating debt relations in Um al Sharayet are folded into (or kept apart from) other obligatory ties that are unequally distributed both socially and spatially. The discussion of gender and obligatory subjectivity illustrated how debt emerges from and reiterates existing inequalities. Such inequalities can be framed as forms of violence, as can other debt-related practices that cause harm. For instance, Im Rami described not buying food because debt repayments limited her family's disposable income (interview with Im Rami, 24 August 2013). Abu Omar said that he did not pay for entertainment in order to pay off debt, which may well have meant missing social events and potentially weakening kinship ties (interview with Abu Omar, 2 June 2013). Mohammad told us he had arguments with friends as a result of borrowing money (interview with Mohammad, 25 August 2013).

In August 2014, the research team shared narratives of debt-related harm with national and municipal policy makers, representatives of the banking industry, and other academic researchers at a Debt Summit that we convened at the Ramallah Municipality. However, national policy makers working for both the Palestinian Authority (PA) and the Palestinian Monetary Authority (PMA) dismissed our narratives. We were told that residents were simply exaggerating or that each case was isolated and not representative of a larger phenomenon. Similar acts of dismissal occurred on other occasions too. Part of the reason policy makers dismissed claims about debt-related harm was because understandings of violence in Palestine are closely tied to Israeli settler-colonial practices. At their most spectacular, such practices include killing, the maiming of bodies, and the destruction of property. Even though debt-related violence is connected to such practices, it is thought about differently. For those in positions of political power, debt was not visible as violence. The relative invisibility of Um al Sharayet as a neighborhood within the larger Ramallah conurbation also contributed to this problem. This chapter seeks to address the challenge of articulating the violence of debt, using Rob Nixon's (2011) concept of slow violence and Lauren Berlant's (2011) work on crisis ordinariness. I will argue that debt can be a form of slow violence: accretive and hardly visible, but not invisible. The slow violence of debt creates conditions of what I term financial crisis ordinariness, a situation of adjudication, adjustment, and improvisation in response to ongoing harm. Developing the book's main argument for understanding debt spatially, the chapter focuses on the geographies of slow violence and financial crisis ordinariness to comprehend its impact. This is largely seen through residents' lived experience of paid and unpaid work, and understandings of time and productivity that emerge in relation to work. In doing so, the chapter demonstrates how the violence of finance is both distinct from, and folded into, existing forms of settler-colonial violence. As the previous chapters have shown, Israeli settler colonialism has played a powerful role in creating the conditions in which finance has emerged and become concentrated in Ramallah. However, finance also draws on practices and rationalities from other places, and thus is somewhat distinct too. Furthermore, while the concept of financial crisis ordinariness helps us understand the slow violence of debt, experiences of work and understandings of productivity also continually point to ways in which debt relations are not inherently violent. Chapter 7 focuses on the ways in which debt can capacitate forms of livable life. Often these forces of slowly violent destruction and capacitation are intimately connected. Therefore, much of the empirical discussion in this and the next chapter foregrounds complex moments in which different forms of work can both be violent and capacitate endurance. Given these complexities, the conclusion to this chapter argues that conceptually, financial crisis ordinariness must be deployed alongside endurance.

Chapter Six

Nixon (2011, 2) describes slow violence as "a violence that occurs gradually and out of sight, a violence of delayed destruction that is dispersed across time and space, an attritional violence that is typically not viewed as violence at all." Slow violence is "incremental and accretive," "long," and "staggered" (Nixon 2011, 2), even as it is caused by fast-paced, short-term capitalist rationalities (Nixon 2011, 17–18). The emphasis on the nonspectacular, incremental, and accretive resonates closely with Berlant's (2011, 95) concept of slow death, "the physical wearing out of a population in a way that points to its deterioration as a defining condition of its experience and historical existence." These conceptual terms draw attention to, and help critique, practices that are not usually thought about or recognized as forms of violence at all. Many of the practices described in the last chapter that I categorized as becoming indebted, managing debt, and wearing debt might be thought about as forms of slow violence. For instance, the compulsory transfer agreement that enables banks in Palestine to withdraw an agreed-upon percentage of the debtor's monthly salary, which can be up to 50 percent of their income, transforms the act of being paid each month into the slow erosion of a family's income by financial institutions. In the case of Im Ghassan, this spread geographically to encompass her brother in Jordan. As the examples cited in the opening paragraph of this chapter show, this violence also spreads socioeconomically as other forms of expenditure are foregone, and intimate relationships are affected.

The adjective "slow" names a particular kind of violence primarily in terms of its temporal rhythm and frame (Nixon 2011; see also Stoler 2016). However, slow violence is also spatial. First, it is dispersed (both temporally and spatially) rather than concentrated. Often it is hard to make visible because it does not cohere in(to) a particular topographic site or event. In Palestine this dispersal occurs through money transfers within families, which are both hard to see and to quantify. However, these topologies become enfolded in topographic urban spaces and objects—multistory apartment buildings, the proliferation of consumer goods, and traffic congestion because of increasing numbers of cars. This dispersal through the topography of the city is related to a second spatiality of slow violence, displacement.

The first example of slow violence Nixon provides in his book—toxic waste that is shipped from export-rich nations to Africa—is one of spatial displacement. The violence of pollution—its ability to degrade environments—is displaced from rich countries to poorer ones, forcing people to leave their land. Innovatively, Nixon expands the idea of displacement to include the loss of land and resources through extraction, theft, and/or degradation. This form of displacement leaves "communities stranded in a place stripped of the very characteristics that made it inhabitable" (Nixon 2011, 19). People are displaced or stripped of place even though they themselves do not move. In the Occupied West Bank, the slow violence of debt displacement works through topological and topographic networks that link urban and rural spaces, and Palestinians in the Occupied Territories with those elsewhere. While debt contracts are concentrated in Ramallah, there were many examples of these debt relations being displaced to other places through kinship ties. By borrowing money, or relying on gifts from relatives elsewhere, residents such as Im Ghassan and Abu Omar rolled over debt repayments spatially and socially. Palestinians in other parts of the West Bank, Jordan, and the United States are folded into the rapidly growing Ramallah debt economy through their relatives living there. If these practices of socio-spatial rollover are moving the consequences of growing financial debt in Ramallah beyond the city, it is also possible to think about displacement where people themselves remain in place. "Poor people may have apartments and cars, but they don't have enough money. They are hungry. Banks cause this poverty. They encourage people to take loans. In fact, when people take loans, they lose everything they have" (interview with Abu Ghassan, 15 September 2013). Abu Ghassan's quote suggests that the financial resources necessary to live in place are extracted by banks, almost from "underneath" families. The families remain while the resources they need to live there dwindle. This example leads to a third spatiality of slow violence: impasse.

Impasse describes slow violence as a form of dynamic capture: a moving around in circles, going nowhere. People and things are stuck, even if they are not imprisoned as such. Such an understanding is drawn from the work of Berlant (2011), who illustrates impasse using the spatial metaphor of the cul-de-sac. Cul-de-sacs are spaces where things keep moving, but do not go anywhere (Berlant 2011, 199). Berlant also describes impasse as a time-space of "animated suspension," like a cartoon character who continues to run even though they are over the edge of the cliff, rather than suspended animation, which would be the same cartoon character frozen in a block of ice (Berlant 2011, 199). The temporality of impasse is slow, but nevertheless dynamic and ongoing. Given its long duration, what is termed the Palestinian-Israeli conflict is often thought about as an impasse (Abu Lughod 2013; Middle East Initiative 2013), a primarily political space in which Palestinians try to move both literally and figuratively but are unable to go anywhere. The growth of financial debt in Ramallah emerges from and contributes to this broader impasse.

The ongoing Israeli Occupation, and the multiple colonial processes that constitute the Occupation, have systematically impoverished Palestinians living in historic Palestine (and elsewhere) since 1948. More recently, the geographic concentration of the Palestinian economy in the Ramallah conurbation, the failure of the PA to realize Palestinian aspirations for an independent national homeland, and increasing levels of inequality within the Occupied Territories have all contributed to the demand for debt, as one kind of response to this impasse.

FINANCIAL CRISIS ORDINARINESS

The three spatialities of slow violence—dispersal, displacement, and impasse—infuse residents' experiences of living with debt. They create a condition that I will term "financial crisis ordinariness." Crisis ordinariness is a concept Berlant (2011, 54) introduces to explore "crisis-shaped subjectivity amid the ongoingness of adjudication, adaptation, and improvisation." Crisis ordinariness is positioned conceptually as a counterpoint to trauma narratives, which narrate responses to crisis as dramatic shifts. This latter frame is often used to describe Palestinian life, given the many ruptures that have occurred across the twentieth and twenty-first centuries, which include the events of '48, the invasion and colonization of the Occupied Territories during and after 1967, and the first and second intifadas (see for example Gregory 2004; Pappe 2006). However, while Israeli colonialism can be narrated as and through these violent spectacles, the slow wearing away of the population is arguably a more pervasive form of violence, precisely because it works over longer time periods to target the population at large. Crisis ordinariness describes practices of living with and through severe forms of violence that are disruptive but become part of people's ongoing lives. Building on Berlant's ideas, financial crisis ordinariness names the practices through which people live with and adjust to finance, particularly the slow violence that financial practices and relations can embody. This way of understanding how people live with/through finance is also different from narratives of financial crisis, which deploy the framing of a decisive break that demands a dramatic response (Roitman 2013). In Palestine, financial crisis ordinariness is folded into, and emerges from, the settler-colonial violence of the Israeli Occupation. However, as noted already, it is very different in form and experience from the types of violence that are usually studied in Palestine. In particular, financial crisis ordinariness in Um al Sharayet is characterized by emotional stress, strained relationships, and exhausted bodies, as the previous chapter began to show. It bears a greater similarity to narratives of living with debt in other parts of the world (e.g., Han 2012; Deville 2015; Davies, Montgomerie, and Wallin 2015) than more conventional analyses of violence in the Occupied Territories. I quote a number of stories to give a sense of the range of experiences of financial crisis ordinariness. The recurrence of these stories also challenges policy-maker dismissals that debt-related harm was isolated to a few cases. "As an experience, if you put pressure on yourself by taking a loan or [paying with] checks you get mad. So, it's better not to ask people for money or to take loans" (interview with Yazan, 12 June 2013). "In general, I feel depressed about my financial situation. I have to pay the loan and because of that I have to take money from my friends. Additionally, problems might occur before I take the money, when I ask my friend to give me money and he says no. That creates a problem between us. I feel depressed all the time. At the beginning of the month, in the middle, and at the end" (interview with Mohammad, 25 August 2013).

> ABU OMAR I'm convinced that my family members will not say anything if I'm not able to pay the money back. When I have enough money, I'll pay it directly to them. And they know that I don't delay the payments if I am able to pay them. The consequences had physiological effects on me.
>
> IM OMAR He couldn't sleep.
>
> ABU OMAR I was worried. It was like a nightmare. I was able to lend money to my relatives and suddenly I became a borrower. I had to pay more than 50,000 JD to my relatives. At that time, I was the only breadwinner in this family, and my kids were at school. I had to pay all the expenses beside the loan payments. My budget was overloaded. I'm just a simple employee who gets a humble salary. I started asking myself different questions about my ability to control my family's financial situation. It was not easy. I got very anxious. I started to get mad about everything. My relationship with my wife was affected too. (Interview with Abu and Im Omar, 12 September 2013)

"Stress doesn't end. People who are involved in loan payments are always worried. I'm less worried because I have relied on less complex financial options since I signed the contract" (interview with Waleed, 4 September 2013).

> I'm lucky. I was able to buy a house without dealing with banks. I didn't take a loan from the bank. My landlord gave me a chance to pay all the house payments over a three-year period. It is not easy to think about this

much debt. The debt is a big problem. I just can't feel calm because I think a great deal about the debt. So, I'm worried even though I didn't take a loan. Sometimes I feel upset and want to commit suicide. Sometimes people have the right to commit suicide due to big debts. (Interview with Hiba, 10 September 2013)

Hiba is a single woman who lives in a rented apartment with four other single women. During our research, she was not in debt herself. Her account, while somewhat hyperbolic, underscores how even imaginaries about living with debt are filled with anxiety and stress. However, it is important to note that even though this was a common experience in Um al Sharayet, it was not universal. Hussein was relaxed about repaying the money he owed, because good family relations meant he did not consider the money he took from his father to be a loan. He told us that he would be forgiven the amount should he not be able to pay it back (interview with Hussein, 27 August 2013). For Ali, a good friendship with his neighbor who had lent him money to buy a laptop included the possibility of forbearance and thus (eventual) repayment without the stress experienced by other residents (interview with Ali, 28 August 2013).

There are two broader points emerging from these accounts. First, financial crisis ordinariness is socially distributed. Whether Mohammad's difficulties with his friends, Abu Omar's relationship with his wife, or Hussein and Ali's more positive relations with family and friends, debt-related stress, anxiety, and difficulties in Palestine are something that is often experienced and distributed (unevenly) through kinship and friendship relationships. This argument builds on the concept of obligatory subjectivity introduced in the previous chapter. The relational nature of responses contrasts with some accounts of debt-related stress elsewhere that emphasize isolation and individualization (Davies, Montgomerie, and Wallin 2015; although see Deville 2015; Stanley, Deville, and Montgomerie 2016). This social distribution also provides further support for a topological understanding of debt tied to obligatory subjectivity, rather than liberal-legal renderings that produce and hold persons individually accountable for their debts.

Second, understanding financial crisis ordinariness as a shared situation, rather than an individual (psychological) problem, is also politically important. It provides a counternarrative to some of the responses we received from policy elites in Ramallah, who dismissed stories of debt-related harm as isolated, individual cases. Such responses drew on liberal understandings of debt as a deliberative economic strategy people employed to improve their lives (cf. Graeber 2011). However, experiences of financial crisis ordinariness in Um al Sharayet stemmed from a shared situation. This was most clearly articulated in accounts of a prior moment, when residents were forced to take debt unwillingly. "I was forced to do it. I need to graduate, and this cannot happen unless I pay all the money for university. The university doesn't give the students their formal educational certification unless they pay, and I need to work after graduation. I guess no company will accept my job application if it doesn't include a copy of my graduation certification" (interview with Ziad, 26 September 2013). "I take the loans because I'm forced to" (interview with Huda, 27 August 2013). "You know, there's no choice. There's no choice. You must go there. You must go to the bank. Because you won't meet anyone who can give you $40,000. No one can give you this amount of money. Your only choice is the bank. The solution is the bank, not the people" (interview with Nasser, 27 August 2013). "Recently, financial liquidity is not available, because of the financial crisis and due to government's economic policies, which are imposed on people. So all financial transactions depend on bank checks, and banks became the only alternative to provide a source of money needed to buy" (interview with Waleed, 4 September 2013). "We are a part of the employees' class who depend on bank loans as a main source of money. It is reality" (interview with Abu Omar, 12 September 2013). I argue that what Ziad and Huda describe as a "force" implicitly names the geopolitical and political-economic processes described in chapter 2. In some ways it is similar to what Susanne Soederberg (2014, 4) describes as debtfare, "a component of neoliberal state intervention that has emerged to mediate, normalize and discipline the monetized relations that inhabit the poverty industry." However, in Palestine, finance is folded into the multiple violences of the Israeli Occupation, and hence recourse to neoliberalism as an explanatory frame is inadequate. Crucially, this force is part of, and mediated by, the lived experience of financial crisis ordinariness. Thinking about financial crisis ordinariness as a geopolitical and political-economic force that is also part of everyday life draws on feminist geographies that have traced the personal and the political through the local and global (Pratt and Rosner 2012; Pain and Staeheli 2014). Such work has convincingly argued that global and intimate scales are not mutually exclusive, as they are often imagined, but "profoundly intertwined" (Pratt and Rosner 2012, 1). This insight is also reflected in narratives emerging from Um al Sharayet.

CHRIS What are your opinions about taking on such a financial obligation?

NADIA Fear, not because of taking on such loans, but the fear is because of the political and financial instability in this country. (Interview with Nadia, 4 September 2013)

To build on these understandings of debt-induced financial crisis ordinariness in Ramallah, the chapter now explores the place where such ideas were articulated most clearly: in accounts of low-paid and unpaid work.

(LOW) PAID WORK

Work and debt are intertwined in a number of ways (cf. Lazzarato 2015). Both are means of paying for the high and rising cost of living, particularly housing, transportation, education, and consumer goods that have come to define modernity in Ramallah (Taraki 2008b). As the cost of living has risen (because salaries have stagnated or decreased for those who used to work in Israel and the Gulf), debt has increasingly taken the place of income derived from work as a means of paying for consumption goods and activities. Nevertheless, paid work is also the primary means through which financial debts are secured and repaid in Palestine (cf. Bylander 2015). As noted earlier in the book, given the significant risks of lending money in Palestine, banks will not extend credit to someone who does not have a salaried job or cannot provide a guarantor who has a salaried job (interview with Rami Al-Najjar, 6 August 2014). Thus, paid work underpins the emerging debt economy, even as debt replaces income derived from work. It is therefore not surprising that in a city where levels of indebtedness have risen rapidly, residents report working a great deal.

Many residents of Um al Sharayet had two jobs, particularly migrants when they first moved to Ramallah. For instance, Abu Ghassan came to Ramallah to work in one of the government ministries but found additional work as a plumber after being encouraged to do so by friends. Poor physical health and the political situation led him to quit plumbing after three years (interview with Abu Ghassan, 30 April 2013). Yazan, a refugee who moved to Um al Sharayet from nearby Al Amari Camp as a child, worked for both the PA and as a part-time teacher at Al Quds University (interview with Yazan, 12 June 2013). Huda worked two separate nursing jobs when she first moved to Ramallah. During this period, she "felt more stable" and sent some of her income to her parents. Because she had quit one of these jobs when we conducted interviews, her parents now sent her money, since she found her single salary insufficient to live on (interview with Huda, 18 June 2013). Nasser, who worked in a full-time salaried job, also co-owned a small retail outlet that he worked in part-time some evenings (interview with Nasser, 20 June 2013). Other participants had to balance paid employment with full-time study. "You know, my wife and I are students. We go to university five days a week, and then she goes to her father's house, and I come to work. Then we meet at midnight in the apartment" (interview with Ziad, 25 May 2013). "I go to university from eight to four and then I go to work at night, and my friend has two jobs. In the morning he works in the bank and in the afternoon he comes to work in this shop . . . I study and work. I only have one day off which is Friday. My wife works too, and because she works in the morning and I work at night we can't attend social obligations together" (interview with Ali, 24 September 2013). While most residents who participated in our research no longer had two jobs, this reflects an unintentional selection bias toward recruiting people who had time to conduct repeat interviews. This became apparent toward the end of the research period, when one participant began a second job. After finishing his paid employment, he began the process of setting up his own business in the evenings. It became very hard to schedule interviews with him. In other cases, additional work was desired but not possible.

ABU SAMIR I wish I had more time so I could get another job.

DAREEN Another job?

ABU SAMIR Yes. I wish.

CHRIS Is it a choice or a necessity?

ABU SAMIR A necessity! (Interview with Abu Samir, 28 September 2013)

While the unemployment rate in the Occupied Territories, which hovered around 27 percent between 2012 and 2015 (PCBS 2017), meant that for some there were no jobs available, in Abu Samir's case the long hours he worked at his retail job prevented him taking another one. Nor was Abu Samir alone in working long hours at one job. Dina reported working for thirteen hours a day in a previous job (interview with Dina, 21 April 2013), while Basma worked 9 A.M. to 9 P.M. shifts in a retail position, six days a week (interview with Basma, 21 May 2013). Mohammad told us he worked ten hours a day in a hotel because of his seniority (interview with Mohammad, 9 June 2013). Residents of Um al Sharayet consistently told us that working long hours, whether in one or two jobs, had become the norm in Ramallah. These stories of working long hours were closely tied to accounts of stress and exhaustion.

DAREEN So you feel so tired after work and you need to rest?

HUSSEIN It is more than tired. I feel more stressed . . . I feel depressed when I work most of the time. (Interview with Hussein, 29 September 2013)

BASMA I submitted my resignation, but my manager didn't accept it.

DAREEN Why?

BASMA I want to find a better job. I feel tired doing two shifts. (Interview with Basma, 4 June 2013)

"I work all day, and come back home late at night and very tired" (interview with Abu Tamer, 18 May 2013). "My life is working and sleeping" (interview with Huda, 28 September 2013). Long hours, tiredness, and stress are all characteristics of financial crisis ordinariness in Ramallah. They reflect ongoing struggles to live with and adjust to the high cost of living in the city. For some but not all participants, these experiences entangle debt repayments. They are familiar embodiments of slow violence for those living on the margins in many places (Berlant 2011, 161–90). Povinelli (2011, 3) argues that this is particularly the case for indigenous peoples living in settler-colonial states, where suffering is "ordinary, chronic, and cruddy rather than catastrophic, crisis-laden, and sublime." Resonating with Nixon's (2011) description of slow violence, Povinelli describes violence toward indigenous communities in Australia as a "noise" that sounds "more like a hum than an explosion," a slow decomposition "according to a rhythm that almost feels natural," or at least comes to be expected and (almost) accepted (Povinelli 2011, 137). In the Palestinian context, this hum of slow violence is heard and interpreted in discussions of being busy and not having enough time due to work.

RAMI Life has changed. People are busy with their jobs. They want to survive. In general, companies and factories are not limited to eight hours a day work. Many people agree to work overtime shifts or to have a second job. People want to earn more money, so they spend most of their time at work. Personally, I don't have fixed working hours. I work in the morning, afternoon, and sometimes until late at night, like 2 or 3 A.M.

DAREEN You work most of the time.

RAMI Yes, and it is not only me. All people work day and night. (Interview with Rami, 3 October 2013)

CHRIS And do you find your colleagues at work don't have enough time?

DINA Yes, many of them say they don't have enough time.

CHRIS But I don't understand. When people finish their work at 3 P.M. what do they do then?

DINA Some people have two jobs; others have to study. Many of my colleagues are MA students. Many of them can't fulfill social obligations because they work and study. (Interview with Dina, 24 September 2013)

In the quote above, Rami alludes to the ways in which work keeps him very busy. However, his account does not necessarily imply that this busy-ness is an experience of violence. Nixon (2011, 2) notes that slow violence largely occurs "out of sight" and is hard to make visible. To address this challenge, I want to follow Dina's observation that the consequences of being busy with work and not having enough time are most commonly evaluated with regard to participants' social relationships and obligations. "It's not easy to have many relationships with neighbors in this building because most of the men and women have jobs. They are busy" (interview with Nadia, 2 May 2013).

DAREEN Do you still have strong relationships like before?

YOUSEF No, they are busy now with their business. (Interview with Yousef, 6 June 2013)

"You know, you want to finish your work and you also want to take care of your family. Also to take care of your social obligations. Always you don't have enough time to finish all these things together" (interview with Khaled, 24 September 2013). "I don't have time to visit people, because we work all the time and I feel that there is not enough time to do anything but work" (interview with Hussein, 29 September 2013). The quotes above suggest that worlds of paid work are colonizing and undermining social life. This is important because, as I will suggest in the next chapter, obligatory subjectivity is one of the key means through which Palestinians capacitate endurance. The need to work a lot is therefore a process of decapacitation. Such an understanding has a spatial and temporal component for many migrant residents. Their evaluations were implicitly drawing on a contrast with other (village) spaces and times, where the work of building and maintaining social relations was more extensive (see next section). Paid work, a means of repaying debt for many residents of Um al Sharayet, can therefore be positioned as a kind of slow violence, as it undoes the social support systems that enable Palestinian society in the West Bank to function. However, this argument requires further nuance, because the line dividing social life and working life is often blurred in practice.

This section positions the labor of building and maintaining social obligations as a form of unpaid work. In doing so, it departs from the views of research participants, who did not consider or term their social activities as work. I position social activities in this way to make the case that forms of unpaid work are folded into rather than neatly divided from forms of paid work. Thinking about social obligations as a form of unpaid work through which social relationships and dependencies are manufactured, maintained, and modified makes clear how different kinds of work co-constitute each other (K. Mitchell, Marston, and Katz 2004). I argue that rather than paid work diminishing social life (unpaid work), both paid and unpaid work are enfolded in the slow violence of debt. This argument builds on residents' recognition that the boundary between financial and social obligations was porous. "Before I was addicted to work. My two boys grew up fast and I didn't recognize that. I worked day and night for the benefit of my family. I don't regret it but today we are frustrated. But someone has to pay the taxes and I pay part of that" (interview with Shadi, 3 June 2013).

As noted in the previous section, being busy due to paid employment was often felt to be problematic because it meant that residents did not have enough time for their social obligations. Initially, this situation might be viewed as an example of capitalist social relations subsuming other forms of social life (Katz 2006, 244; Lazzarato 2012, 2015). Such an understanding places a divide between the economic or financial and the social, in ways echoed by some participants. "I have escaped from financial obligations, but I am committed to the social ones" (interview with Abu Mahmoud, 28 August 2013).

YOUSEF It is harder to meet [social obligations] than the financial.

CHRIS Why is that?

YOUSEF Because I'm busy most of the time, and my relatives live far away from here. The financial is not hard to meet. I can manage the expenses. I wish I could solve all of my problems through financial obligations. (Interview with Yousef, 3 September 2013)

However, the categories financial and social are performatives, instantiating and re-creating a conceptual division through which practices are understood, acted upon, and regulated (T. Mitchell 2002; Latour 2005; Mackenzie, Muniesa, and Siu 2007; Muniesa 2014; Gudeman 2016). These divisions are always at risk of dissolution. In the following account, Waleed both maintains and dissolves the division between the social and the financial (or economic) at various points.

> The social obligations don't stop. I think of them all day and night. I can postpone a financial obligation, and this will not affect my social life, but I can't postpone the social obligation, which is connected to financial obligations at the same time . . . Social commitment requires providing more things than money, such as psychological support, moral and cultural development. And because social commitment is linked to the culture of the community, it is the most difficult to meet because it requires a true representation of the identity of this community. I can stop thinking about the bills, but I just can't stop thinking about social obligation because it reflects my daily life. The family demands I don't stop. Large families' obligations are harder to meet rather than small families. Social obligations are the basic obligations, and financial obligations are just a means to facilitate social life. (Interview with Waleed, 4 September 2013)

The dissolution of the division between economic and social obligations, such as when Waleed acknowledges that social commitments require money and psychological support as well as moral and cultural development, is important because it demonstrates how debt-related slow violence enfolds everyday life practices in ways that make the distinction between the social and the economic unhelpful. Everyday practices are both economic and social simultaneously. The division performed by these latter terms is nevertheless effective as a means through which participants evaluated their own practices and decisions. Waleed's, Yousef's, and Abu Mahmoud's assessment of their social and financial obligations, and their standing relative to each other, map on to accounts that cite paid work as responsible for a lack of time—time that was needed for social obligations. However, many residents from refugee families suggested that it was the social work of fulfilling obligations that kept them busy in ways that exhaust them physically and financially. The reason such accounts emerge from refugee families in particular is because these families tend to have lived in Um al Sharayet longer, and thus in most cases own their homes outright. Their financial obligations in this regard are therefore significantly smaller than those many migrant residents face. "Some time I would like to go out on Friday. But there is a wedding and I have to go. There are weddings I can escape, but others I can't. Also, other social obligations. When there are many, time will be tight" (interview with Shadi, 23 September 2013). "We have relatives who live in a city far away, and there are many occasions and deaths in particular during the year, most of the time. We have to visit them and we can't avoid these occasions" (interview with Rami, 7 September 2013). "Social events take a lot of time, especially if the events are in the camp and I visit many friends there. But I don't feel sorry about the time I spend there at all" (interview with Fadi, 25 September 2013). These narratives show that nondebt social events are also thought about as obligatory, and they are critically interrogated. While Shadi does not want to attend so many events, Fadi is happy to do so. Space plays a key role in constructing social activities as time sinks. For both Rami and Fadi in the quotes above, it is the combination of close social ties and lack of physical proximity that makes honoring their obligations take time. The spatialities of social obligations combine with the cyclical temporalities of celebrations (e.g., Eids, the holy month of Ramadan, weddings in the summer months) and more discrete, punctual temporalities (such as mourning someone's death) to shape social work. Similar to representations of paid work, residents' accounts of their social obligations frequently mentioned how exhausting such obligations were. "It's exhausting, financially and physically. Mostly financially, but we can't get rid of this habit" (interview with Fadi, 29 May 2013). "It's really exhausting but it's just the three months in the summer. We are forced to go every Thursday, Friday, and Saturday. Then after the summer, there are fewer events" (interview with Fadi, 28 August 2013). "You get tired because people also visit you" (interview with Ibrahim, 29 May 2013).

Residents' accounts of not having enough time span both paid and unpaid (i.e., social) work. Therefore, it is hard to establish a causal chain between debt, work, and the destruction of the social. Rather, financial crisis ordinariness is folded into and emerges from differential intersections of paid and unpaid (social) work. For financially indebted residents, the slow violence of these topologies is both dispersed and distributed through these different kinds of work, which are themselves enfolded in obligatory subjectivity. Fadi's reference to continuing to engage in practices that exhaust him ("we can't get rid of this habit") also provides an illustration of slow violence as impasse.

Lacking Time and Being Busy

At this point in the chapter, we must begin to critically interrogate claims that different forms of work, both paid and unpaid, are forms of slow violence that contribute to financial crisis ordinariness. While this argument resonates with residents' accounts of their lives, it misses the nuanced ways in which debt and work can capacitate as much as decapacitate. To develop this argument, I return to residents' discourses and contestations around the slow violence of debt and its consequences. These emerged primarily through their evaluations of other people's claims about lacking time and being busy. "In general, we have enough time. I am responsible for the employees. They always come late and say we don't have time. But that is just an excuse" (interview with Mohammed, 1 October 2013).

CHRIS If people don't have enough time, what takes up their time?

ABU MAHMOUD As I said before, this is not true. What activities are they doing?

REEMA Besides working, what do you think it is that takes up their time?

ABU MAHMOUD Nothing, just talking with each other. What kind of stuff will they be busy with here? In the past they planted. Today they don't do agriculture, or look after the trees, so this is not true . . . People have got used to saying we don't have time. (Interview with Abu Mahmoud, 25 September 2013)

"Yes, some people are busier than others. Other people say they don't have enough time in order to escape social obligations" (interview with Abu Ghassan, 26 September 2013). "Only 5 percent of the people who said that they don't have any time are telling the truth" (interview with Yazan, 25 September 2013). "Many people say they don't have time because they want to rest or just want to escape social obligations . . . I spend most of the daytime at work, and after work I just want to relax and get rid of stress, so I say I don't have enough time in order have some relaxation" (interview with Hussein, 29 September 2013). Earlier in the chapter I quoted residents who suggested that paid work is the root cause of lacking time. However, many residents, such as Yazan, Abu Mahmoud, and Mohammad, simply do not believe such claims. Abu Ghassan interprets claims about lacking time as a means of escaping social obligations rather than paid work. Hussein's admission that he says he is busy to avoid attending social obligations supports this idea. However, his tactic is also tied to, and a result of, spending most of the day at work. Such evaluations build on the argument that financial crisis ordinariness is folded into different forms of work, and not simply embedded in paid work. These evaluations also point to the ways in which residents negotiate financial crisis ordinariness, and particularly exhaustion stemming from being busy. The claim to be busy itself becomes a means of creating time to relax and recuperate. Other residents affirmed the role of socially extensive forms of obligatory subjectivity in the face of financial crisis ordinariness.

According to our traditions we can't say that social obligations are without benefit or if it is or is not productive. It's part of our life. We can't ignore it.

But there are people who are abnormal. I have a brother who works for very long time, and because of his work he can't attend family events. So, he feels isolated from the family. He feels bad that he can't attend. We have strong family relations in Palestine. Even though people sometimes feel that this is a waste of time they still do it. And if you don't do it, you will be isolated. There are things that we do even though I am personally not convinced . . . but I do it. Because of our traditions. (Interview with Shadi, 23 September 2013)

Shadi's comment illustrates the complexity of lacking time, which threads through paid work, but also the social work of maintaining family relations. His ambivalence about social work is set alongside a belief that such work is beneficial. His framing of work in relation to time wasting, and its counterpoint, productivity, was one that other residents used to make sense of financial crisis ordinariness. Given the general perception that people lack time in Ramallah, because of both paid and unpaid work, the frames of wasting time and being productive are crucial interpretative tools with which residents evaluate social action.

Wasting Time and Being Productive

There were a variety of social activities that were said to constitute time wasting. Often, these were activities that residents themselves engaged in. For instance, Huda and Im Ala, both keen Facebook users, suggested that spending too much time on the social networking site led to time wasting. When asked to define time wasting, Ziad and Ali, who were both students who also worked full-time jobs, mentioned spending time in coffee shops with friends—something students commonly do. Other participants echoed Shadi and suggested that social activities like visiting family and neighbors, or even offering condolences to the relatives of someone who had died, could constitute time wasting. "There are some social commitments that feel like I am wasting my time. And there are no results from doing it. Like if somebody dies. They take three days to accept condolences and you must stay for three days. Why not just one day? They might be right, but we are in a fast-paced world, and this wastes time. Also wedding parties" (interview with Mohammad, 1 October 2013). "[To husband:] Can I say an example? [To interviewers:] Like when my brother-in-law's wife prolongs a talk on a subject of little value. I don't like useless chats! It's a part of reality. Many people like to talk about subjects of little value" (interview with Nour, 29 September 2013).

NADIA It is nice to meet the neighbors in the morning, but it became bor-ing after a while. These visits constitute time wasting. The neighbors in this building don't visit each other in the morning.

CHRIS Why do you consider that these activities constitute time wasting?

NADIA Because they stay for a long time. Therefore, I feel I'm forced to postpone and cancel many duties that day.

DAREEN Many duties and less time?

NADIA Exactly. Wasting time happens when relatives come to visit us and stay in the house for several days. This will cause defects in the entire home system. House chores are another cause of time wasting especially when the kids become hyperactive. (Interview with Nadia, 29 September 2013)

While these examples relate to forms of unpaid work, other residents sug-gested that paid work constituted time wasting. "Some people who have jobs waste their time too. They have to benefit themselves or benefit others" (inter-view with Im Samir, 28 September 2013).

FADI We have a driving problem and also the unemployment (problem). Just 5 to 8 percent of people in the government are working. The others are disguised unemployment. Most (of them) work in the service ministries like [Ministry of] Interior and Finance. All the revolutions started because of unemployment . . .

REEMA How many hours a day do you work?

FADI None. (Interview with Fadi, 29 May 2013)

Fadi himself works in a PA ministry. His comment illustrates how the PA is thought of as one part of the Israeli Occupation. Rather than regarding the PA as a productive government that works for the benefit of the Palestinian people, Shadi positions it as an institution that prevents revolutions by em-ploying people. His analysis provides another example of how the violence of the Israeli Occupation is folded into the lived experience of financial crisis ordinariness. Julie Peteet (2008) argues that the control and theft of time is one of the most pervasive forms of colonial violence in Palestine. "The direct corollary of Israeli freedom of movement and expansion through space and control of time is that Palestinian space shrinks, time slows and mobility is constricted. Palestinians wait at checkpoints for hours before being allowed to pass with no explanation as to why they are being delayed. Soldiers take their identity cards and simply walk away" (Peteet 2008, 15). This theft of time is coupled with the uncertainty of not knowing how long something like passing through a checkpoint will take. Given the ways in which the PA fits within the broader Occupation, Fadi's analysis of being present but not working each day might be thought about as another means through which settler-colonialism steals Palestinians' time. However, in the accounts of Mohammad, Nadia, and Nour, residents' understandings of time wasting revolve around ideas about productivity that are not tied to settler-colonialism directly.

For some people, such as Yazan, Ali, Nasser, and Yousef, being unemployed was the primary way in which people were not productive and wasted time. Such an understanding links productivity with paid work and has clear gender implications. Given the gendered division of labor that prevails in Palestine (see previous chapter), the primarily female labor of working at home is occluded from discussions of productivity altogether. However, even understandings of productivity as paid work were often grounded in a broader social conception of usefulness, which might extend to unpaid work. "People waste time when they do not offer anything useful for people, but those who produce good things feel that they are always busy" (interview with Yousef, 24 September 2013). "Being of benefit to others is like gaining benefit from others. This is a basic rule for understanding time benefit and time wasting. Excessive self-love leads to time wasting because we don't live alone, and we have many obligations. And those who worry about their share of time are lost human beings" (interview with Abu Tariq, 26 September 2013). As Abu Tariq's quote illustrates, for most participants productivity was a category that spanned paid and unpaid work, economic and social activities.

> YAZAN I'm an employee. I work from eight till three. What is wasting time? Not working. Our economy is not developed.
>
> REEMA Why do you consider it wasting time?
>
> YAZAN Anything that's not productive, and if you don't have goal. Like I have a goal to educate my children. So, the two hours I spend with them I don't consider wasting time. If people just sit and talk and smoke, I consider it wasting time. Cultural activities are not wasting time. I see in Israel and many other countries that people always read on the train, everywhere. Here people don't worry if they waste time. (Interview with Yazan, 25 September 2013)

"In this fast world, anything without a result is considered lost. Or if it makes your community better. Maybe you will have a relationship without any effect on economic or social life" (interview with Shadi, 23 September 2013). "My definition of time wasting is when you waste productive opportunities in order to do useless things. Young people should benefit from their ability to be productive . . . When the impact of wasting time is so great that it affects your community, your country and your family. Entertainment after being productive is a bonus and not a waste of time. Productivity is the way to have an independent economy" (interview with Abu Omar, 3 October 2013). The value of productivity for residents of Um al Sharayet was connected with the broader flourishing of others, whether this was the family, the community, or the nation. I argue that this is an affirmation of obligatory subjectivity. Where and when work—both paid and unpaid—is productive, it enables the endurance of the family, community, and nation. This in turn enables certain futures to be realized. Abu Omar's aspiration for an independent economy echoes long-held Palestinian aspirations for future political and economic independence. Abu Tariq's comment that "being of benefit to others is like gaining benefit from others" suggests that forms of collective life are valued because they enable the flourishing of obligated subjects. A contrasting example is Fadi's understanding of paid work. Fadi suggests that most PA employees, including him, sit and drink tea all day. PA employees are not productive. Understanding productivity in its broadest sense as that which enables the endurance of the Palestinian community is the topic of the next chapter.

CONCLUSION: ANTI-CRISIS

I have argued that the slow violence of debt in Ramallah emerges through durative or ongoing practices, rather than crisis events that create moments of rupture and trauma. This leads to a situation that can be termed financial crisis ordinariness. Debt is tied to forms of work—both paid and unpaid—through which people are exhausted and stressed. Extensive social obligations also contribute to financial crisis ordinariness. Building on this argument in the next chapter, I suggest that while debt can be a form of slow violence, there are also situations in which it can capacitate endurance. This is because debt is not exterior to social life, but (becomes) part of it (Roitman 2003). It is productive, in the sense that it coproduces subjects, space-times, and broader political economies. Such productive relations might be violent, particularly when they are folded into practices of settler-colonialism. However, debt relations can also be nonviolent in the sense of building or capacitating time-spaces. The reason I introduce this argument here is because it troubles the case I have made for understanding life in Um al Sharayet through the concept of financial crisis ordinariness. To address this concern, I want to reflect on crisis as an analytical lens for understanding lives lived amid multiple forms of violence.

In her book *Anti-Crisis*, Janet Roitman (2013) suggests that the use of crisis is inherently conservative because it reaffirms a norm (e.g., business as usual) against which crisis (disruption, diversion) is defined. In the context of Palestine, it is tempting to refer to the growth of debt since 2008 as a financial crisis (rupture), given the rapidity with which debt has expanded. However, this framing positions the era before 2008 as the norm. This was when banking was very limited for reasons closely tied to settler-colonial violence (see chapter 2). A return to the past therefore does not offer a progressive resolution to the slow violence of debt identified earlier in the chapter.

Roitman also argues that crisis is used to secure or "frame" a world that the narrator (who may be an intellectual, policy maker, or politician) can then act in and/or on. This maneuver risks overlooking the capacities of those living through the crisis, and the forms of endurance that are crafted alongside forms of violence. In response, she seeks a form of analysis that is explicitly "anti-crisis." In her text, this takes the shape of deconstruction, which attends to the blind spots created when crisis is declared (Roitman 2013, 94), such as the ways in which people are always already adapting, adjusting, and enduring. In this chapter, I argued that a feminist geographical approach that ties together the local and the global discloses not only how (geo)political processes are enfolded in intimate lives, but also how people are already enduring. This chapter sought to illustrate some aspects of everyday life in Um al Sharayet pertaining to debt, social obligations, and work, which are obscured by narratives of Israeli settler-colonialism and financial crisis as dramatic events that require or lead to dramatic responses (e.g., Soederberg 2014). There was no evidence of any dramatic finance-related ruptures, such as home dispossessions or bankruptcy. Residents negotiate the emergence of debt through everyday, often banal practices, such as avoiding social events. These practices are continually evaluated and critiqued, and subject to adjustment. As the next chapter argues more fully, such practices demonstrate how residents' lives are not simply the residual of a crisis, whether Occupation- or debt-related. This argument contrasts with Berlant's concept of slow death, mentioned at the beginning of this chapter, which positions deterioration as a defining condition of a population's experience and historical existence. I mention slow death here because it is a crisis ordinariness narrative, which risks reducing complex lives and experiences to the status of an object or residue of powerful and extensive forms of violence. Consequently, even using crisis ordinariness as a conceptual lens is risky. Crisis ordinariness usefully frames the ways people experience slow violence. However, it potentially writes out much of the liveliness one encounters in Um al Sharayet, which cannot be adequately thought about as simply the result of violence. Such liveliness is found in the range of evaluations of work, productivity, and time wasting (and often in animated arguments when such evaluations are discussed publicly). Writing out this liveliness also risks universalizing what are in fact quite particular, situated ideas about what makes life livable. This argument has implications for how we use Nixon's work on slow violence.

In his book, Nixon (2011, 3) seeks forms of intervention that "turn the long emergencies of slow violence into stories dramatic enough to rouse public sentiment and warrant political intervention." In other words, he advocates a politics of representation that mitigates or diminishes slow violence. This maneuver turns slow violence into a crisis story. In doing so, it risks obliterating the precise nature of such violence or trivializing it (Povinelli 2011, 152–53). As I argue in the next chapter, it may also be politically ineffective because residents often deal with forms of slow violence through practices that are "quiet" (Bayat 2010) or "camouflaged" (Povinelli 2011). Such practices only work because they fall below the threshold of governmental visibility. Drawing attention to them not only risks romanticizing practices of survival, to the point where such practices can be hijacked as evidence of "resilience" (Nixon 2011, 21). It may also expose those engaging in such practices to forms of governmental intervention that prevent, subsume, and/or evacuate their political or practical potential (Bayat 2010; A. Simone and Rao 2012). This means that writing about them in this book also risks exposing them. This is tricky terrain to navigate. In the Debt Summit we convened in 2014, we were very careful to avoid telling stories about endurance. However, this may have contributed to the unsympathetic response we received from policy elites to stories of debt-related harm. Learning from this situation, the next chapter therefore seeks to amplify practices of endurance, in the knowledge that residents themselves are best placed to articulate solutions to debt. Such solutions may include state- or municipal-led actions, as much as practices embedded in everyday neighborhood life. These practices of endurance are important to consider because they demonstrate how accounts of indebted or obligated subjects as passive victims are inadequate. They provide a supplement that enables more nuanced renderings of (financial) crisis ordinariness, which reflect the ways in which capacitation and slow, violent destruction are intimately connected in people's lives.

politics as endurance

In the previous chapter I examined how debt is a form of slow violence. This kind of violence contributes to what I termed financial crisis ordinariness, where crisis is not spectacular and discrete, but rather ongoing, mundane, and embedded within people's everyday lives. As I noted in the chapter's conclusion, there are some dangers with framing life in Um al Sharayet using the concept of financial crisis ordinariness. While it draws attention to accretive forms of harm that are barely visible, it risks missing ways in which residents live and deal with debt. In the process, indebted life is transformed from a quasi-event to an event. What does this mean? When everyday practices are made the object of intellectual enquiry, this process can discursively transform the very nature of those practices. What are general conditions of "human social life . . . widespread . . . [and thus] confound response ([the practices'] slightness occurs below any level of accountability)" (Povinelli 2011, 144) can become magnified and reified as a result of social science critique. They become events, in the following sense: "If events are things that we can say happened such that they have a certain objective being, then quasi-events never quite achieve the status of having occurred or taken place . . . They are, or are not, aggregated and thus apprehended, evaluated, and grasped as ethical and political demands in specific late liberal markets, publics and states, as opposed to catastrophes and crises that seem to necessitate ethical reflection and political and civic engagement" (Povinelli 2011, 13). Povinelli defines quasi-events as ongoing conditions or daily practices that are often not significant enough to warrant political or ethical concern. They can become transformed into "events" of social scientific critique (through aggregation), and in so doing take on a significance and import that they never actually had as part of the "quiet" ongoingness of the everyday (Bayat 2010). In effecting this transformation, social scientific accounts risk both misrepresenting the everyday and missing much of what is actually happening in the world.

> Models of thinking that slide over the live surface of difference at work in the ordinary to bottom-line arguments about "bigger" structures and underlying causes obscure the ways in which a reeling present is composed out of heterogeneous and noncoherent singularities. They miss how someone's ordinary can endure or can sag defeated; how it can shift in the face of events like a shift in the kid's school schedule or the police at the door. How it can become a vague but compelling sense that something is happening, or harden into little mythic kernels. How it can be carefully maintained as a prized possession, or left to rot. How it can morph into a cold, dark edge, or give way to something unexpectedly hopeful. (Stewart 2007, 4)

In the Palestinian context, academic analysis often transforms the quasi-events of everyday life into an event of Israeli Occupation: a crisis. Furthermore, there is always an incentive to do this, since the language of crisis determines what counts (and what does not) as matters of political concern (Povinelli 2011, 144). Crisis secures a world for social scientific observation (Roitman 2013). However, this mode of framing is often conservative in that it posits (and can even implicitly reaffirm) a comparative noncrisis, and thus implicitly a norm against which crisis is measured. In Palestine, crises are often described as eruptions of violence, a phrase that almost always refers to moments of military violence (Said 2003). This framing is politically disabling for Palestinians and their allies because it almost always situates eruptions of violence as two opposing forces (one Palestinian, one Israeli). In so doing, it occludes the profound asymmetries and inequalities of power that characterize all colonial situations. More insidiously, a focus on momentary eruptions of violence implicitly positions everyday performances of colonial violence that are cloaked in bureaucracy, law, and security discourse as a norm. The ongoing, slow violence of the Israeli Occupation is thus hidden when military forms of violence become crises. Building on the previous chapters, we might add the slow violence of financial debt to this mix. Furthermore, efforts to turn quasi-events (such as the harm of living with debt) into crises or catastrophes can also make a problem seem trivial (Povinelli 2011, 144).

This chapter explores the problem of how to write about and respond to the quasi-event of living with debts and other obligations. While "quasi-event" is a slightly awkward neologism, it helps move us away from crisis talk. Quasi-events are problematic for those who experience them, but they are also lived with and through in ways that open up futures. It is important that quasi-events are not turned into crises, a process that evacuates such situations of what makes them problematic. Kathleen Stewart (2007) proposes a form of witnessing that seeks to mark what is forceful in the ordinary (comparable to Povinelli's quasi-events), without fully inhabiting and exhausting it. This is done by following the "heterogeneous and noncoherent singularities" of specific lives, while actively resisting the urge to "add up" such differences and thus reduce or transform them into something else. Such an approach is useful for following Palestinian lives in Um al Sharayet, which continually refuse to be placed in neat conceptual boxes. Any attempt to do so is easily dismissed, as policy officials and bankers demonstrated at the Ramallah Debt Summit when we positioned residents as victims of debt (see previous chapter). In response they outlined all the ways in which debt enabled people to buy homes and consumer goods "necessary" for work and education. Their insistence that becoming indebted would ultimately benefit residents also occludes a great deal. One overly simplistic frame (victimhood) was replaced with another (future flourishing). The witnessing method Stewart advocates demands that lives are reducible to neither of these, nor other archetypes. Throughout this book I have tried to draw attention to the specificity of lives, and how migrant history, gender, age, and kinship networks shape participants' experiences of debt in different ways. However, while recognizing the complex and heterogeneous circumstances of participants' lives, it is also necessary to account for the homogenizing force of financial debt. This is similar to the ordering force of colonial violence that creates a homogeneous, "native" them (Fanon 2005; Said 2003). What Ann Laura Stoler (2016, 7) terms duress, "a relation to a condition, a pressure exerted, a troubled condition borne in the body, a force exercised on muscles and mind," captures both the protracted temporalities and intangible aspects of this force. Recognizing its homogenizing properties is important because it not only shapes subjectivity (creating a shared group identity), but consequently becomes a means through which such violence can be challenged and resisted collectively. "Personal interests are now the collective interest, because in reality *everyone* will be discovered by the French legionnaires and consequently massacred or else *everyone* will be saved" (Fanon 2005, 11–12; original emphasis). In Ramallah, there were no signs of a collective debtor identity at the time of the research. This stands in contrast to the long-standing national identity (i.e., being Palestinian) in the face of colonial occupation. However, while the homogenizing force of debt's slow violence has not (yet) drawn together those who experience it, this lack of collective identity does not mean that those who live with debt in Um al Sharayet do so passively. Residents are continually adapting, getting by, and occasionally getting out. These practices do not equate to the sorts of flourishing imagined by Ramallah's policy and banking elites. They are also different from the form of resistance alluded to by Franz Fanon, which I elaborate more fully in relation to the concept of *sumud* later in this chapter. I want to think about practices of continually adapting, getting by, and getting out through the concept of endurance. I argue that endurance offers a better understanding of the agency of obligated subjects and forms of action that can emerge from such subject formations without necessarily coalescing into forms of more extensive collectivity (cf. Bayat 2010). The concept of endurance seeks to heed Stewart's concern with the heterogeneity of the ordinary, while recognizing that homogenizing forces, including colonial violence and financial debt, do create alignments that infuse diverse everyday practices.

ENDURANCE

"In contrast to survival, endurance is a means of continuing to continue that is not attributable to some inner force or underlying proposition. It is not the unfolding of a plan or a well-put-together personality, full of fortitude, able to roll with the punches and flexibly duck and dive, avoiding all threats. Endurance depends on the continuing efforts of people to discover and reach each other. It is the willingness to suspend the familiar and even the counted-on in order to engage something unexpected" (A. Simone 2014, 213). Endurance, as articulated by Abdoumaliq Simone, is different from concepts of survival (Povinelli 2011, 31–33) and resilience, the increasingly popular idea he alludes to as rolling with the punches. Resilience is often understood as the ability of systems and increasingly individuals to recover or bounce back from shocks (crisis). Genealogies and critiques of resilience are plentiful, and it is not my intention to review them here (see Walker and Cooper 2011; MacKinnon and Derickson 2012). Instead, I want to elaborate on Simone's definition of endurance, which is far more useful for understanding what is happening in Um al Sharayet. First, endurance is an activity done by large numbers of people, but not necessarily in a coordinated or collective fashion (see also Bayat 2010 on social nonmovements). It is speculative, in that efforts to "reach each other" are never assured beforehand. The language of reaching others also invokes subjectivity that is, or seeks to become, obligated in certain ways, although this may mean forms of obligation, like "business," that are short in duration or limited in spatial extent.

Second, endurance has a particular temporality and spatiality. Temporally, endurance is characterized by ongoingness (Stoler 2016, 7), which may resonate with "the hum" of everyday life (see Povinelli 2011, 137) or may disrupt the routine. In both cases, endurance enables a continued relationship with a future, in situations where no future is a lived possibility. This is different from the reactive temporality of survival and resilience. As I will discuss in detail later, debt in Ramallah opens up a future of material consumption in place of a political future of national liberation that is rapidly diminishing, and for some no longer exists as a real possibility. Endurance is a mode of enabling the ability to capacitate oneself—"continuing to continue"—where one may be an obligated subject rather than an individual. As Simone's phrase "reaching out" makes clear, endurance is spatially extensive in that it involves moving beyond the familiar. However, while this suggests moving around, endurance may also mean staying in place (but ensuring you can move on at some point in the future). Given the specific histories of colonial dispossession in Palestine, residents may endure a great deal to capacitate staying in place, while simultaneously ensuring they can "get out" in the future (e.g., by obtaining foreign passports or visas). These are forms of experimentation that seek alternatives without risking everything (A. Simone 2014, 210).

Third, while Simone (2014) describes endurance as efforts by people to reach each other, I want to argue that it also involves efforts by people to reach out and create certain nonhuman relations too (cf. Povinelli 2016). In the context of Ramallah, this includes debt. Debt enables staying put in the face of colonial processes that seek to forcibly displace, whether through violence that is spectacular and momentary, or corrosive and more dissipated spatiotemporally. As Stoler (2016, 7) notes, endurance can countermand colonial duress "and its damaging and disabling qualities." Debt can become a means of bridging the present and the future, and staying put in a particular place, surrounded and connected to a particular community. For those living in other parts of the West Bank, debt may enable the move to a place (i.e., Ramallah) where there are more opportunities to make a living, and thus possibilities for a "less bad" experience (Berlant 2011, 117). The latter response, pursued by many residents of Um al Sharayet, also involves investing in home spaces and topologically less extensive relations with family and friends. Debt has become a site of experimentation, which residents use to fulfill aspirations for a better life (James 2015), even as this experimentation may increase their exposure to new risks and, as the previous chapter demonstrated, cause additional harm. To develop this argument further, it is necessary to discuss endurance in relation to sumud.

Sumud *and Endurance*

Any argument about endurance as politics in the Palestinian context immediately brings to mind the concept of sumud (Shehadeh 1982). Usually translated as steadfastness, sumud is closely linked with standing one's ground, literally and figuratively. The meaning of sumud has broadened over time to encapsulate an entire way of life that traces a path between passive submission and violent resistance (Rijke and van Teeffelen 2014, 89). Lena Meari (2014, 549–50) argues that "*sumud,* translated roughly as 'steadfastness,' has no fixed meaning; it incarnates a multiplicity of significations and practices. It can only be approximated through an assemblage of the singular practices of Palestinians-in-*sumud* . . . This steadfastness constitutes a Palestinian relational political-psycho-affective subjectivity. It becomes an indefinable force representing the possibility of political praxis outside the space of normalized forms of politics. Under conditions of oppression it is a constant revolutionary becoming, opening up a possibility for an alternative regime of being, for an ethical-political relational selfhood." While endurance is a form of reaching out, this is more prosaic than what Meari describes as the "constant revolutionary becoming" of sumud, or what Alexandra Rijke and Toni van Teeffelen (2014, 89) term "everyday heroism." At its most extreme, the concept of sumud has been equated with the refrain "existence is resistance" (Rijke and van Teeffelen 2014, 91). This understanding of sumud is overinflated, to the point where the idea loses all meaning. However, it underscores the avowedly affirmative moral framing of sumud while also illustrating the contrast with the concept of endurance, which is politically ambivalent and ethically ambiguous. Endurance is neither the realm of best practices nor even of good practice.

The second area of contrast is the spatiotemporality of sumud, captured in the word "steadfastness," and its common association with practices of remaining on the land. Sumud maybe dynamic in terms of the forms of politics/resistance—a "constant revolutionary becoming"—but its goal is maintenance (e.g., of land, or of the self under conditions of torture) rather than the experimentalism and change of endurance. Again, it is important to emphasize that despite common understandings, the term "experimentation" is not intended to carry either positive or negative connotations, but simply describe a way of creating a different future.

Endurance and Agency

Simone's (2014, 213) reference to "continuing efforts" also clearly frames endurance as a form of agency. It is useful to return to Mahmood's (2012) work to specify the sorts of agency and capacity that endurance involves. Mahmood (2012, 29) understands agency as (1) capacities and skills needed to undertake particular kinds of moral action, and (2) bound up with historically and culturally specific disciplines through which subject is formed. Consequently, it is not possible to establish a single theory of agency. "If the ability to effect change in the world and in oneself is historically and culturally specific (both in terms of what constitutes 'change' and the means by which it is effected), then the meaning and sense of agency cannot be fixed in advance, but must emerge through an analysis of the particular concepts that enable specific modes of being, responsibility and effectivity" (Mahmood 2012, 14–15; see also 188). There are two implications to this approach that I would like to draw out further. The first is that the capacities that characterize or infuse subjects do not precede power but are the product of operations of power (Mahmood 2012, 17; see also McNay 2014). In the Palestinian context, such operations of power span the Israeli Occupation, the Palestinian Authority (PA), the banking sector, and family practices, including discourses that affirm the priority of the family over other subject forms and relations (including individuality). So, for example, Rita Giacaman (2017) argues that ideas around health need to be framed as "social suffering" to recognize the impact of political violence on Palestinians at large, in ways that go well beyond biomedical understandings of health. Endurance operates within such power relations. The second implication is that Mahmood's understanding of agency is implicitly geographical. In other words, it is not just power, history, and culture that determine "specific modes of being, responsibility and effectivity," but also space and spacing. Endurance as a form of agency emerges through the creation of particular spaces and spatial relations. This is very clearly borne out in the accounts of obligatory subjectivity emerging from Um al Sharayet.

There are parallels here with Lazzarato's (2012) concept of the indebted man, which is an involuntary condition (in that we are made indebted through public debt and taxation) and yet one that specific subjects actively inhabit. However, Lazzarato's analysis (and normative political imaginary) describes passive actors determined by subjection and undone by subjugation, unless they engage in heroic acts of refusal (to repay and/or work). Lazzarato's theory assumes an identity, or at least a close correspondence, between biopolitical governance and everyday life, when in fact there is a gap. The subject as conceived in and by governmental practice is not a lived experience, even if there may be close correspondences in some contexts. As I will elaborate in the next section, the gap between governance and lived experience contains a far wider range of possibilities for agency and action. A binary (active-passive) conception of agency does not and cannot account for the blurred space where much of life in Ramallah (and elsewhere) actually happens, where capacities to endure and their capacitation are unevenly distributed, embodied, and performed. In Ramallah, endurance and the forms of agency this term invokes emerge from intersections of obligatory subjectivity, debt, and work.

ENDURANCE, DEBT, WORK

In the previous chapter, I argued that paid work underpins the emerging debt economy, while residents experience the harm of debt primarily through low-paid and unpaid work. Productive work and debt also fill the temporal void created by the Israeli Occupation and the foreclosure of a political future of Palestinian national liberation. In other words, work and debt enable obligated subjects to capacitate themselves. This is in contrast to the prevailing political-economic and geopolitical scene in Palestine, in which a particular past, present, and future (of national liberation) are being worn down and worn away, as Palestine itself has been increasingly enfolded by Israeli colonialism since 1948. Productive work is sometimes framed as something that resists this foreclosure, when it leads (or is believed to lead) to building the community or the nation, such as in Abu Omar's claim that "productivity is the way to have an independent economy" (interview, 3 October 2013). At other times, productive work capacitates obligatory subjectivity, as Yazan suggests when discussing the importance of educating his children (interview, 25 September 2013). Obligatory subjectivity in turn capacitates community and nation building and offers an alternative future focused primarily on family.

Debt also offers a means of endurance that opens up an alternative future that is not clearly aligned with nation or community building. Within the impasse of the Israeli Occupation, debt promises a better present as a replacement for a political future of national liberation and the end of the Occupation, which has been closed down and denied by that Occupation (which includes the PA and the international community). In some accounts, the alternative present that debt offers is one that is imposed on residents from above or by outside forces. Journalists such as Amira Hass (2012) and Dalia Hatuqa (2013) suggest that debt-fueled consumption in Ramallah has become an economic peace initiative (cf. Gordon 2008). Israel, Palestinian elites, and international investors are said to have encouraged ordinary residents to become indebted. In a context of colonial occupation, debt becomes a form of pacification that replaces communal political struggles for future national liberation with the promise to individuals of a present-day good life defined by capitalism. Just as Lazzarato (2012) suggests that debt reduces the uncertainty of time and behavior of the governed, the growth of private debt in Palestine is said to shape the conduct of the Palestinian population so as to render them politically docile. Debt creates a future (of repayment) in the present, which displaces struggles for national liberation that embody a present without a future. Those who must repay debt must work to do so, and therefore do not have time to resist ongoing colonialization. In this scenario, debt as an economic peace initiative becomes another way in which life under settler-colonial occupation resembles an impasse (Berlant 2011, 199–200) and is experienced through financial crisis ordinariness.

The growth of the financial debt economy, centered on Ramallah, clearly owes much to the policies and decisions made by the PA, the Palestinian Monetary Authority (PMA), and international organizations and investors, as well as to highly mobile ideas about the power of finance to enhance people's prosperity (Haddad 2016). However, accounts of debt as pacification miss the ways in which it also capacitates endurance. As Povinelli (2011, 130) notes, "Conditions of excess always sit side by side with conditions of exhaustion and endurance that put into question the neat capture of substance by capital and other biopolitical projects."

To suggest that there is something else besides the machinations of colonial governance (whether practiced by the PA, Israel, or the international community) is not a claim that enduring the slow violence of the Israeli Occupation and growing financial debt is a "picturesque scene . . . of glorious resistance" (Povinelli 2011, 99). However, nor does everyday life in Um al Sharayet involve a passive acceptance of the situation. Thus, while analyses like Hass's and Haquta's may seem easy to accept on the face of it, the use of debt to buy a home, car, or other commodities does not necessarily imply a lack of desire for a national homeland or liberation, or the ability to work toward such a goal. This is complex and nuanced terrain, and it is important to critically interrogate such practices. The recently completed Rawabi housing development just to the north of Ramallah positions its construction activities as a form of national activism, in which Palestinians are creating their own "facts on the ground" before the land is stolen (Buck 2012). In this case, such claims are masking capital accumulation at the expense of local village residents (Grandinetti 2015). Nevertheless, home ownership more broadly remains an important form of security given the extensive history of home destruction and theft in Palestine (Falah 1996; Harker 2009b). Car and commodity ownership signify access to modernity (Taraki 2008b), something Israeli colonialism has denied. And while debt contracts create individual (legal) subjects, as I have shown, the experience of being in debt is intensely social, as these legal subjects are entangled with obligated subjectivity that enfolds immediate and extended family members, guarantors, neighbors, and employers (see also Roitman 2003; Schuster 2014; Kar 2018).

While becoming indebted clearly is not an act of sumud, it is an act of endurance. Just as numerous studies of microfinance demonstrate that most loans are not used for the entrepreneurial activity for which they are intended (Elyachar 2005; Guerin, Morvant-Roux, and Villarreal 2014; Estes and Green 2019), growing levels of debt do not automatically render a population apolitical, because debt is used in all sorts of ways. Again, nuance is needed. In Ramallah the growth of debt may resonate with processes that have curtailed certain forms of political protest and resistance, such as the failure of the Oslo Accords and the sharp increase in Palestinian security forces tasked with policing their own population. However, debt also enables residents to capacitate their ability to continue living amid the conditions of long-term de-development. As Povinelli (2011, 78) notes, "The social worlds of the impractical and disagreeable remain in durative time. They persist. But do not persist in the abstract." This capacity to endure can open up different futures from the Israeli Occupation. Exploring the contingent capacities of debt—to curtail and/or open up different futures—requires greater geographic sensitivity, which is to say attending to both time and space.

In the Palestinian context, debt does directly foreclose some present-futures. The most obvious future is one in which debtors choose not to pay their debts to banks. The ability to say no to repaying a bank loan has been removed from the present and placed out of reach in the past. The enforced automatic monthly deductions—a condition of becoming indebted to a bank—from a borrower's or guarantor's monthly salary, and the digital infrastructure for transferring funds, enables the foreclosure of a future of non-repayment. In so doing, the future as a site of particular forms of potentiality and novelty is closed down (cf. James 2015). "People say that we get money with our right hands and spend it with our left hands, but I guess the money I get doesn't

Chapter Seven

reach my right hand at all. It just goes straight to the left hand!" (interview with Im Samir, 19 June 2013). This is particularly problematic given the novelty of bank credit in Palestine, and thus the lack of existing personal and shared knowledge about what life with debt might entail. The foreclosure of a future in which debt is rejected mirrors the past moment, which reoccurs continually in the present, in which residents became indebted. As noted in the previous chapter, many residents of Um al Sharayet suggest that they had no choice but to become indebted, and thus the "choice" to become indebted was no choice at all.

Should one say no to a bank debt in the present, then participants were also clear that this would result in a deferred and intensified present of later repayment, rather than a different future. "People will continue paying back all their lives. A [US$]10,000 loan will become $20,000 if the borrower postpones his payments" (interview with Abu Ghassan, 15 September 2013). "The bank procedures are not the same . . . They have the right to take [repayments] from the salary. Basically, the bank does not lose anything. Even if the salaries are delayed, the bank will increase the interest on the loan. In the past there was a delay in paying the employees' salaries, and the loan's interest increased. We were forced to pay double" (interview with Im Ghassan, 31 August 2013). "The banks can easily reclaim the mortgages, even if this process takes a long time. I know a person who has been involved in mortgage redemption since his great-grandfather was alive. The bank has taken the mortgage payments for a long time and still the grandsons are trying to pay off their great-grandfather's mortgage. The grandsons can't take new loans until they are able to pay off the former mortgage" (interview with Abu Tariq, 15 September 2013). "My friend took a loan from the bank in order to help her brother get married, and she took another loan in order to pay the debt . . . She was forced to take the loan from the bank to pay another loan she took from people. They threatened to take her to the police if she didn't pay" (interview with Huda, 27 August 2013).

ABU OMAR A friend of mine took a big loan in order to get married, buy a house and buy a car.

DAREEN In order to marry his wife.

ABU OMAR Yes. I told him if he was not able to repay the loan that he took to marry, the bank will take his wife back. (Interview with Abu Omar, 12 September 2013)

Huda's story makes clear that it is not only banks that enforce future repayment, but people too. This is another example of how different debt topologies become entangled. In this case, the enfoldment of people, the bank, and the police intensifies and enforces debt repayment. As Abu Omar's joke indicates, not repaying debt is imagined as a future of (further) loss. This indebted future of loss is often imagined because of compound interest payments, which both Abu and Im Ghassan allude to. This is a particularly acute problem in Palestine because there have been a number of periods in recent years when public employees (who constitute approximately 25 percent of the entire workforce in the Occupied Territories) did not receive salaries. This occurred when Israel withheld tax transfers, which the PA relies on to fulfill its budgetary obligations (Reuters 2011; Beck 2015; MEMO 2017). This caused so much hardship that in 2012 the PMA instructed banks to postpone debt repayments and not to charge additional interest during such periods (PMA 2012b). Consequently, such periods enable a kind of non-repayment of debt, although this unchosen act did not constitute a rejection of an indebted present. More broadly, if debt offers a form of endurance in Ramallah, it is an emaciated one in which various kinds of future are closed down.

However, this argument focuses on the temporal aspects of endurance. A more spatial account of debt-enabled endurance in Ramallah may have a different tone. While home, car, and commodity ownership are key ways in which residents of Um al Sharayet access the modern (i.e., the present/future), they also enable material occupation of, and thus endurance on, a land that is being constantly colonized. This is demonstrated in discussions of owned housing, and the greater security it provides, in comparison with rented housing (see also Harker 2009b). "Why should I rent if I can buy a home? The rent payments I paid for two or three years are the same as the cost of buying" (interview with Khaled, 14 April 2013). "No, we were all convinced that building our own house and living in it was better than living in a rented house" (interview with Abu Kareem, 8 May 2013). "They [i.e., your family] are happy. They will not ask you anything. They won't ask you anything about the cost because you're buying. So, at first they are happy you are buying. They are satisfied that you are buying, whatever condition the apartment is in. Whatever the condition of the apartment is, it's our apartment" (interview with Waleed, 5 May 2013). Here it is important to remember that some debts related to purchasing a home do not involve banks. Residents including Mohammad, Abu Ghassan, and Abu Samir bought directly from the owner after renting. In many of these cases the amount of money paid as rent was deducted from the sale price. Mohammad and Abu Omar borrowed money from relatives. Many research participants who owned houses, rather than apartments, were refugees who had bought the land and built their own home in the 1980s and 1990s. For these residents, endurance enabled through the ownership of land and the material occupation of a particular place has been heightened by their prior experiences of dispossession and the subsequent precarity of living in nearby refugee camps (Abourahme 2011; Woroniecka-Krzyzanowska 2017). For residents who had moved from other parts of the West Bank, usually after 2000, their evaluations about the importance of (not) buying homes in Ramallah are made in relation to homes elsewhere. "Life in a city is better than living in a village. The services are better for sure. Education, medical treatment, entertainment, all of these things are better. I don't care about Ramallah. It's not Ramallah versus my village. Rather it's city versus village" (interview with Dina, 5 May 2013). "If I want to buy an apartment here [in Ramallah], I'll have to pay $130,000 or $150,000 now. But by the time I finish paying the bank, the cost will exceed [$]200,000. It's very, very costly. For this amount of money, I can build a palace in my hometown. The second thing is that after a long time, or when I retire, I will have no reason to stay here. So I will go back to home. That's another reason. But a lot of my colleagues bought here. Everyone has their own ideas" (interview with Ahmad, 14 April 2013).

Enduring presence on the land must also be seen alongside another spatial practice of endurance—moving abroad. While those who have engaged in such practices are by definition not present in Um al Sharayet, they maintained a spectral presence through stories told by their relatives who remained (Harker, Shebeitah, and Sayyad 2014). Some residents had second passports or visas that would allow them (and often their small or nuclear family) to endure by living somewhere else if needed. For migrants who have moved to Ramallah and whose big families (*hamula*) live elsewhere in Palestine, buying property in Um al Sharayet with a mortgage can be comparable to moving abroad. However, home ownership in a particular place, even in a neighborhood such as Um al Sharayet known for its weak social ties, produces forms of sociality that construct broader communities and ultimately the nation. This occurs in part, as Hussein speculates, because of the shared experience of heightened forms of colonial violence. "I think that social obligations will improve in wars. During the first and second intifada, there was a social solidarity between people" (interview with Hussein, 14 September 2013). This comment discloses how imaginaries of endurance are closely connected with social ties and the continued importance of obligatory subjectivity in particular places. In light of the PA's failure to become an effective national institution that ends the Occupation, obligatory subjectivity becomes the key means for enabling a different future. "Young men and young parents don't have enough time for social obligations, but getting old makes people feel they need to keep their social obligations. I'm a father and have the physical ability to work and work, to take care of my family expenses. So I'm interested in working and taking care of my family's expenses. In the future I'll lose my energy and I'll have enough time for social obligations then" (interview with Yousef, 10 September 2013).

IM ALA Personally, my family relationships are better than in the past.

DAREEN What played a role in this positive change?

IM ALA I don't know exactly, but it seems it was due to the local and regional situations. My family is maintaining its social ties. My sister came to visit me last week and it was the first time she stays at my home for a whole week. It has been a long time, more than twenty years, since she came to visit me. (Interview with Im Ala, 8 September 2013)

For migrants whose families live in other parts of the West Bank, the endurance of obligatory subjectivity often involves forms of experimentation. Im Ala notes that social media may enable the endurance of existing social networks across increasingly large topographic distances, by enabling forms of regular contact such as sharing pictures and commenting on each other's time lines. The use of "social" technologies, including the letter and the telephone, is strongly embedded in Palestinian society given the history of dispossession. However, her son, Faris, was less sanguine about the role contemporary forms of social media might play in maintaining sociality at a distance. In his opinion, the regular contact it enabled was superficial, and did not reflect meaningful relationships.

IM ALA Social media is very important in strengthening and maintaining social relationships. For instance, my son's cousin was very excited when she saw his pictures for the first time using the Internet. Speaking with relatives on social media makes them know more about each other. My son's cousin thinks that he is very cute and she didn't know that before. Social visits are not enough to maintain social obligations.

FARIS In the past my family and friends used to call and come to my birthday party. Now many friends just write greetings on my Facebook wall, and I only get many "likes" . . . On social media people have 1,000 friends on their lists, but in reality they only talk with five people. (Interview with Im Ala and Faris, 8 September 2013)

Chapter Seven

What empirical research makes clear, in contrast to accounts that position debtors as passive objects of change, is that residents were constantly evaluating these changing practices, and by implication emerging forms of endurance. Various residents commented on changes in social obligations: "With the continued concentration of jobs in some cities and due to the poor economic conditions and because individuals have more than one job in order to be able to pay their debts. All of these facts will cause the limitation of social obligations in the future . . . The original people of the city will continue maintaining their social obligations, while the migrants who moved to live in the city will not be able to maintain their social obligations because they have to travel and pay for social obligations" (interview with Abu Omar, 12 September 2013). "Social obligations always change. They are not the same as in the past. People invited the entire village to their weddings and occasions, but now they only invite close relatives and friends. Social occasions were public. Everyone in the city was able to attend weddings and other occasions. Invitations are limited now because the increase of population causes less social relationships" (interview with Abu Tamer, 16 September 2013).

> ALI Traditions and habits don't stay the same. There is always constant social change. For example, people used to call relatives and friends to dinner on the occasion of marriage, while today, due to bad economic conditions, many people cancelled this habit. In the past, it was impossible to cancel inviting people to eat dinner on the occasion of weddings. Also, in the past the groom was forced to build a house for his family but now he only rents a house.
>
> DAREEN So the social change is a result of economic change?
>
> ALI Yes, it is related to financial situations. (Interview with Ali, 9 September 2013)

The evaluations above take account of changing social and economic conditions, and how those are folded into everyday lives. All three men foresee or already note a decline in the extensiveness of people's social obligations. Such actions are shaped by economic changes but might also be understood as the means through which evolving forms of obligatory subjectivity continue to be capacitated. Experiments with endurance in Um al Sharayet, tied closely to the importance of obligatory subjectivity, are dynamic. They often take on similar forms because of widely circulating ideas about the importance of obligatory subjectivity, and also because of the shared condition of living under colonial occupation. However, as residents' evaluations demonstrate, while they observe and learn from each other, endurance is not a coordinated practice. It may be something done by many people, but it is not a form of collective action. Nor are such capacities a realm of good—let alone best—practices. Endurance may mean inviting fewer guests to a wedding or renting rather than buying a house. Neither capacitates resistance, but both enable residents to continue to continue. Endurance is politically ambivalent, an argument that provides the springboard for rethinking the Palestinian present.

THEORIZING THE PALESTINIAN PRESENT

The final section of this chapter explores how practices of endurance might help rethink the Palestinian present geographically. Spatially, Palestine is most often represented through a geopolitical lens, an epistemic frame that foregrounds the Israeli Occupation through the practices and policies of politicians, national and international institutions, various types of militarized forces, and the effects all these things have on the ground (e.g., Falah 1996; Weizman 2007; Raja Khalidi and Samour 2011). Many of these geopolitical practices have resulted in forms of legal (Forman and Kedar 2004; Jones 2015), bureaucratic (Abu-Zahra 2008), and material (Halper 2009; Abu-Zahra, Leech, and MacNeil 2016) separation, which enable Israel to control as much land as possible, while being responsible for as few Palestinian people as possible. This settler-colonial dynamic of inclusion/exclusion has meant that Palestine is also often conceptualized as a space of exception (Gregory 2004; Weizman 2007; Ophir, Givoni, and Hanafi 2009; Abujidi 2014), an idea that seeks to capture the ways in which Palestinians are included within colonial power relations by means of their exclusion. It is important to note that the use of the term "exception" should not be interpreted as claiming that such spaces are exceptional. Indeed, many of these theorists claim that spaces of exception are currently proliferating across the globe (Agamben 1998).

Geopolitical approaches to Palestine function collectively to create and reinforce a particular representation of Palestine as a place of violence and (geo) politics (Harker 2011). Not only can this representation, through its repetition, take on the shape of a stereotype, but it also overlooks many aspects of Palestinian life. In particular, the Palestinian everyday passes from view entirely in some cases, while in other studies the disparate activities of Palestinians are crudely summed together through and as the figure of the population or masses. For instance, Weizman's (2007) widely read examination of the Israeli Occupation highlights the role of not only politicians and acts of military violence, but also the work of Israeli planners, architects, agricultural specialists, and settler colonists in shaping Palestinian lives and spaces. However, the ways in which Palestinians also co-constitute their spaces and lives, even if asymmetrically, are largely ignored.

There are more nuanced analyses that approach the spatial politics of everyday life through the lens of resistance to various forms of dominance and oppression, whether Israeli or Palestinian (Gordon 2008). Such analyses resonate productively with critiques of growing levels of inequality between Palestinian ruling elites and the majority of the Palestinian population in the Occupied Territories (Raja Khalidi and Samour 2011; Haddad 2016). However, they still risk conceptualizing Palestinian life as little more than a derivative of the Israeli Occupation. This should not be surprising, given the extensiveness and pervasiveness of Israeli control of Palestinian lives. Few studies capture the nuances and complexities of the lives of nonelite Palestinians, who are forced to act amid the Israeli Occupation, but are not defined by it (although see Hammami 2004, 2015, 2019; L. Allen 2008; Kelly 2008; Abourahme 2011; Harker 2011; Joronen 2017). These efforts to think Palestinian life as more than a derivative of Israeli Occupation resonate with broader theorizations of political action beyond protest and confrontation, particularly relevant in contexts where subordinate classes do not have the luxury or capacity to politically organize in the open (Bayat 2010; Scott 2014; McNay 2014). Such studies have generated a rich conceptual vocabulary for describing muted forms of agency (e.g., "getting by," "quiet encroachment," "everyday resistance"), which I have drawn on at various points in this book. What the concept of endurance adds to this discussion is a language for describing capacitation in contexts such as the Israeli Occupation, where the possibility for agency is severely constrained. This language, built using the accounts of Um al Sharayet's residents, may also prove effective for augmenting the Palestinian story more generally.

Many accounts of settler-colonial violence in Palestine (e.g., Gregory 2004; Salamanca et al. 2012), including the one I offered in chapter 2, tell a chronological story structured by events, which acquire the proper names 1948/nakba, 1967, first and second intifada, and Oslo. Such an approach to narrating colonial violence is structured by the economies of attention that organize liberal biopolitics. As Povinelli (2011, 134) notes, "Liberal modes of making die, letting die and making live are organized within and through a specific imaginary of the event and eventfulness." Eventfulness is used to make sense of the social distribution of life and death.

As I argued in the previous chapter, many forms of violence escape critical theoretical attention because they are not eventful (Povinelli 2011; see also Berlant 2011). These forms of violence wear down and wear out bodies slowly.

People are "let" or left to die, rather than made to die. Povinelli (2011, 137) uses the analogy of water draining from a bath, rather than a tidal wave; a "noise" that sounds more like a hum than an explosion; suffering as "ordinary, chronic, and cruddy rather than catastrophic, crisis-laden, and sublime" (Povinelli 2011, 3). Such is the pace and rhythm of this kind of violence that it can come to feel natural. It is also carefully distributed so that particular bodies, particularly indigenous bodies in liberal settler colonies, feel its full force. "Indigenous communities are often cruddy, corrosive, and uneventful. An agentless slow death characterizes their mode of lethality. Quiet deaths. Slow deaths. Rotting worlds. The everyday drifts toward death . . . Any claim that these forms of decay matter can be referred back to the general condition of human life—everyone is slowly dying!" (Povinelli 2011, 145). Povinelli's use of the terms "cruddy," "corrosive," and "uneventful" here resonates with the discussion of slow violence in the previous chapter. Such violence may appear as "agentless" because it is hard to make visible, and thus so are its causes. Much political-economic violence in Palestine takes this shape, including the long delays both people and goods experience when traveling around the West Bank because of Israeli checkpoints and barriers (Hammami 2004, 2015), the labyrinthine permit system that governs who can do what (e.g., build, get married), where, when, and with whom (Abu-Zahra 2008; Griffiths and Joronen 2019), and the legal machinery through which Palestinians are dispossessed of their land (Forman and Kedar 2004; Joronen 2017). All of these situations are relatively dispersed temporally and spatially, even as they include moments of greater or lesser intensity. In each case, the Occupation creates an impasse in which acting in particular ways is not necessarily prohibited. Instead, certain actions and decisions are made very difficult, until people become exhausted and give up. Residents of Um al Sharayet mentioned visiting family members who live in other cities far less frequently than they would like to. Visiting their relatives is for the most part possible, but very difficult because of the time, stress, and cost caused by Israeli movement restrictions. This kind of corrosive violence includes the theft of land, water, and air, the mass imprisonment of the Palestinian population (particularly young men), and growing authoritarianism and inequality since the PA came to power. These practices combine to make the very act of earning a living one of the ways in which Palestinian life is slowly worn down and worn out. Consequently, for many Palestinians, politics may involve finding ways to endure, and capacitating a will to endure until material supports are in place (Povinelli 2011, 112; McNay 2014). Endurance becomes an important means through which Palestinians continue to continue, in the face of an increasingly pervasive assemblage of colonial violence that wears them down and out. Such processes are interrupted by moments of lethal and spectacular violence that kill and maim. But much of Palestinian life in Um al Sharayet involves building and maintaining obligatory subjectivity that in turn enables endurance. Too little existing scholarship is attuned to such practices, which are not well characterized through the language of resistance and sumud. Those interested in Palestinian geo/politics might learn a great deal by moving beyond a focus on large organizations (e.g., political parties, resistance groups) and large-scale territorial transformations to explore the everyday geographical contestations through which endurance is practiced, valued, and evaluated. This means building on feminist geographical approaches to the local-global discussed in the previous chapter (Pratt and Rosner 2012; Pain and Staeheli 2014), which attend to both the ways in which "events" are enfolded in the quasi-events of everyday life and the excessiveness of the everyday that eludes biopolitical capture. Such an approach promises more nuanced and fully fleshed out accounts of Palestinian subjects, who are neither passive objects nor heroic subjects.

8   dealing with debt?

"IT'S NOT POSSIBLE TO DISSOLVE ANY MORE SUGAR IN THE TEA"

We are living in a financial crisis, but people continue living their ordinary lives. They are used to it.
—Interview with Basma, 10 September 2013

It's not possible to dissolve any more sugar in the tea.
—Interview with Riyad Abu Shehadeh, 25 May 2014

When I interviewed Riyad Abu Shehadeh in May 2014, he was director of the Supervision and Inspection Department at the Palestinian Monetary Authority (PMA). He was responsible for overseeing banks in Palestine. His sugary tea metaphor summarized the Palestinian debt economy at the time we spoke. It conveys the idea that Palestinians could not continue becoming more indebted to banks. There are limits. However, since our interview, the amount of private credit issued by banks in Palestine has continued to grow. Basma's reflection that people "continue living their ordinary lives" because they are used to "financial crisis" helps us understand why this expansion of debt has continued (cf. Kelly 2008). In Ramallah, financial hardship has become normalized to the point where it is part of ordinary life. This may be true of the Occupied Territories more generally. Numerous economic indicators depict a situation that has barely improved—even during the so-called boom period after the second intifada (PMA 2015, 2016, 2017b)—as the Israeli Occupation continues to de-develop Palestinian economic lives. However, residents endure, drawing on a range of kinship and friendship networks, many of which expand beyond the topographic space of Ramallah itself. As this book has shown, for some endurance is enabled or capacitated by folding debt relations into broader ecologies of obligation. Since 2008, debt from banks has not only become far easier to obtain, but increasingly necessary, as land prices have inflated and demand for the trappings of modernity has proliferated (Taraki 2008b).

In chapter 1 I argued that none of these changes can be adequately understood unless we conceptualize debt spatially. Debt is a topological spatial relation. It binds obligated subjects, sometimes across significant topographic distances, connecting families with banks, relatives, friends, employers, and landlords. The resulting geographies stretch well beyond the Ramallah conurbation and even the West Bank in some cases. These topological relations are folded into a series of topographies that includes housing, consumer goods including cars, the physical infrastructure of occupation that marks the borders of Palestinian legislative and political influence (i.e., Areas A and B), and communication networks that enable families to support and reproduce themselves without being physically copresent. I conceptualized topological and topographic entanglements that are orientated around debt as ecologies. Debt ecologies are forms of coherence—or practical achievements—that have dynamic but nevertheless specific temporal durations and spatial extents. This book has tried to illustrate one such coherence, which I call the Ramallah debt ecology, from the perspective of Um al Sharayet's residents. This debt ecology enfolds different aspects of urban space, including flows of money, cultures, and imaginaries. It is coproduced through forms of obligated subjectivity, primarily the family but also friendship relations and "business" relations. It is threaded through forms of work, both paid and unpaid, and the geopolitics of colonial occupation.

A spatial approach significantly extends existing theoretical understandings of debt, which conceive debt through registers of temporality and power. The experiences and descriptions provided by ordinary residents of Um al Sharayet have been crucial in building this approach (cf. Bear 2015; James 2015; Kar 2018). Their insights demand a theoretical frame that can account for how debt is wrapped up in broader ecologies of obligation, the (geo)politics and economics of Israeli colonialism, and sociocultural dynamics within Palestinian society in the central West Bank after the second intifada. The spatial approach that this book has built is therefore specific to the context through which it was developed. However, it also seeks to be "dislocated" (Ananya Roy 2009), speaking to, and with, other ways of thinking about debt elsewhere. This approach does not ignore "boundaries and nationalities" (cf. Lazzarato

2012, 162), while still recognizing the circulation of debt practices and theories beyond specific territories. It is important to state too that the circulation of both practices and theories follows and reproduces conduits of power rooted in deeply inequitable colonial histories and geographies (Chakrabarty 2000; Connell 2007; Comaroff and Comaroff 2012). While arguments about the epistemic and practical legacies of colonialism are now fairly widespread across some parts of the social sciences, this book puts them to work in relation to debt and finance, where postcolonial critique has yet to have a substantive and sustained effect.

A postcolonial critique of finance challenges existing epistemologies that produce debt as an object of knowledge without acknowledging the differences and heterogeneity that emerge if the analysis (as well as the analyst) leaves global financial centers. Existing knowledge formations of debt, finance, and economy are still largely grounded in colonial presences that persist, endure, recur, and recede from the worlds we differently inhabit (Stoler 2016, 33; T. Mitchell 2002). Other scholars have begun to outline the sorts of detailed historical work necessary to understand "centers" in this way (Graeber 2011; Kish and Leroy 2015; Bourne et al. 2018). This book focuses on geography. It contributes to decolonizing knowledge about debt by foregrounding different practices, spaces, and entanglements beyond Euro-America.

However, to think about postcolonizing debt as merely a process of challenging and broadening Eurocentric knowledge formations is inadequate. Such an approach ignores decolonial critique. In an important intervention, Eve Tuck and Wayne Yang (2012) argue that many projects that seek to decolonize something (e.g., school or university curricula, research methods) treat decolonization as a metaphor. This evacuates the term of its radical, critical potential. Following Fanon (2005, 9), they argue that decolonization is first and foremost a struggle by indigenous people for sovereignty and land. A partial conceptualization of decolonization focused only on knowledge production ignores this crucial dimension. This can also recenter nonnative theorists and their conceptual framework, and thus sideline indigenous scholars and scholarship too. One of the ways I have tried to address this concern is through coproducing knowledge with residents of Um al Sharayet, my research assistants Dareen and Reema, and the many other critical friends and conversation partners mentioned in the acknowledgments. The second response is to return this conceptual discussion of decolonization back to the connections between debt and Palestinian life and land amid Israeli settler-colonialism. Here, life must not be understood as an abstraction or a categorical frame, but as fleshy, excessive, and differently inhabited. In the context of this study, this means focusing on how Palestinians living in Ramallah are actually addressing the growth of debt.

DEBT AND DECOLONIAL STRUGGLES IN RAMALLAH

In Palestine, struggles over and around debt must be, by necessity, de-colonial. However, beyond understandings that debt is a colonial strategy designed to decapitate Palestinian resistance (Hass 2012; Hatuqa 2013), there are few signs that existing forms of anticolonial resistance are connected to debt relations and struggles. Nevertheless, I think it is possible to identify two links. The first is that the growth of debt can be a form of slow violence (see chapter 6). It is causing harm, which is hard to capture because it is dispersed throughout everyday life and often displaced outside the topographic boundaries of Ramallah (and sometimes the West Bank). Debt does not block or imprison people as such but creates an impasse in which people can still move without going anywhere in particular. The slow violence of debt is different from many other forms of violence inflicted by the Israeli Occupation, but it is also connected. As I argued in chapter 2, the emergence of financial debt in the Occupied Territories is intimately entwined with Israeli colonialism, even if this complex relationship is not one that is well described by simple accounts of causation.

Second, as I have argued in chapter 7, debt also capacitates forms of endurance that enable residents to stay on the land and craft better lives (even if such lives are never "good" as such; see Berlant 2011). Other forms of socioeconomic provisioning would undoubtedly have had more positive outcomes had they been put in place. However, now that debt has become widespread in Palestine, what should be done? Is it possible to accentuate those aspects of debt that capacitate endurance, while downplaying those that cause harm? What combination of transformations and regulations might achieve this? Would it be better to simply pursue the abolition of financial debt entirely?

As noted in chapter 6, debt is not exterior to social relations, but rather is itself a social relation, characterized by asymmetry. "The productivity of debt can also be understood in terms of a primary relation that puts debtor-creditor relations at the very base of social relations more generally, and hence at the heart of productive associations. This means positing debt as a fundamental social fact, as *already there*" (Roitman 2003, 212; original emphasis). Therefore, calling for the end of debt is tantamount to calling for the end of sociability. The more pertinent question is, How does debt become a mode of affirming and denying particular kinds of sociability (Roitman 2005, 73)? A full and meaningful answer to this question in the context of Ramallah will only ever come from Palestinians themselves. Furthermore, the noun "Palestinians" itself names a heterogeneous multiplicity. The elite actors—representatives from the Palestinian Authority (PA), the Palestinian Monetary Authority, the banking industry, the Ramallah conurbation municipalities, local think tanks, and academics—who attended the Debt Summit we organized in 2014 discussed and proposed a range of responses to the growth of financial debt. These can be summarized as follows:

— *Financial Regulation:* Lower the maximum percentage of a person's wage that can be claimed by banks for debt repayments from 50 percent to 30 percent. Limiting individual borrowing protects individuals' incomes, brings Palestine in line with regional standards, and enables banks to lend to more people and grow the credit market in a sustainable fashion.

— *Financial Infrastructure:* Develop a national investment and savings scheme that Palestinian citizens can contribute to. The capital raised by the scheme will be used for development projects in Area C, where private actors are least likely to intervene because the risk is greatest. These investments in agriculture should be supported through a rebalancing of the PA budget. To increase their trust in the scheme, citizens should be able to support specific projects.

— *Employment:* Change (and increase) the minimum wage into a living wage, which is calculated according to the cost of living. To promote income equality, introduce a law that creates a maximum ratio between the maximum and minimum salary in any one organization.

— *Housing:* Develop new zoning laws that prioritize the construction of smaller-sized units in places where there is pressing need for housing. Develop new regulations that enable all residential developments built primarily for resale to include low-income units.

— *Taxation:* Tax all unused nonarable land as a percentage of the value, which will encourage deflation of land prices and the use of nonarable land. Increase property taxes and develop measures for enforcing the payment of property taxes, particularly by those who can afford to pay them.

— *Municipalities:* Give local government increased powers to enable tax collection, while continuing to increase transparency to encourage payment of taxes.

— *Law:* Implement legal reform in relation to debt repayment, forgiveness, and foreclosure to support Palestinian citizens and the banking system.

— *Public Awareness:* Create an advisory body that gives Palestinian citizens independent financial advice.
— *Social Policy:* To limit the need to take a loan, the PA may recommend a dowry and bride-price that takes into account geographical and social difference.

It is important to note that even within this group of "elite" actors, there were differences of opinion, and certainly not all participants agreed with all the proposed suggestions.

While we were not able to conduct a survey to find out whether residents of Um al Sharayet support some or all of these proposed ideas, their practices are forging additional, "quiet" (Bayat 2010) alternatives. Amid the quasi-events of everyday life, residents nurture particular connections and repel others through their obligatory relations. Some residents, particularly women in paid employment, choose to become indebted as a means of refusing particular practices of patriarchal power. Dina's relatively well-paid job and occasional IOUs to her flatmates enabled her continued residence in Ramallah, which was simultaneously a refusal to return to Tulkarem, get married, and live there. Similarly, the dynamics of a rapidly growing population and rapidly shrinking land due to colonization, in a place where land ownership has always had a private component, means that for residents like Mohammed, Abu and Im Omar, and Abu and Im Tamer, debt enables continued residence in Um al Sharayet. It is through practices of endurance such as these that debt ecologies intersect long-standing decolonial and antipatriarchal struggles (and probably more besides). Such actions may not appear as forms of liberal agency (Povinelli 2011, 33; Mahmood 2012), and thus risk being missed by analytical frameworks that only look for particular types of action. However, understanding these practices is crucial if we are to fully comprehend how ordinary residents are already responding to the problems they live with and through. Such insights support Mahmood's (2012, 36) call to "[untether] the concept of agency from that of progressive politics for the purposes of analytical clarity."

These insights into the escape routes Palestinians are forging also highlight, once again, the importance of thinking debt geographically. In the European context from which he writes, Lazzarato (2012, 161–62) argues that new forms of collective debt refusal are required to end the harm that financialized debt is causing. However, this argument does not account for how automatic repayment is a condition of becoming indebted and could only be refused by voluntary unemployment. In Palestine, where unemployment hovers just above 25 percent (PCBS 2017, 2018) and ongoing colonialism has de-developed many of the support systems that make life livable, a politics of debt refusal and work refusal (cf. Lazzarato 2015) borders on the suicidal. Even in more prosaic situations where residents could refuse to take small amounts of debt, such an act of refusal might in practice mean the denial of, or turning away from, sociability (Roitman 2005). This sociability is a key resource in a context where so few other resources exist. Furthermore, even if refusal were possible and effective, it would do nothing to address connected forms of violence rooted in and routed through patriarchal (gendered and age-related) power. Such forms of violence can be clearly seen in processes of becoming, managing, and embodying debt (see chapter 5). A geographical approach demands understandings of indebtedness (and its politics) that are sensitive to the spatiality of the debt ecology in question.

In Ramallah, the enfolding of debt relations with colonial and patriarchal power relations has resulted in obligated subjects whose relationships with debt topologies are complex. Even in a context where the experience of mass refusal during the first intifada remains an important part of the collective memory, advocating the mass refusal of debt may ultimately not be effective. While some residents prefer to borrow from friends and family, others, like Waleed, prefer banks precisely as a means of avoiding the "social methods" used to ensure repayment. While it is possible to envision a society without formal banks in Palestine, since those that currently operate there only returned recently, the more complex reality I have tried to illustrate in this book may mean that such a measure is not popular. Alternatives that begin with the modes of endurance found in residents' everyday lives may prove far more effective, both in Palestine and elsewhere.

BIBLIOGRAPHY

Aalbers, Manuel. 2009. "The Sociology and Geography of Mortgage Markets: Reflections on the Financial Crisis." *International Journal of Urban and Regional Research* 33, 2: 281–90.

———. 2017. "Geographies of Mortgage Markets." In *Handbook on the Geographies of Money and Finance*, edited by Ron Martin and Jane Pollard, 298–322. Cheltenham: Edward Elgar Publishing.

Abed, George. 1991. "The Palestinians and the Gulf Crisis." *Journal of Palestine Studies* 20, 2: 29–42.

Abourahme, Nasser. 2009. "The Bantustan Sublime: Reframing the Colonial in Ramallah." *City* 13, 4: 499–509.

———. 2011. "Spatial Collisions and Discordant Temporalities: Everyday Life between Camp and Checkpoint." *International Journal of Urban and Regional Research* 35, 2: 453–61.

Abu Jazar, Lutfi. 2015. Untitled presentation at Ramallah Debt Summit, Ramallah Municipality, 10 August 2015.

Abujidi, Nurhan. 2014. *Urbicide in Palestine: Spaces of Oppression and Resilience.* London: Routledge.

Abu Lughod, Lila. 2013. "Pushing at the Door: My Father's Political Education, and Mine." In *Seeking Palestine: New Palestinian Writing on Exile and Home*, edited by Penny Johnson and Raja Shehadeh. Northampton, MA: Olive Branch Press.

Abu-Zahra, Nadia. 2008. "Identity Cards and Coercion in Palestine." In *Fear: Critical Geopolitics and Everyday Life*, edited by Rachel Pain and Susan Smith, 175–192. Aldershot, UK: Ashgate.

Abu-Zahra, Nadia, Philip Leech, and Leah MacNeil. 2016. "Emancipation versus Desecuritization: Resistance and the Israeli Wall in Palestine." *Journal of Borderlands Studies* 31, 3: 381–94.

Agamben, Giorgio. 1998. *Homo Sacer: Sovereign Power and Bare Life.* Stanford, CA: Stanford University Press.

Al Bireh Society. 2017. http://www.albirehsociety.org/.

Allen, John. 2011. "Topological Twists: Power's Shifting Geographies." *Dialogues in Human Geography* 1, 3: 283–98.

Allen, Lori. 2008. "Getting by the Occupation: How Violence Became Normal during the Second Palestinian Intifada." *Cultural Anthropology* 23, 3: 453–87.

Allon, Fiona. 2014. "The Feminisation of Finance." *Australian Feminist Studies* 29, 79: 12–30.

Alqasis, Amjad. 2013. "The Ongoing Nakba: The Forcible Displacement of the Palestinian People." *Jadaliyya*, 15 May. http://www.jadaliyya.com/pages/index/11732/the-ongoing-nakba_the-forcible-displacement-of-the.

American Federation of Ramallah Palestine. 2017. http://www.afrp.org/.

Amin, Ash, and Nigel Thrift. 2002. *Cities: Reimagining the Urban*. Cambridge: Polity.

Anderson, Ben, Matthew Kearnes, Colin McFarlane, and Daniel Swanton. 2012. "On Assemblages and Geography." *Dialogues in Human Geography* 2, 2: 171–89.

Arab Bank. 2017. Our History. http://www.arabbank.com/en/history.aspx.

Arafeh, Nur. 2017. "The Myth of a 'Palestinian Economy.'" *Al Jazeera*, 6 July. https://www.aljazeera.com/indepth/features/2017/07/myth-palestinian-economy-170706060337109.html.

Bayat, Asef. 2010. *Life as Politics: How Ordinary People Change the Middle East*. Stanford, CA: Stanford University Press.

BBC. 2007. "Profile: Salam Fayyad." *BBC News*, 17 June. http://news.bbc.co.uk/1/hi/world/middle_east/6757273.stm.

Bear, Laura. 2015. *Navigating Austerity: Currents of Debt along a South Asian River*. Stanford, CA: Stanford University Press.

Beaumont, Peter. 2017. "Palestinian Authorities Arrest Activist in Growing Free Speech Crackdown." *Guardian*, 5 September. https://www.theguardian.com/world/2017/sep/05/palestinian-authorities-arrest-activist-issa-amro-in-growing-free-speech-crackdown.

Beck, Jonathan. 2015. "Israel Transfers Withheld Tax Money to Palestinians." *Times of Israel*, 20 April. https://www.timesofisrael.com/israel-transfers-withheld-tax-money-to-palestinians/.

Berlant, Lauren. 2011. *Cruel Optimism*. Durham, NC: Duke University Press.

Bishara, Azmy. 1989. The Uprising's Impact on Israel. In *Intifada: The Palestinian Uprising against Israeli Occupation*, edited by Zachary Lockman and Joel Beinin, 217–30. Boston: South End Press.

Blyth, Mark. 2013. *Austerity: The History of a Dangerous Idea*. Oxford: Oxford University Press.

Bourdieu, Pierre. 1977. *Outline of a Theory of Practice*. Cambridge: Cambridge University Press.

Bourne, Clea, Paul Gilbert, Max Haiven, and Johnna Montgomerie. 2018. "Focus: Colonial Debts, Imperial Insolvencies, Extractive Nostalgias." *Discover Society*, 4 September. https://discoversociety.org/2018/09/04/focus-colonial-debts-imperial-insolvencies-extractive-nostalgias/.

Bow, Michael. 2016. "Council Faces Probe into 'Time-Bomb' Lobo Loans from City amid Cuts in Children's Services." *Evening Standard*, 9 March.

Brenner, Neil, David Madden, and David Wachsmuth. 2011. "Assemblage Urbanism and the Challenges of Critical Urban Theory." *City* 15, 2: 225–40.

B'Tselem. 2008. "Ofra: An Unauthorized Outpost." http://www.btselem.org /publications/summaries/200812_ofra.

———. 2014. "The West Bank: Settlements and Separation Barrier, November 2014." https://www.btselem.org/download/201411_btselem_map_of_wb_eng.pdf.

———. 2017. "Statistics on Settlements and Settler Population." http://www.btselem.org /settlements/statistics.

Buck, Tobias. 2012. "Investor Creates Palestinian Facts on the Ground." *Financial Times*, 17 September. http://www.rawabi.ps/uploads/file/Financial%20Times%20 _17-09-12_%20final.pdf.

Busbridge, Rachel. 2018. "Israel-Palestine and the Settler Colonial 'Turn': From Interpretation to Decolonization." *Theory, Culture and Society* 35, 1: 91–115.

Bylander, Maryann. 2015. "Credit as Coping: Rethinking Microcredit in the Cambodian Context." *Oxford Development Studies* 43, 4: 533–53.

Central Bank of Jordan. 2014. *Jordan Financial Stability Report 2014*. Amman: Central Bank of Jordan. http://www.cbj.gov.jo/EchoBusV3.0/SystemAssets/PDFs/EN /FINANCIAL%20STABILITY%20REPORT%202014.pdf.

Cerwonka, Allaine, and Liisa Malkki. 2007. *Improvising Theory*. Chicago: University of Chicago Press.

Chakrabarty, Dipesh. 2000. *Provincializing Europe: Postcolonial Thought and Historical Difference*. Princeton, NJ: Princeton University Press.

Christophers, Brett. 2013. *Banking across Boundaries: Place Finance in Capitalism*. London: Wiley.

Collier, Stephen. 2011. *Post-Soviet Social: Neoliberalism, Social Modernity, Biopolitics*. Princeton, NJ: Princeton University Press.

Comaroff, Jean, and John Comaroff. 2012. "Theory from the South: Or, How Euro-America Is Evolving toward Africa." *Anthropological Forum* 22, 2: 113–31.

Connell, Raewyn. 2007. *Southern Theory*. Cambridge: Polity Press.

Connolly, William. 2005. "The Evangelical-Capitalist Resonance Machine." *Political Theory* 33, 6: 869–86.

Cooper, Melinda. 2008. *Life as Surplus: Biotechnology and Capitalism in the Neoliberal Era*. Seattle: University of Washington Press.

Corbridge, Stuart. 1993. *Debt and Development*. Oxford: Blackwell.

Dana, Tariq. 2013. "Palestinian Civil Society: What Went Wrong?" *Al Shabaka*, 14 April. https://al-shabaka.org/briefs/palestinian-civil-society-what-went-wrong/.

———. 2015. "Corruption in Palestine: A Self-Enforcing System." *Al Shabaka*, 18 August. https://al-shabaka.org/briefs/corruption-in-palestine/.

Datta, Kavita, and Camille Aznar. 2019. "Challenging the Poverty Industry: Lessons from London's Transnational Migrants' Credit and Debt Practices and Institutions." *Geoforum* 98: 300–308.

Davey, Ryan. 2019. "Mise en scène: The Make-Believe Space of Over-Indebted Optimism." *Geoforum* 98: 327–34.

Davies, Will, Johnna Montgomerie, and Sara Wallin. 2015. *Financial Melancholia: Mental Health and Indebtedness*. London: Goldsmiths, University of London.

Debt Resistance UK. 2017. "Reclaim Local Democracy from the Clutches of the Financial Sector." http://lada.debtresistance.uk/.

Derrida, Jacques. 1992. *Given Time: 1. Counterfeit Money*. Chicago: University of Chicago Press.

Deville, Joe. 2015. *Lived Economies of Default*. London: Routledge.

Deville, Joe, and Greg Seigworth. 2015. "Everyday Debt and Credit." *Cultural Studies* 29, 5–6: 615–29.

Dodd, Nigel. 2014. *The Social Life of Money*. Princeton, NJ: Princeton University Press.

Elyachar, Julia. 2005. *Markets of Dispossession: NGOs, Economic Development, and the State in Cairo*. Durham, NC: Duke University Press.

Estes, Jennifer, and W. Nathan Green. 2019. "Precarious Debt: Microfinance Subjects and Intergenerational Dependency in Cambodia." *Antipode* 51, 1: 129–47.

European Commission. 2016. "EU Renews Its Support to Palestinian Authority and Palestinian Refugees with a first 2016 Assistance Package Totalling €252.5 million." Brussels, 1 March. http://europa.eu/rapid/press-release_IP-16-464_en.htm.

Falah, Ghazi-Walid. 1996. "The 1948 Israeli-Palestinian War and Its Aftermath: The Transformation and De-signification of Palestine's Cultural Landscape." *Annals of the Association of American Geographers* 86, 2: 256–85.

———. 2005. "The Geopolitics of 'Enclavisation' and the Demise of a Two-State Solution to the Israeli-Palestinian Conflict." *Third World Quarterly* 26, 8: 1341–72.

Fanon, Franz. 2005. *The Wretched of the Earth*. New York: Grove Press.

Farsakh, Leila. 2005a. "Independence, Cantons, or Bantustans: Whither the Palestinian State?" *Middle East Journal* 59, 2: 230–45.

———. 2005b. *Palestinian Labour Migration to Israel*. New York: Routledge.

———. 2008. "The Political Economy of Israeli Occupation: What Is Colonial about It?" *Electronic Journal of Middle Eastern Studies* 8: 41–58.

———. 2016. "Palestinian Economic Development: Paradigm Shifts since the First Intifada." *Journal of Palestine Studies* 45, 2: 55–71.

Flaherty, Jan, and Sarah Banks. 2013. "In Whose Interest? The Dynamics of Debt in Poor Households." *Journal of Poverty and Social Justice* 21, 3: 219–32.

Forman, Geremy, and Alexandre Kedar. 2004. "From Arab Land to 'Israel Lands': The Legal Dispossession of the Palestinians Displaced by Israel in the Wake of 1948." *Environment and Planning D: Society and Space* 22, 6: 809–30.

Foucault, Michel. 2008. *The Birth of Biopolitics: Lectures at the Collège de France, 1978–1979*. London: Palgrave Macmillan.

French, Shaun, Andrew Leyshon, and Nigel Thrift. 2009. "A Very Geographical Crisis: The Making and Breaking of the 2007–2008 Financial Crisis." *Cambridge Journal of Regions, Economy and Society* 2, 2: 287–302.

French, Shaun, Andrew Leyshon, and Thomas Wainwright. 2011. "Financializing
   Space, Spacing Financialization." *Progress in Human Geography* 35, 6: 798–819.
Friedman, Thomas. 2009. "Green Shoots in Palestine?" *New York Times*, 4 August.
   https://www.nytimes.com/2009/08/05/opinion/05friedman.html.
Gazit, Shlomo. 1995. *The Carrot and the Stick: Israel's Policy in Judea and Samaria,
   1967–68*. Washington, DC: B'nai B'rith Books.
Ghabra, Shafeeq. 1988. "Palestinians in Kuwait: The Family and the Politics of Sur-
   vival." *Journal of Palestine Studies* 17, 2: 62–83.
Giacaman, Rita. 2017. "Social Suffering, the Painful Wounds Inside." *American Journal
   of Public Health* 107, 3: 357.
Gibson-Graham, J.-K. 2014. "Rethinking the Economy with Thick Description and
   Weak Theory." *Cultural Anthropology* 55, S9: S147–S153.
Gordon, Neve. 2008. *Israel's Occupation*. Berkeley: University of California Press.
Graeber, David. 2011. *Debt: The First 5,000 years*. London: Melville House.
Graham, Stephen. 2004. "Constructing Urbicide by Bulldozer in the Occupied Ter-
   ritories." In *Cities, War and Terrorism: Towards an Urban Geopolitics*, edited by
   Stephen Graham, 192–213. Oxford: Blackwell.
———. 2010. *Cities under Siege: The New Military Urbanism*. London: Verso.
Grandinetti, Tina. 2015. "The Palestinian Middle Class in Rawabi: Depoliticizing the
   Occupation." *Alternatives* 40, 1: 63–78.
Gregory, Derek. 2004. *The Colonial Present*. Oxford: Blackwell.
Griffiths, Mark, and Mikko Joronen. 2019. "Marriage under Occupation: Israel's Spou-
   sal Visa Restrictions in the West Bank." *Gender, Place and Culture* 26, 2: 153–72.
Gudeman, Stephen. 2016. *Anthropology and Economy*. Cambridge: Cambridge Univer-
   sity Press.
Guerin, Isabelle, Solène Morvant-Roux, and Magdalena Villarreal, eds. 2014. *Microfi-
   nance, Debt and Over-Indebtedness*. London: Routledge.
Hackworth, Jason. 2007. *The Neoliberal City: Governance, Ideology, and Development
   in American Urbanism*. Ithaca, NY: Cornell University Press.
Haddad, Toufic. 2016. *Palestine Ltd.: Neoliberalism and Nationalism in the Occupied
   Territory*. London: I. B. Tauris.
Hall, Sarah Marie. 2016. "Everyday Family Experiences of the Financial Crisis: Getting by
   in the Recent Economic Recession." *Journal of Economic Geography* 16, 2: 305–30.
Halligan, Neil. 2015. "Banking on Peace: Bank of Palestine's Hashim Shawa." *Arabian
   Business*, 23 January. www.arabianbusiness.com/banking-on-peace-bank-of
   -palestine-s-hashim-shawa-579560.html.
Halper, Jeff. 2009. "Dismantling the Matrix of Control." Middle East Research and
   Information Project (MERIP), 11 September. http://www.merip.org/mero
   /mero0911091.
Hammami, Rema. 1995. "NGOs: The Professionalisation of Politics." *Race and Class* 37,
   2: 51–63.
———. 2000. "Palestinian NGOs since Oslo: From NGO Politics to Social Movements?"
   Middle East Report 214: 16–19, 27, 48.

———. 2004. "On the Importance of Thugs: The Moral Economy of a Checkpoint." *Middle East Report* 231: 26–34.

———. 2015. "On (Not) Suffering at the Checkpoint: Palestinian Narrative Strategies of Surviving Israel's Carceral Geography." *borderlands e-journal* 14, 1: 1–17.

———. 2019. "Destabilizing Mastery and the Machine: Palestinian Agency and Gendered Embodiment at Israeli Military Checkpoints." *Current Anthropology* 60, S.19: S87–S97.

Hammami, Rema, and Salim Tamari. 2001. "The Second Uprising: End or New Beginning?" *Journal of Palestine Studies* 30, 2: 5–25.

Han, Clara. 2012. *Life in Debt: Times of Care and Violence in Neoliberal Chile*. Berkeley: University of California Press.

Hanafi, Sari. 2013. "Explaining Spacio-cide in the Palestinian Territory: Colonization, Separation, and State of Exception." *Current Sociology* 61, 2: 190–205.

Hanieh, Adam. 2013. *Lineages of Revolt: Issues of Contemporary Capitalism in the Middle East*. Chicago: Haymarket Books.

Harel, Amos. 2013. "13-Year High: Number of Work Permits Issued to Palestinians Highest since Second Intifada." *Haaretz*, 17 September. https://www.haaretz.com /israel-news/.premium-1.547555.

Harker, Christopher. 2009a. "Student Im/mobility in Birzeit, Palestine." *Mobilities* 4, 1: 11–35.

———. 2009b. "Spacing Palestine through the Home." *Transactions of the Institute of British Geographers* 34, 3: 320–32.

———. 2011. "Geopolitics and Family in Palestine." *Geoforum* 42, 3: 306–15.

———. 2012. "Precariousness, Precarity, and Family: Notes from Palestine." *Environment and Planning A* 44, 4: 849–65.

———. 2014. "The Only Way Is Up? Ordinary Topologies of Ramallah." *International Journal of Urban and Regional Research* 38, 1: 318–35.

———. 2017. "Debt Space: Topologies, Ecologies and Ramallah, Palestine." *Environment and Planning: Society and Space* 35, 4: 600–619.

Harker, Christopher, Reema Shebeitah, and Dareen Sayyad. 2014. "Ghosts of Jerusalem: Ramallah's Haunted Landscapes." *Jerusalem Quarterly* 58: 7–11.

Harrison, Paul. 2007. "'How Shall I Say It?': Relating the Nonrelational." *Environment and Planning A* 39, 3: 590–608.

Harvey, David. 1982. *The Limits to Capital*. Oxford: Blackwell.

———. 2008. "The Right to the City." *New Left Review* 53: 23–40.

Hass, Amira. 2012. "Don't Burst the Bubble." *Haaretz*, 9 April. https://www.haaretz .com/1.5212534.

Hatuqa, Dalia. 2013. "Banking on West Bank Prosperity." AlJazeera.com, 12 September. http://www.aljazeera.com/indepth/features/2013/09/201391275625391674 .html.

Hever, Shir. 2010. *The Political Economy of Israel's Occupation*. London: Pluto Press.

ICJ. 2004. "Legal Consequences of the Construction of a Wall in the Occupied Palestinian Territory: Summary of the Advisory Opinion of 9 July 2004." International Court of Justice, 9 July. http://www.icj-cij.org/files/case-related/131/1677.pdf.

IMF. 2016. "Debt: Use It Wisely." *IMF Fiscal Monitor*, October. Washington, DC: International Monetary Fund.

———. 2017. "Debt: Glossary of Selected Financial Terms." http://www.imf.org/external/np/exr/glossary/showTerm.asp#93.

Ismail, Salwa. 2013. "Urban Subalterns in the Arab Revolutions: Cairo and Damascus in Comparative Perspective." *Comparative Studies in Society and History* 55, 4: 865–94.

Issacharoff, Avi. 2012. "Despite Fiscal Crisis, PA Increases Stipends to Palestinian Prisoners." *Haaretz*, 4 September. https://www.haaretz.com/middle-east-news/despite-fiscal-crisis-pa-increases-stipends-to-palestinian-prisoners-1.462526.

Jad, Islah. 1990. "From Salons to the Popular Committees: Palestinian Women, 1919–1989." In *Intifada: Palestine at the Crossroads*, edited by Jamal Nassar and Roger Heacock, 125–42. New York: Praeger.

———. 2011. "The Post-Oslo Palestine and Gendering Palestinian Citizenship." *Ethnicities* 11, 3: 360–72.

James, Deborah. 2015. *Money from Nothing: Indebtedness and Aspiration in South Africa*. Stanford, CA: Stanford University Press.

Jean-Klein, Iris. 2000. "Mothercraft, Statecraft, and Subjectivity in the Palestinian Intifada." *American Ethnologist* 27, 1: 100–127.

———. 2003. "Into Committees, out of the House? Familiar Forms in the Organization of Palestinian Committee Activism during the First Intifada." *American Ethnologist* 30, 4: 556–77.

Johnson, Penny. 2006. "Living Together in a Nation in Fragments." In *Living Palestine: Family Survival, Resistance, and Mobility under Occupation*, edited by Lisa Taraki, 51–102. Syracuse, NY: Syracuse University Press.

Jones, Craig. 2015. "Frames of Law: Targeting Advice and Operational Law in the Israeli Military." *Environment and Planning D: Society and Space* 33, 4: 676–96.

Joronen, Mikko. 2017. "'Refusing to Be a Victim, Refusing to Be an Enemy': Form-of-Life as Resistance in the Palestinian Struggle against Settler Colonialism." *Political Geography* 56: 91–100.

Joseph, Miranda. 2014. *Debt to Society: Accounting for Life under Capitalism*. Minneapolis: University of Minnesota Press.

Kar, Sohini. 2018. *Financialising Poverty: Labor and Risk in Indian Microfinance*. Stanford, CA: Stanford University Press.

Karim, Lamia. 2008. "Demystifying Micro-credit: The Grameen Bank, NGOs, and Neoliberalism in Bangladesh." *Cultural Dynamics* 20, 1: 5–29.

Kashti, Or. 2017. "Israel Admits Palestinian Laborers Are Often Exploited to Receive Work Permits." *Haaretz*, 21 July. https://www.haaretz.com/israel-news/.premium-1.802739.

Katz, Cindi. 2006. "Messing with 'the Project.'" In *David Harvey: A Critical Reader*, edited by Derek Gregory and Noel Castree, 234–46. Oxford: Blackwell.

Kear, Mark. 2016. "Peer Lending and the Subsumption of the Informal." *Journal of Cultural Economy* 9, 3: 261–76.

Kelly, Tobias. 2008. "The Attractions of Accountancy: Living an Ordinary Life during the Second Palestinian Intifada." *Ethnography* 9, 3: 351–76.

Khalaf, Issa. 1997. "The Effect of Socioeconomic Change on Arab Societal Collapse in Mandate Palestine." *International Journal of Middle East Studies* 29, 1: 93–112.

Khalidi, Raja. 2017. "What Is the 'Palestinian Economy'?" In *Between State and Non-state*, edited by Gülistan Gürbey, Sabine Hofmann, and Ibrahim Seyder, 123–39. New York: Palgrave Macmillan.

Khalidi, Raja, and Sobhi Samour. 2011. "Neoliberalism as Liberation: The Statehood Program and the Remaking of the Palestinian National Movement." *Journal of Palestine Studies* 40, 2: 6–25.

Khalidi, Rashid. 1997. *Palestinian Identity*. New York: Columbia University Press.

Khatam, Azam, and Oded Haas. 2018. "Interrupting Planetary Urbanization: A View from Middle Eastern Cities." *Environment and Planning D: Society and Space* 36, 3: 439–55.

Kish, Zenia, and Justin Leroy. 2015. "Bonded Life: Technologies of Racial Finance from Slave Insurance to Philanthrocapital." *Cultural Studies* 29, 5–6: 630–51.

Lai, Karen. 2016. "Financial Advisors, Financial Ecologies and the Variegated Financialisation of Everyday Investors." *Transactions of the Institute of British Geographers* 41, 1: 27–40.

Langley, Paul. 2008. *The Everyday Life of Global Finance: Saving and Borrowing in Anglo-America*. Oxford: Oxford University Press.

———. 2014. *Liquidity Lost*. Oxford: Oxford University Press.

Langley, Paul, and Andrew Leyshon. 2017. "Capitalising on the Crowd: The Monetary and Financial Ecologies of Crowdfunding." *Environment and Planning A* 49, 5: 1019–39.

Lata, Iulian, and Claudio Minca. 2016. "The Surface and the Abyss / Rethinking Topology." *Environment and Planning D: Society and Space* 34, 3: 438–55.

Latour, Bruno. 2005. *Reassembling the Social*. Oxford: Oxford University Press.

Lazzarato, Maurizio. 2012. *The Making of Indebted Man*. Los Angeles: Semiotext(e).

———. 2015. *Governing by Debt*. Los Angeles: Semiotext(e).

LeBaron, Genevieve. 2014. "Reconceptualizing Debt Bondage: Debt as a Class-Based Form of Labor Discipline." *Critical Sociology* 40, 5: 763–80.

Lee, Roger. 2006. "The Ordinary Economy: Tangled Up in Values and Geography." *Transactions of the Institute of British Geographers* 31, 4: 413–32.

Lefebvre, Henri. 2003. *The Urban Revolution*. Minneapolis: University of Minnesota Press.

Levine, Mark. 2009. *Impossible Peace: Israel/Palestine since 1989*. London: Zed Books.

Leyshon, Andrew, Dawn Burton, David Knights, Catrina Alferoff, and Paola Signoretta. 2004. "Towards an Ecology of Retail Financial Services: Understanding the Persistence of Door-to-Door Credit and Insurance Providers." *Environment and Planning A* 36, 4: 625–46.

Leyshon, Andrew, and Nigel Thrift. 1997. *Money/Space: Geographies of Monetary Transformation*. London: Routledge.

Lury, Celia, Luciana Parisi, and Tiziana Terranova. 2012. "Introduction: The Becoming Topological of Culture." *Theory, Culture and Society* 29, 4–5: 3–35.

Mackenzie, Donald, Fabian Muniesa, and Lucia Siu, eds. 2007. *Do Economists Make Markets? On the Performativity of Economics*. Princeton, NJ: Princeton University Press.

MacKinnon, Danny, and Kate Derickson. 2012. "From Resilience to Resourcefulness: A Critique of Resilience Policy and Activism." *Progress in Human Geography* 37, 2: 253–70.

Mahmood, Saba. 2012. *Politics of Piety: The Islamic Revival and the Feminist Subject*. Rev. ed. Princeton, NJ: Princeton University Press.

Marron, Donncha. 2012. "Producing Over-Indebtedness." *Journal of Cultural Economy* 5, 4: 407–42.

Martin, Lauren, and Anna Secor. 2014. "Towards a Post-Mathematical Topology." *Progress in Human Geography* 38: 420–38.

Massey, Doreen. 2005. *For Space*. London: Sage.

Maurer, Bill. 2006. *Pious Property: Islamic Mortgages in the United States*. New York: Russell Sage Foundation.

Mauss, Marcel. 1954. *The Gift: The Form and Reason for Exchange in Archaic Societies*. Eastford, CT: Martino Fine Books.

McFarlane, Colin. 2011a. "Assemblage and Critical Urbanism." *City* 15, 2: 204–24.

———. 2011b. "The City as Assemblage: Dwelling and Urban Space." *Environment and Planning D: Society and Space* 29, 4: 649–71.

———. 2016. "The Geographies of Urban Density: Topology, Politics and the City." *Progress in Human Geography* 40, 5: 629–48.

McNay, Lois. 2014. *The Misguided Search for the Political*. Cambridge: Polity Press.

Meari, Lena. 2014. "*Sumud*: A Palestinian Philosophy of Confrontation in Colonial Prisons." *South Atlantic Quarterly* 113, 3: 547–78.

MEMO. 2017. "Israel Approves Cut to PA Tax Transfer." *Middle East Monitor*, 15 June. https://www.middleeastmonitor.com/20170615-israel-approves-cut-to-pa-tax -transfer/.

Mendel, Yonatan. 2013. "New Jerusalem." *New Left Review* 81: 35–56.

MERIP. 2014. "Primer on Palestine, Israel and the Arab-Israeli Conflict." https://www .merip.org/primer-palestine-israel-arab-israeli-conflict-new.

Mian, Atif, and Amir Sufi. 2014. *House of Debt: How They (and You) Caused the Great Recession, and How We Can Prevent It from Happening Again*. Chicago: University of Chicago Press.

Middle East Initiative. 2013. Transcript of Breaking the Impasse Keynote Luncheon. http://www.mei.edu/content/transcript-breaking-impasse-keynote -luncheon.

Mitchell, Katharyne, Sallie Marston, and Cindi Katz, eds. 2004. *Life's Work: Geographies of Social Reproduction*. Oxford: Blackwell.

Mitchell, Timothy. 2002. *Rule of Experts: Egypt, Techno-Politics, Modernity*. Los Angeles: University of California Press.

Mitter, Sreemati. 2014. "A History of Money in Palestine: From the 1900s to the Present." Doctoral diss., Harvard University.

Monterescu, Daniel, and Dan Rabinowitz. 2007. *Mixed Towns, Trapped Communities*. Aldershot, UK: Ashgate.

Montgomerie, Johnna. 2013. "America's Debt Safety-Net." *Public Administration* 91, 4: 871–88.

Montgomerie, Johnna, and Daniela Tepe-Belfrage. 2017. "Caring for Debts: How the Household Economy Exposes the Limits of Financialisation." *Critical Sociology* 43, 4–5: 653–68.

Moody's. 2017. "US Municipal Bond Defaults and Recoveries, 1970–2016." Moody's Investor Service, 27 June. https://www.researchpool.com/download/?report_id =1412208&show_pdf_data=true.

Morris, Benny. 2003. *The Birth of the Palestinian Refugee Problem Revisited*. Cambridge: Cambridge University Press.

Muhanna-Matar, Aitemad. 2013. *Agency and Gender in Gaza: Masculinity, Femininity and Family during the Second Intifada*. London: Routledge.

Muniesa, Fabian. 2014. *The Provoked Economy*. London: Routledge.

Munn, Nancy. 1986. *The Fame of Gawa*. Durham, NC: Duke University Press.

Myers, Garth. 2014. "From Expected to Unexpected Comparison: Changing the Flows of Ideas about Cities in a Post-Colonial Urban World." *Singapore Journal of Tropical Geography* 35, 1: 104–18.

Nadan, Amos. 2005. "The Competitive Advantage of Moneylenders over Banks in Rural Palestine." *Journal of the Economic and Social History of the Orient* 48, 1: 1–39.

Nethercote, Megan, and Ralph Horne. 2016. "Ordinary Vertical Urbanisms: City Apartments and the Everyday Geographies of High-Rise Families." *Environment and Planning A* 48, 8: 1581–98.

Nixon, Rob. 2011. *Slow Violence and the Environmentalism of the Poor*. Cambridge, MA: Harvard University Press.

OED. 2017. "Obligation." *Oxford English Dictionary*. oed.com.

Oldfield, Sophie, and Parnell, Susan. 2014. "From the South." In *The Routledge Handbook on Cities of the Global South*, edited by Susan Parnell and Sophie Oldfield, 1–4. London: Routledge.

Ong, Aihwa. 2007. "Neoliberalism as a Mobile Technology." *Transactions of the Institute of British Geographers* 32, 1: 3–8.

Ophir, Adi, Michal Givoni, and Sari Hanafi, eds. 2009. *The Power of Inclusive Exclusion: Anatomy of Israeli Rule in the Occupied Palestinian Territories*. Cambridge, MA: MIT Press.

PA (Palestinian Authority). 2009. *Palestine: Ending the Occupation, Establishing the State*. Ramallah: Palestinian Authority. https://unispal.un.org/pdfs/PA _EndingOccupation-Statehood.pdf.

Pain, Rachel, and Lynn Staeheli. 2014. "Introduction: Intimacy-Geopolitics and Violence." *Area* 46, 4: 344–60.

Pappe, Ilan. 2006. *The Ethnic Cleansing of Palestine*. Oxford: Oneworld.

Parry, Nigel. 2004. "Blaming Arafat for Israel's Torpedoing of Oslo." *Electronic Intifada*, 11 November. http://electronicintifada.net/content/blaming-arafat-israels-torpedoing-oslo/5311.

PCBS (Palestinian Central Bureau of Statistics). 2013. *Palestinians at the End of 2013*. http://www.pcbs.gov.ps/Downloads/book2028.pdf.

———. 2017. "Labour Force Participation Rate." http://www.pcbs.gov.ps/site/lang__en/881/default.aspx#Labour.

———. 2018. "Main Statistical Indicators in the West Bank and Gaza Strip." http://www.pcbs.gov.ps/Portals/_Rainbow/StatInd/StatisticalMainIndicators_E.htm.

Peck, Jamie. 2012. "Austerity Urbanism." *City* 16, 6: 626–55.

Peebles, Gustav. 2010. "The Anthropology of Credit and Debt." *Annual Review of Anthropology* 39: 225–40.

———. 2012. "Whitewashing and Leg-Bailing: On the Spatiality of Debt." *Social Anthropology* 20, 4: 429–43.

Peteet, Julie. 2008. "Stealing Time." *Middle East Report* 248: 14–15.

Pike, Andy, and Jane Pollard. 2010. "Economic Geographies of Financialization." *Economic Geography* 86, 1: 29–51.

PMA (Palestinian Monetary Authority). 2010. *Palestine Monetary Authority 2009 Annual Report*. Ramallah: Palestine Monetary Authority. http://www.pma.ps/Portals/1/Users/002/02/2/Publications/English/Annual%20Reports/PMA%20Annual%20Reports/Annual_Report_2009_English.pdf.

———. 2011. *Palestine Monetary Authority 2010 Annual Report*. Ramallah: Palestine Monetary Authority. http://www.pma.ps/Portals/1/Users/002/02/2/Publications/English/Annual%20Reports/PMA%20Annual%20Reports/Annual_Report_2010_English.pdf.

———. 2012a. "Report on the Credit Risk Management Lending Practices in the West Bank." 5 December. http://www.pma.ps/Default.aspx?tabid=205&ArtMID=793&ArticleID=185&language=en-US.

———. 2012b. "PMA Requested Banks Not to Exceed 70% of the Discount from the Value of Due Installments." Palestine Monetary Authority, 13 August 2012. http://www.pma.ps/Default.aspx?tabid=205&ArtMID=793&ArticleID=8&language=en-US.

———. 2014a. "Distribution of Total Facilities by Region." *Quarterly Statistical Bulletin: Fourth Quarter 2014*, vol. 7. Ramallah: Palestine Monetary Authority. https://tinyurl.com/rdom8u2.

———. 2014b. *Palestine Monetary Authority 2013 Annual Report*. Ramallah: Palestine Monetary Authority. http://www.pma.ps/Portals/1/Users/002/02/2/Publications/English/Annual%20Reports/PMA%20Annual%20Reports/Annual_Report_2013_Final_En.pdf.

———. 2015. *Palestine Monetary Authority 2014 Annual Report*. Ramallah: Palestine Monetary Authority. http://www.pma.ps/Portals/1/Users/002/02/2/Publications

/English/Annual%20Reports/PMA%20Annual%20Reports/Annual_Report
_2014_Final_En.pdf.pdf.

———. 2016. *Palestine Monetary Authority 2015 Annual Report*. Ramallah: Palestine
Monetary Authority. http://www.pma.ps/Portals/1/Users/002/02/2/Publications
/English/Annual%20Reports/PMA%20Annual%20Reports/AR2015_en.pdf.

———. 2017a. "Distribution of Credit Facilities by Economic Sector." Ramallah:
Palestine Monetary Authority. http://www.pma.ps/Portals/1/Users/002/02/2
/Monthly%20Statistical%20Bulletin/Banking%20Data/table_23_facilities_by
_economic_sectors.xls.

———. 2017b. *Palestine Monetary Authority 2016 Annual Report*. Ramallah: Palestine
Monetary Authority. http://www.pma.ps/Portals/1/Users/002/02/2/Publications
/English/Annual%20Reports/PMA%20Annual%20Reports/Annual_Report
_2016.pdf.

———. 2017c. "PNA Revenues, Expenditures and Financing Sources." Ramallah:
Palestine Monetary Authority. http://www.pma.ps/Portals/1/Users/002/02/2
/Monthly%20Statistical%20Bulletin/Public%20Finance/table_35.xls.

———. 2018. "PNA Revenues, Expenditures and Financing Sources (Cash Basis)." Ramallah: Palestine Monetary Authority. http://www.pma.ps/Portals/1/Users/002
/02/2/Monthly%20Statistical%20Bulletin/Public%20Finance/table_35.xls.

Pollard, Jane, Cheryl McEwan, Nina Laurie, and Alison Stenning. 2009. "Economic
Geography under Postcolonial Scrutiny." *Transactions of the Institute of British
Geographers* 34, 2: 137–42.

Povinelli, Elizabeth. 2011. *Economies of Abandonment*. Durham, NC: Duke University
Press.

———. 2016. *Geontologies*. Durham, NC: Duke University Press.

Pratt, Gerry, and Victoria Rosner. 2012. *The Global and the Intimate: Feminism in Our
Time*. New York: Columbia University Press.

Protocol on Economic Relations. 1994. *Protocol Gaza-Jericho Agreement. Annex IV—
Protocol on Economic Relations between the Government of the State of Israel and
the P.L.O., Representing the Palestinian People*. Paris, 29 April. http://www.incore
.ulst.ac.uk/services/cds/agreements/pdf/is23.pdf.

Rabie, Kareem, 2013. "Ramallah's Bubbles." *Jadaliyya*, 18 January. https://www.jadaliyya
.com/Details/27839/Ramallah%E2%80%99s-Bubbles.

Ramallah Friends School. 2017. "History." http://www.rfs.edu.ps/en/page/history?p
=history.

Rankin, Katharine. 2001. "Governing Development: Neoliberalism, Microcredit, and
Rational Economic Woman." *Economy and Society* 30, 1: 18–37.

Reuters. 2011. "Israel Maintains Block on Tax Transfers to PA." Ma'an News Agency, 14
November. http://www.maannews.com/Content.aspx?id=436667.

Rijke, Alexandra, and Toni van Teeffelen. 2014. "To Exist Is to Resist: Sumud, Heroism
and the Everyday." *Jerusalem Quarterly* 59: 84–99.

Roberts, Adrienne, and Susan Soederberg. 2014. "Politicizing Debt and Denaturalizing
the 'New Normal.'" *Critical Sociology* 40, 5: 657–68.

Robinson, Jennifer. 2006. *Ordinary Cities: Between Modernity and Development.* London: Routledge.

Roitman, Janet. 2003. "Unsanctioned Wealth; or, The Productivity of Debt in Northern Cameroon." *Public Culture* 15, 2: 211–37.

———. 2005. *Fiscal Disobedience: An Anthropology of Economic Regulation in Central Africa.* Princeton, NJ: Princeton University Press.

———. 2013. *Anti-Crisis.* Durham, NC: Duke University Press.

Rose, Gillian. 1997. "Situating Knowledges: Positionality, Reflexivities and Other Tactics." *Progress in Human Geography* 21, 3: 305–20.

Ross, Andrew. 2014. *Creditocracy: And the Case for Debt Refusal.* New York: OR Books.

———. 2017. "Calculating the Debt Gap." *Antipode* 49, S1: 19–33.

Roy, Ananya. 2009. "The 21st-Century Metropolis: New Geographies of Theory." *Regional Studies* 43, 6: 819–30.

Roy, Ananya, and Aihwa Ong, eds. 2011. *Worlding Cities.* Oxford: Blackwell.

Roy, Arpan. 2016. "Reimagining Resilience." *City: Analysis of Urban Trends, Culture, Theory, Policy, Action* 20, 3: 368–88.

Roy, Sara. 1999. "De-development Revisited: Palestinian Economy and Society since Oslo." *Journal of Palestine Studies* 28, 3: 64–82.

Saʾdi, Ahmad, and Lila Abu-Lughod, eds. 2007. *Nakba: Palestine, 1948, and the Claims of Memory.* New York: Columbia University Press.

Said, Edward. 1989. "Intifada and Independence." In *Intifada: The Palestinian Uprising against Israeli Occupation*, edited by Zachary Lockman and Joel Beinin, 5–25. Boston: South End Press.

———. 1992. *The Question of Palestine.* 2nd ed. New York: Vintage Books.

———. 1993. "The Morning After." *London Review of Books* 15, 20: 3–5.

———. 2001. *The End of the Peace Process: Oslo and After.* London: Penguin.

———. 2003. *Orientalism.* Classics Edition. London: Penguin.

Salamanca, Omar, Mezna Qato, Kareem Rabie, and Sobhi Samour. 2012. "Past Is Present: Settler Colonialism in Palestine." *Settler Colonial Studies* 2, 1: 1–8.

Saqfalhait, Yara. 2015. "الفراغ المعماري في رام للة" [The architectural vacuum in Ramallah]. *Bidayat* 12, summer/fall: n.p. https://www.bidayatmag.com/node/631.

Sayigh, Yusif. 1986. "The Palestinian Economy under Occupation: Dependency and Pauperization." *Journal of Palestine Studies* 15, 4: 46–67.

Schuster, Caroline. 2014. "The Social Unit of Debt: Gender and Creditworthiness in Paraguayan Microfinance." *American Ethnologist* 41, 3: 563–78.

Scott, James. 2014. *Two Cheers for Anarchism: Six Easy Pieces on Autonomy, Dignity, and Meaningful Work and Play.* Princeton, NJ: Princeton University Press.

Searle, Beverley, and Stephan Köppe. 2015. "The Geographies of Debt." In *Handbook of the Geographies of Money and Finance*, edited by Ron Martin and Jane Pollard, 323–47. Cheltenham: Edward Elgar.

Secor, Anna. 2013. "Topological City." *Urban Geography* 34, 4: 430–44.

Seigworth, Greg. 2016. "Wearing the World Like a Debt Garment: Interface, Affect, and Gesture." *Ephemera* 16, 4: 15–31.

Shalhoub-Kevorkian, Nadera. 2000. "Women Victimization in Palestinian Society."
In *The Palestinians in the Twentieth Century: An Inside Look*, edited by Adel
Manna, 153–204. Jerusalem: Van Leer Jerusalem Institute.

Shalhoub-Kevorkian, Nadera, and Adrien Wing. 2015. "Violence against Palestinian
Women in the West Bank." In *Comparative Perspectives on Gender Violence:
Lessons from Efforts Worldwide*, edited by Rashmi Goel and Leigh Goodmark,
59–69. Oxford: Oxford University Press.

Shehadeh, Raja. 1982. *The Third Way: A Journal of Life in the West Bank*. London:
Quartet Books.

———. 2012. *Occupation Diaries*. London: Profile Books.

Sherwood, Harriet. 2013. "Palestinians Celebrate Mohammed Assaf's Arab Idol
Triumph." *Guardian*, 23 June. http://www.theguardian.com/world/2013/jun/23
/palestinians-mohammed-assaf-arab-idol.

Shipton, Parker. 2007. *The Nature of Entrustment: Intimacy, Exchange, and the Sacred
in Africa*. New Haven, CT: Yale University Press.

Shweiki, Omar. 2014. "Before and Beyond Neoliberalism: The Political Economy of
National Liberation, the PLO and *'amal ijtima'i*." In *Decolonizing Palestinian
Political Economy*, edited by Mandy Turner and Omar Shweiki, 220–37. London:
Palgrave Macmillan.

Simone, Abdoumaliq. 2010. *City Life from Jakarta to Dakar: Movements at the Crossroads*. London: Routledge.

———. 2014. *Jakarta: Drawing the City Near*. Minneapolis: University of Minnesota Press.

———. 2016. "It's Just the City after All!" *International Journal of Urban and Regional
Research* 40, 1: 210–18.

Simone, Abdoumaliq, and Vyjayanthi Rao. 2012. "Securing the Majority: Living
through Uncertainty in Jakarta." *International Journal of Urban and Regional
Research* 36, 2: 315–35.

Simone, Dylan, and Alan Walks. 2019. "Immigration, Race, Mortgage Lending, and
the Geography of Debt in Canada's Global Cities." *Geoforum* 98: 286–99.

SJTP (*Singapore Journal of Tropical Geography*). 2003. "50th Anniversary Issue on
Geography and Postcolonialism." *Singapore Journal of Tropical Geography* 24, 3:
269–90.

———. 2014. "Advancing Postcolonial Geographies." *Singapore Journal of Tropical
Geography* 35, 1: 1–159.

Soederberg, Susanne. 2014. *Debtfare States and the Poverty Industry*. London:
Routledge.

Stanley, Liam, Joe Deville, and Johnna Montgomerie. 2016. "Digital Debt Management: The Everyday Life of Austerity." *New Formations* 87: 64–82.

Stasavage, David. 2015. "Why Did Public Debt Originate in Europe?" In *Fiscal Regimes
and the Political Economy of Premodern States*, edited by Andrew Monson and
Walter Scheidel, 523–33. Cambridge: Cambridge University Press.

Stein, Kenneth. 1987. "Palestine's Rural Economy, 1917–1939." *Studies in Zionism* 8, 1:
25–49.

Stewart, Kathleen. 2007. *Ordinary Affects*. Durham, NC: Duke University Press.

Stoler, Ann Laura. 2016. *Duress: Imperial Durabilities in Our Times*. Durham, NC: Duke University Press.

Strathern, Marilyn. 1988. *The Gender of the Gift*. Berkeley: University of California Press.

Tamari, Salim. 1981. "Building Other People's Homes: The Palestinian Peasant's Household and Work in Israel." *Journal of Palestine Studies* 11, 1: 31–66.

———. 2008. *Mountain against the Sea: Essays on Palestinian Society and Culture*. Berkeley: University of California Press.

Tamari, Vera, and Yazid Anani. 2010. "Ramallah—The Fairest of Them All?" *Nafas Art Magazine*. https://universes.art/nafas/articles/2010/ramallah/.

Taraki, Lisa. 2008a. "Enclave Micropolis: The Paradoxical Case of Ramallah / al-Bireh." *Journal of Palestine Studies* 37, 4: 6–20.

———. 2008b. "Urban Modernity on the Periphery: A New Middle Class Reinvents the Palestinian City." *Social Text* 26: 61–81.

———. 2013. Personal communication, 6 September.

Taraki, Lisa, and Rita Giacaman. 2006. "Modernity Aborted and Reborn: Ways of Being Urban in Palestine." In *Living Palestine: Family Survival, Resistance, and Mobility under Occupation*, edited by Lisa Taraki, 1–50. Syracuse, NY: Syracuse University Press.

Taussig, Michael. 1993. *Mimesis and Alterity*. London: Routledge.

Terranova, Tiziana. 2014. "Debt and Autonomy: Lazzarato and the Constituent Powers of the Social." *New Reader* 1: n.p. http://thenewreader.org/Issues/1 /DebtAndAutonomy.

Thrift, Nigel. 2006. "Space." *Theory, Culture and Society* 23, 2–3: 139–55.

Toscano, Alberto. 2014. "Alien Mediations: Critical Remarks on the Making of the Indebted Man." *New Reader* 1: n.p. http://thenewreader.org/Issues/1 /AlienMediations.

Toukan, Hanan. 2014. "On Delusion, Art, and Urban Desires in Palestine Today: An Interview with Yazid Anani." *Arab Studies Journal* 22, 1: 208–29.

Tuck, Eve, and Wayne Yang. 2012. "Decolonization Is Not a Metaphor." *Decolonization: Indigeneity, Education and Society* 1, 1: 1–40.

Turner, Mandy. 2014. "The Political Economy of Western Aid in the Occupied Palestinian Territory since 1993." In *Decolonizing Palestinian Political Economy*, edited by Mandy Turner and Omar Shweiki, 32–52. London: Palgrave Macmillan.

Ulrichsen, Kristian. 2015. *The Gulf States in International Political Economy*. Basingstoke: Palgrave Macmillan.

UN (United Nations). 2016. "Israel's Settlements Have No Legal Validity, Constitute Flagrant Violation of International Law, Security Council Reaffirms." 23 December. https://www.un.org/press/en/2016/sc12657.doc.htm.

UNCTAD (United Nations Conference on Trade and Development). 1989a. *Palestinian External Trade under Israeli Occupation*. New York: United Nations.

———. 1989b. *The Palestinian Financial Sector under Israeli Occupation*. New York: United Nations.

———. 1995. *Developments in the Economy of the Occupied Palestinian Territory*. New York: United Nations.

———. 2012. *The Palestinian Economy: Macroeconomic and Trade Policymaking under Occupation*. New York: United Nations.

———. 2014. *Palestinian Fiscal Revenue Leakage to Israel under the Paris Protocol on Economic Relations*. New York: United Nations.

———. 2018. *Report on UNCTAD Assistance to the Palestinian People: Developments in the Economy of the Occupied Palestinian Territory*. New York: United Nations.

UNRWA (United Nations Relief and Works Agency for Palestine Refugees in the Near East). 2015. "Where We Work." http://www.unrwa.org/where-we-work/west-bank/.

Walker, Jeremy, and Melinda Cooper. 2011. "Genealogies of Resilience: From Systems Ecology to the Political Economy of Crisis Adaptation." *Security Dialogue* 42, 2: 143–60.

Walks, Alan. 2013. "Mapping the Urban Debtscape: The Geography of Household Debt in Canadian Cities." *Urban Geography* 34, 2: 153–87.

Ward, Kevin. 2017. "Policy Mobilities, Politics and Place: The Making of Financial Urban Futures." *European Urban and Regional Studies* 25, 3: 266–83.

Weizman, Eyal. 2007. *Hollow Land: Israel's Architecture of Occupation*. London: Verso.

Weszkalnys, Gisa. 2013. *Berlin, Alexanderplatz: Transforming Place in a Unified Germany*. Oxford: Berghahn Books.

Wilkis, Ariel. 2017. *The Moral Power of Money: Morality and Economy in the Life of the Poor*. Stanford, CA: Stanford University Press.

Wirth, Louis. 1938. "Urbanism as a Way of Life." *American Journal of Sociology* 44, 1: 1–24.

Wolfe, Patrick. 1999. *Settler Colonialism and the Transformation of Anthropology*. London: Continuum.

———. 2012. "Purchase by Other Means: The Palestine Nakba and Zionism's Conquest of Economics." *Settler Colonial Studies* 2, 1: 133–71.

Woroniecka-Krzyzanowska, Dorota. 2017. "The Right to the Camp: Spatial Politics of Protracted Encampment in the West Bank." *Political Geography* 61: 160–69.

Wyly, Elvin, Marcus Moos, Daniel Hammel, and Emanuel Kabahizi. 2009. "Cartographies of Race and Class: Mapping the Class-Monopoly Rents of American Subprime Mortgage Capital." *International Journal of Urban and Regional Research* 33, 2: 332–54.

Yazbak, Mahmoud. 2000. "From Poverty to Revolt: Economic Factors in the Outbreak of the 1936 Rebellion in Palestine." *Middle Eastern Studies* 36, 3: 93–113.

Zelizer, Viviana. 2013. *Economic Lives: How Culture Shapes the Economy*. Princeton, NJ: Princeton University Press.

Zureik, Elia. 1977. "Toward a Sociology of the Palestinians." *Journal of Palestine Studies* 6, 4: 3–16.

Bank of Palestine, 94–96, 101, 107
bankruptcies, bond markets and, 63–64
Banks, Sarah, 45
Bear, Laura, 2
Ben Gurion, David, 23
Berlant, Lauren, 122–25, 141
biopolitics, credit-debt relation and, 97–98, 118
Bourdieu, Pierre, 42–43
British Mandate, 22–24
B'Tselem, 25
built environment: debt-based transformation of, 66–74; growth of, 4; second intifada and, 35–37. *See also* homeownership and housing
Busbridge, Rachel, 11
business, Ramallah as center for, 76–80, 99–100

Canada: debt data in, 44; urban housing prices in, 65
capital flight, remittances as, 68–71
capitalism: social relations under, 133–40; urbanization and, 64–66
checkpoint infrastructure (West Bank): development of, 31; post-second intifada increase in, 35–37
class structure: free city ideology and, 82–83; resident imaginaries and, 89–91
collective resistance, to nakba, 29
commodities, debt topology and, 55–57
community groups, donor influence on, 34
Consolidated Consultants-Jafar Tukan Architects, 84–87
construction industry: mortgage industry and, 66–74; urban geographies and, 64–66
consumer debt, 44
consumption: debt management and, 111–14; as economic peace initiative, 150–51; growth of, 56–57; Palestinian economic shift to, 4, 32–34; topology of debt and, 49–52

credit: capitalist urban (re)development and, 65–66; in cities, 63; debt management and, 114–16; distribution in Occupied Territories of, 2–3; gender dynamics in indebtedness and, 109–11; growth in Palestine of, 7–8; mobility and, 43; post-Oslo resumption of, 33; in pre-1948 Palestine, 22–23; spatial theory of debt and, 42
credit-collection practices, 44
crisis ordinariness: debt-related harm and, 122; endurance and, 143–46; financial debt and, 11, 125–29, 140–42; under Israeli Occupation, 144–46; obligatory subjectivity and, 135–37; stress of multiple jobs and, 130–32
culture: debt topology and, 56–57; money and, 4, 62–63, 80–83; social relations as unpaid work and, 134–40
curfews, post-second intifada increase in, 35–37
currency control, debt economy in Palestine and, 8–9

Datta, Kavita, 65
debt: business relations and, 77–80; concentration in Ramallah of, 4–5; decolonization and, 165–68; distribution in Occupied Territories, 2–3; endurance and, 150–58; Fayyadism and growth of, 38–40; gender dynamics and, 108–14; geography of, 11–13; growth in Ramallah of, 7–11; mobility and, 43; mortgage increases and, 41–42; obligatory subjectivity concerning, 96; post-Oslo resumption of, 33; in pre-1948 Palestine, 22–23; prevalence of, 1–2; slow violence and, 18–19; social theories of, 95–96; subjectivity and, 96–100; topology of, 4–5; urbanization and, 64–66; work entanglement with, 129–32. *See also* consumer debt; credit; ecologies of debt; family debt; financial debt; spatial theory of debt

debt garment, gender dynamics and. *See* wearing of debt

debt-related harm, research on, 121–22

Debt Resistance UK, 64

Debt: The First 5,000 Years (Graber), 43

decolonization: debt theory and, 19, 164–65; Ramallah debt burden and, 165–68. *See also* settler colonialism (Israel)

de-development: continuation of, 162–63; Israeli settler colonialism and, 7, 28–29; Ramallah indebtedness and, 71–74

dependency, Israeli settler colonial creation of, 27–29

Derrida, Jacques, 43

Deville, Joe, 44, 49, 95

donor economy: freezing of, 36–40; geography of debt and, 61–63; investment in Ramallah and, 71–74; post-Oslo growth of, 33–34. *See also* aid programs; foreign donor governance

duress, debt and, 145–46. *See also* endurance

ecologies of credit: bank debt and, 10–11; topologies and, 47–49

ecologies of debt: defined, 5; financial ecologies and, 47–49, 59; obligatory subjectivity and, 104–7, 118–20; in Ramallah, 5–7, 92–93

economic enclavization, post-Oslo shift to, 32

economic peace: consumpton as initiative for, 150–51; Israeli attempted creation of, 27; topology of debt and, 49–52

economic self-sufficiency, Palestinian goal of, 29

Elyachar, Julia, 76

emigration, endurance through, 155–58

empirical research, debt theory and, 14–17

employment. *See* labor (employment); unemployment

endurance: agency and, 149–50; debt as means of, 6, 19, 150–58, 165–68; geopolitics of, 158–61; migration as tool of, 155–58; ordinariness and, 143–46; properties of, 146–47; *sumud* and, 148

environmental degradation, violence of, 123–124

Ersal Center, 4, 84–88

ethics of care, 103

Euro-American spatial context: debt theory and, 43–46; geography of debt and, 119–20; global debt and, 12–13; postcolonial critique of debt and, 164–65

European city-states, debt and credit in, 45, 63

European colonialism, geography of debt and, 119–20

European Commission, 73–74

European Union (EU), foreign donor governance and, 5–6

expropriation, Israeli settler colonialism and, 28–29

extended family, debt as means of support for, 10

externalization, Israeli settler colonialism and, 28–29

family debt: entanglements of, 67; management of, 112–14; negotiation of obligatory subjectivity and, 103–7; obligatory subjectivity of, 101–3, 107–16, 116–18; redistribution of burden of, 107–8; subjectivity and, 96–100; topology of, 4–5, 46–47, 52–54, 100–101

family geographies: debt management and, 113–14; remittances and, 67–71, 92–93; social obligations as unpaid work and, 134–40. *See also* geography of debt

Fanon, Franz, 146, 164–65

Fatah, 36–38

Fayyad, Salam, 37–40, 98

Fayyadism: business policies and, 77; operational unity of, 37–40, 98 financial crisis of 2008: debt theory and, 43–46; global debt burden and, 1; impact in Occupied Territories of, 10; urban bankruptcies and, 63–64

financial debt: crisis ordinariness of, 11, 125–29; endurance of, 143–46; global pervasiveness of, 2; growth of, 151–58; ordinariness, 11; postcolonial critique of, 164–65; social obligations linked to, 133–40

financial sector: debt theory and, 13; ecologies in, 48–49, 94–96; infrastructure of, 166; Israeli settler-colonialism and absence of, 28–29; obligatory subjectivity and, 62–63, 104–7; Palestinian Monetary Authority and, 40; regulation, 166

first intifada, as response to nakba, 29

Flaherty, Jan, 45

foreign donor governance: financial debt economy and, 151; investment in Ramallah and, 71–74; in Occupied Territories, 5–6

free city, Ramallah's identity as, 80–83, 99–100, 111

French, Shaun, 48–49

friendship, family debt and, 4–5, 101

Gaza Strip: Oslo Accords division of, 31; private credit/debt in, 7–8

gender dynamics: debt management and, 111–14; family debt and dynamics of, 108–16; free city ideology and, 81–83; housing investment and, 64; indebted subjectivity and space and, 18; microfinance and, 65–66; remittances and role of, 68–71; wearing of debt and, 114–16. See also women

The Gender of the Gift (Strathern), 118–19

generational dynamics, debt management and, 112–14

geographic inequality: resident imaginaries and, 89–91; second intifada and growth of, 35

geography of debt, 2–3, 11; debt ecologies and, 59–60; family entanglements and, 67–71, 92–93; financial ecologies and, 48–49; future research and, 167–68; obligation and, 61–63; remittances and, 68–71; scholarship on, 119–20. See also family geographies

geopolitical theory: endurance and, 158–61; Israeli Occupation and, 11; Palestine in context of, 6; topology of debt and, 49–52

German Agency for Technical Cooperation (GTZ), 83–84

Giacaman, Rita, 149

gift exchange: foreign aid as, 73–74; remittances as, 70–71; spatial theory of debt and, 42

Given Time: 1. Counterfeit Money (Derrida), 43

global debt burden: growth of, 11–13; pervasiveness of, 1–2; spatial distribution and, 44–46

globalization ethos, urban imaginary and, 85–87

governance, in cities, 62–63

Graeber, David, 43–46

Green Line, Israeli creation of, 31

gross domestic product (GDP): fiscal austerity and deficit reduction and, 38; private debt as percentage of, 7–8

Gudeman, Stephen, 117

Gulf states, Palestinian workers in, 72–74

Haddad, Toufic, 33, 36

Halper, Jeff, 25

Hamas, 36

Hanafi, Sari, 25

Harvey, David, 64, 67

Hass, Amira, 150–51

Hatuqa, Dalia, 150–51

hire-purchase agreements, 111–14

homeownership and housing: in cities, 62–63; credit-based purchases of, 66–74; debt ecologies and,

intifada economic boom in, 9–10; second intifada impact in, 35–37; settler-colonization of, 25–29; terminology of, 19–20; topology of debt in, 4–5; West Bank, 1. *See also* Israeli Occupation

Oslo Accords, 3; banking sector reinvigoration under, 7; debt accumulation as response to, 152; negotiations of 1993–2000 and, 30–34; Palestinian debt ecology and, 5–6; topological and topographical entanglements and, 54–57; topology of debt in Ramallah and, 49–52. *See also* Protocol on Economic Relations

Ottoman Empire, 22–23

Outline of a Theory of Practice (Bourdieu), 42–43

Palestine: land and sovereignty dispossession, 1948–1967, 23–25; pre-1948 history of, 22–23; terminology of, 19–20

Palestine: Ending the Occupation, Establishing the State, 37

Palestine Liberation Organization (PLO), 19–20, 24; negotiations of 1993–2000 by, 30–34; support for Saddam Hussein by, 29

Palestinian Authority (PA): banking sector and, 54–57; borrowing by, 8; business relations and, 78–80; creation of, 30; criticism of, 138–40; debt-related harm dismissed by, 121–22; donor influence on, 33–34, 73–74; financial debt economy and, 151; foreign donor governance and, 5–6; formation of, 19–20; free city ideology promoted by, 83; geography of debt and, 61–63; Israeli withholding of funds for, 154; jobs created by, 32; ministries of, 1; Ramallah as government center for, 4; topology of debt in Ramallah and, 49–52

Palestinian economy, Israeli settler colonialism and, 5, 30–34

Palestinian Legislative Council (PLC), 36–37

Palestinian Monetary Authority (PMA): banking sector and influence of, 39–40; creation of, 32–33; debt ecology and, 59; debt incentivization by, 55; debt-related harm dismissed by, 121–22; debt statistics of, 4, 8–9; financial debt economy and, 151; Israeli withholding of funds for, 154

Palestinian nakba: banking sector under, 23–25; de-development and political repression and, 29

Palestinian nationalism, 24

Paris Protocol. *See* Protocol on Economic Relations

patriarchy, money management and, 108–11

Peck, Jamie, 64

Peebles, Gustav, 42, 44–45

personhood, obligatory subjectivity and, 102

Peteet, Julie, 138

place, debt and creation of, 43–44

political repression of Palestinians: debt accumulation and, 152–53; family debt and, 101; Israeli settler colonialism and, 29; second intifada as response to, 35–37

pollution, violence of, 123124

postcolonialism: debt theory and, 13–17; decolonial critique and, 19; financial debt and, 164–65; global debt growth and, 12–13

poststructuralist theory, debt and, 44

Povinelli, Elizabeth, 102–3, 131, 143–44, 151–52, 159

power: agency and endurance and, 149–50; debt as apparatus of, 98–100

predatory nature of debt, 2

private credit: banking sector and, 39–40; growth in Palestine of, 7–8, 151, 162–63; research on, 2–3

private schools, credit-based support of, 67

private sector, Palestinian economy
and weakness of, 32
productivity, work linked to, 139–40
profit generation, cultural shift to, 4
property ownership: debt and loss of,
22–23; dispossession in post-1948
period, 23–25; endurance through,
154–58; family debt and, 101; geopolitics of, 158–61; remittances and,
69–70; as security, 151–52; slow violence in loss of, 123–25; topological
and topographical entanglements
and, 55–57
Protocol on Economic Relations,
30, 32–34
public debt to GDP ratio, in Palestine,
7–8
public sector workers: debt burden
of, 9; increase in, 35; migration to
Ramallah of, 4, 35–37; salaries withheld for, 154

Qaddora Refugee Camp, 24
Qalandia Refugee Camp, 24
quasi-events, debts and obligations in
context of, 145–46

race, housing investment and, 64
Ramallah: bubble metaphor concerning, 3–5; as business center, 76–80;
census taking in, 14–15; conurbation
growth in, 23; debt levels in, 41–42;
decolonization and debt struggle
in, 165–68; ecology of debt in, 5–7,
92–93; free city status of, 80–83;
gender dynamics of indebtedness
in, 111, 119–20; growth of debt in,
7–11; history of, 17–18; increased
migration into, 35–37; investments
in, 71–74; Israeli settler colonialism in, 25–29; money, culture and
imaginaries in, 62–63, 80–83; obligatory subjectivity of debt in, 102–3;
Palestinian Authority relocation to,
34; post-second intifada economic
boom in, 9–10; refugee migration

into, 74–83; research methods in,
13–17; resident imaginaries in, 87–91;
topology of debt in, 49–52; urban
imaginaries in, 83–87
Ramallah-Al Bireh conurbation:
culture of, 74–83; development
in, 4; formation of, 23–24; Israeli
encroachment in, 35; neighborhoods
in, 1
Ramallah Debt Summit, 121–22,
145–46, 166–68
Ramallah Friends School, 23–24
Rao, Vyjayanthi, 15–16
Rawabi development, 4, 151–52
real estate debt, 44, 66–74
refugee camps: establishment of, 24;
urban migration and rise of, 74–83
regulatory bodies, debt boundaries
and, 44–45
remittances, urban economy and,
67–71
resident imaginaries, urbanization and,
87–91
resilience, endurance and, 146–47
Rijke, Alexandra, 148
Roitman, Janet, 141
rollover practices, debt management
and, 112–14
rotating savings and credit associations
(ROSCAS), 65–66
Roy, Sara, 28–29

Said, Edward, 30
Samour, Sobhi, 37
savings patterns, gender dynamics in
indebtedness and, 109–11
Sayigh, Yusif, 27
Sayyad, Dareen, 16–17
Second Annual Child and Youth
Banking Week, 40
second intifada, economic conditions
following, 35–37, 162–63
Secor, Anna, 46, 48
Seigworth, Greg, 114–16
self-imposed pressure, topology of
debt, 52

separation, forms of, 41–43, 104–7
service sector employment, urban
    concentration of, 4
settler colonialism (Israel): control
    and theft of time in, 138–40; crisis
    ordinariness and, 125–29; debt
    ecology and, 5; economic de-
    development under, 7, 28–29; family
    relations and, 108; Fayyadism and,
    38–40; geography of debt and, 61–63;
    land expropriation under, 31–34;
    of Occupied Territories, 25–29;
    Palestinian space and, 6; productive
    work and debt as response to, 151–58;
    Ramallah indebtedness and, 71–74;
    slow violence of, 11; temporality of
    endurance and, 154–58; violence
    linked to, 26–29, 122, 159–61. See also
    Israeli Occupation
Shawa, Hashim, 40
Shebeitah, Reema, 16–17
Shehadeh, Riyad Abu, 162–63
Shipton, Parker, 119
Simone, Abdoumaliq, 15–16, 146, 149
slave trade, credit arrangements
    and, 44
slow violence: characteristics of,
    123–25; debt and, 18–19, 122, 140–42,
    165–68; endurance through debt
    of, 151–58; forms of work as, 135–37;
    stress of multiple jobs and, 130–32.
    See also violence
social conflict resolution, debt obliga-
    tions and, 105–7
social media, 137–40, 156–58
social redistribution: debt management
    and, 112–14; financial crisis ordinari-
    ness and, 127–29
social relations: business orientation of
    Ramallah and, 77–80; debt manage-
    ment and, 114; debt topologies and,
    52–54, 165–68; geographic and social
    differences in, 167; obligatory ties
    and experience of, 107–16, 118–20;
    stress of multiple jobs and, 130–32;
    topologic and topographic entangle-

ments, 54–57; unpaid social work
    and, 133–40
social subjection, debt and, 98–100
sovereign debt, creation of, 63
spaciocide, Israeli settler colonialism
    as, 25
spatial theory of debt, 2–3, 18; de-
    development and, 29; endurance
    and, 147; future research and,
    163–64; gender dynamics and,
    110–11; Palestinian framework for,
    6; remittances and, 68–71; scholar-
    ship on, 42–46; second intifada
    destruction in Occupied Territo-
    ries and, 35–37; slow violence and,
    124–25; social obligations as unpaid
    work and, 135–40; sumud and, 148;
    topology of debt and, 47; urbaniza-
    tion and, 18, 63–66
Stasavage, David, 45, 63
state-building policies, in post-second
    Intifada period, 36–37
Stein, Kenneth, 22
Stewart, Kathleen, 145–46
Stoler, Ann Laura, 145–46
Strathern, Marilyn, 118–19
structural adjustment policies, global
    debt growth and, 12–13
subjectivity: debt and, 96–100; sumud
    and endurance and, 148. See also
    obligatory subjectivity
subprime lending, 64–65
suburbanization, financial markets
    and, 65
sumud, Palestinian concept of, 146,
    148, 152

Taabo (land registration agency), 55–57
Taraki, Lisa, 15, 23, 56, 74, 85
taxation reforms, 166
temporality: of endurance, 147, 154–58;
    slow violence and, 123–25; social
    activities as time wasting, 137–40;
    spatial theory of debt and, 42–46;
    sumud and, 148; topology of debt
    and, 47

Terranoa, Tiziana, 99–100

Thai migrant workers, influence in Israel of, 36

time wasting, social activities as, 137–40

topographies: debt topology and, 55–57; slow violence of debt and, 124–25; of urban debt, 66–74

topology of debt, 4–5; baking sector and, 105–7; connection and disconnection and, 58–60; ecologies of debt and, 41–42, 47–49; entangled relations and, 52–54, 153–54; in Ramallah, 49–52; research on, 46–47; slow violence of, 124–25; topographic entanglements and, 54–57

Toscano, Alberto, 99–100

trade with Israel, Palestininan dependency in, 27–29, 32

trust, debt boundaries and, 44–45

Tuck, Eve, 164–65

Turner, Mandy, 33

Um al Sharayet neighborhood, 1; business orientation of Ramallah and, 76–80; debt experiences in, 96–100; debt management and social redistribution in, 112–14; debt-related harm in, 122; endurance in, 146–47, 155–58; family debt negotiations in, 103–7; financial crisis ordinariness in, 125–29; geography of debt and, 61–63; housing costs in, 41–42; indebted subjectivity and space in, 18; land and housing ownership in, 70–71; migrant population in, 67–71; mobility issues in, 57; obligatory subjectivity of debt in, 116–18; population demographics in, 15–16; refugee camps near, 75–83; research in, 14–17; resident imaginaries and, 87–91; spatial theory of debt and, 163–64

unemployment: debt as replacement for income and, 130–32; gender

dynamics in, 139–40; intifada impact on, 29; post-Oslo increase in, 31–34. See also labor (employment)

United Kingdom (UK): debt and credit in, 44–46; urban bankruptcies and, 64; urbanization in, 65–66

United Nations (UN): foreign donor governance and, 5–6; two-state proposal by, 23

United Nations Relief and Works Administration for Palestine Refugees in the Near East (UNRWA), 24

United States (US): foreign donor governance and, 5–6; municipal bond markets in, 63; Palestinian family ties to, 70–71; Palestinian migration to, 71–72, 74

urban imaginaries, 83–87

urbanization: capitalist urban (re)development and, 65–66; city bankruptcies and, 63–64; city landscape and lifestyle and, 56–57; culture and, 74–83; debt and, 61–63; governance and, 62–63; migrant remittances and, 67–71; refugee camps and, 74–83; resident imaginaries and, 87–91; spatial theory of debt and, 18, 63–66; urban imaginary and, 83–87

value, space-time and creation of, 47

van Teeffelen, Toni, 148

variegated financialization, 59–60

violence: debt-related harm and, 121–22; as financial crisis ordinariness, 138–40; geopolitics of, 158–61; obligated subjectivity and, 18–19; in post-second Intifada period, 36–37; of settler colonialism, 26–29. See also slow violence

visiting practices, family debt and, 4–5

wages: debt as replacement for income and, 129–32; employment and, 166; post-Oslo increase in, 32–34

www.ingramcontent.com/pod-product-compliance
Lightning Source LLC
Chambersburg PA
CBHW071103280326
41928CB00051B/2775